KAGEROU DAZE 9
CONTENTS

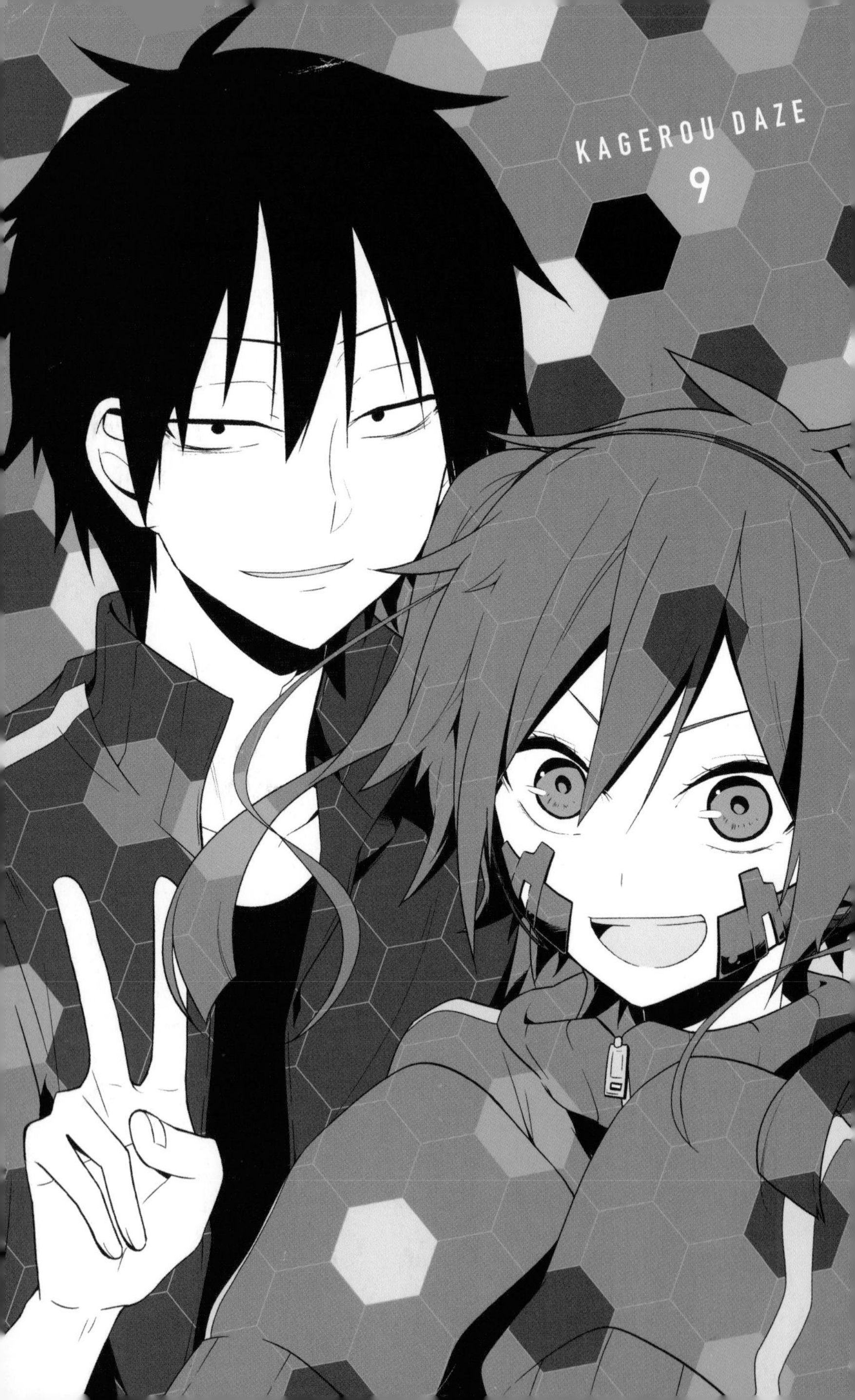
KAGEROU DAZE
9

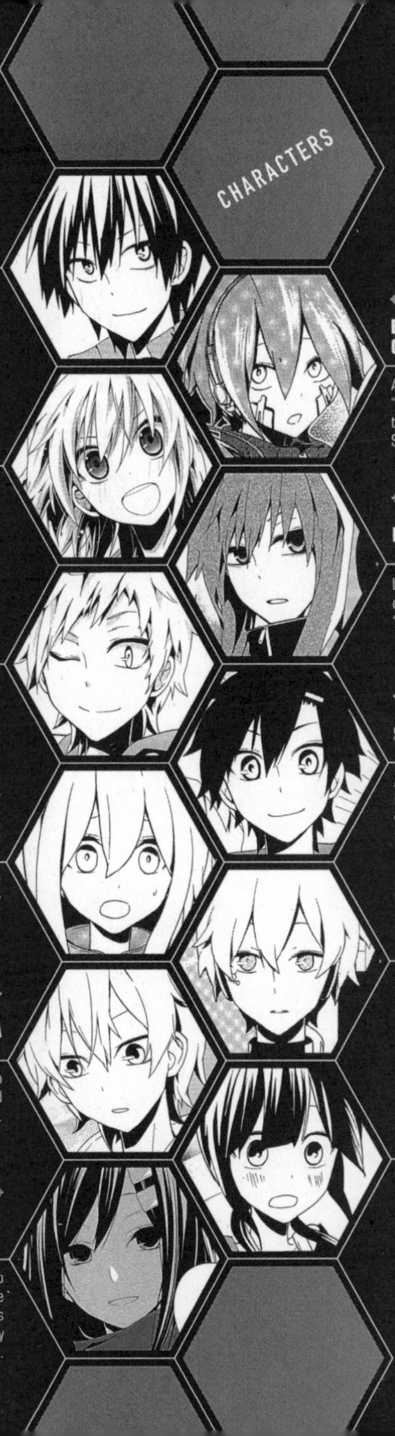
CHARACTERS

>>>

SHINTARO

A teenage boy who's been holed up in his house for the past two years.

<<<

ENE (Takane Enomoto)

An innocent, naive "digital girl" who's taken up residence in Shintaro's computer.

>>>

MOMO

An ultra-popular singer with the "drawing eyes" ability. Shintaro's sister.

<<<

KIDO

Leader of the Mekakushi-dan. Possesses the "concealing eyes" ability.

>>>

KANO

Friends with Kido and Seto since childhood. Possesses the "deceiving eyes" ability.

<<<

SETO

A young man engaged in assorted part-time work. Possesses the "stealing eyes" ability.

>>>

MARIE

A young Medusa whose "locking eyes" ability lets her freeze people in their tracks.

<<<

KONOHA (Haruka Kokonose)

A young man who's lost his memory.

>>>

HIBIYA

A boy who's come to visit the neighborhood with Hiyori.

<<<

HIYORI

A girl who's come to visit Shintaro's neighborhood. A big fan of Momo.

>>>

???

A mysterious girl who approached Hibiya. Capable of projecting memories and emotions directly into people's brains.

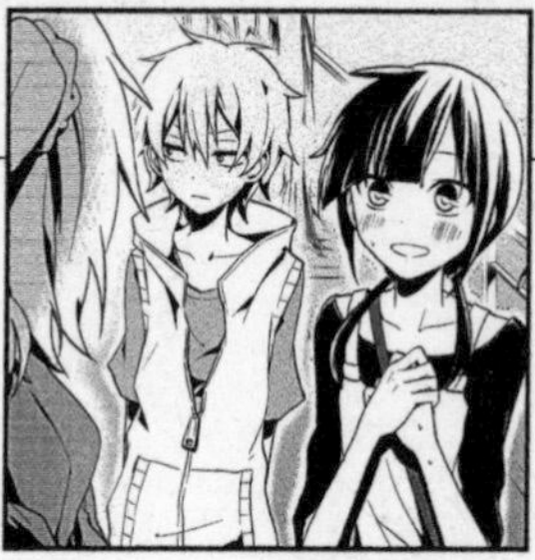

STORY

The tale of the events of August 14 and 15.

Shintaro and Momo run into a pair of children, Hibiya and Hiyori. They soon become friends, but after relaying a cryptic message to Momo over the phone, Hiyori disappears. They later discover Hibiya alone and unconscious, but he has lost his memory of the past little while. On the same day, Shintaro and Momo come across Kido and Kano, who claim to be part of a secret organization. They are also pursuing Hibiya and Hiyori, and soon the entire group's goals, destinies, and anxieties crisscross each other—and it's all connected by a supernatural phenomenon known as "Kagerou Daze."

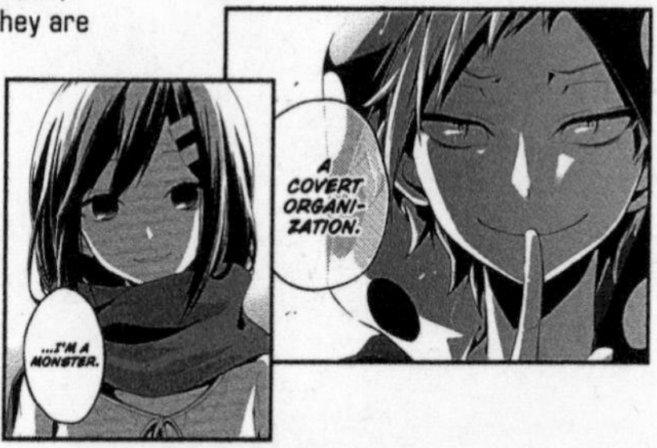
A COVERT ORGANIZATION.
...I'M A MONSTER.

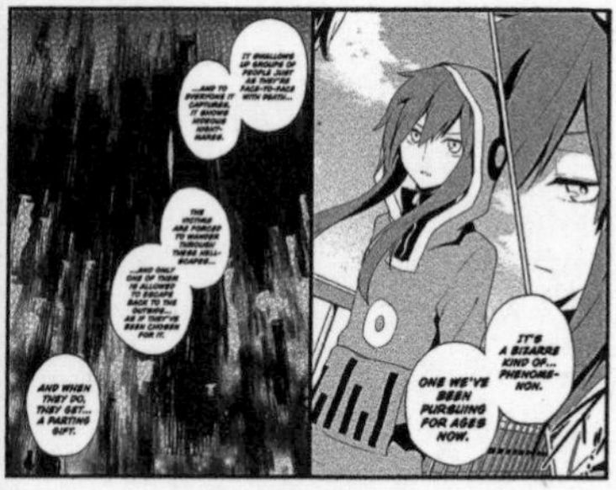
IT'S A BIZARRE KIND OF... PHENOMENON.
ONE WE'VE BEEN PURSUING FOR AGES NOW.
IT SWALLOWS UP GROUPS OF PEOPLE JUST AS THEY'RE FACE-TO-FACE WITH DEATH...
...AND TO EVERYONE IT CAPTURES, IT SHOWS HIDEOUS NIGHTMARES.
THE VICTIMS ARE FORCED TO WANDER THROUGH THESE HELLSCAPES...
...AND ONLY ONE OF THEM IS ALLOWED TO ESCAPE BACK TO THE OUTSIDE... AS IF THEY'VE BEEN CHOSEN FOR IT.
AND WHEN THEY DO, THEY GET... A PARTING GIFT.

As Hibiya searches for the missing Hiyori, a mysterious girl approaches him. Using her ability to impart memories and emotions directly into anyone she wants, she reveals the truth behind the Kagerou Daze. She fears a snake with the "clearing eyes" ability is attempting to unite all the snakes that gave the rest of this group their own eerie skills into a single entity—and now it might be here, in the "worst possible form."

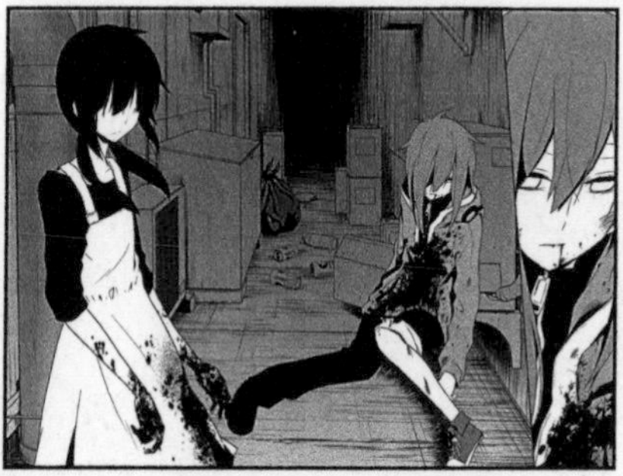

When Kano and Momo do find Hiyori, the scene is like something out of their worst nightmares: Hiyori, covered in blood, standing in front of a lifeless Kido. As he carries the fainted Momo back, Kano tells Ene about the lives of the Mekakushi-dan and how the snake has affected all of them.

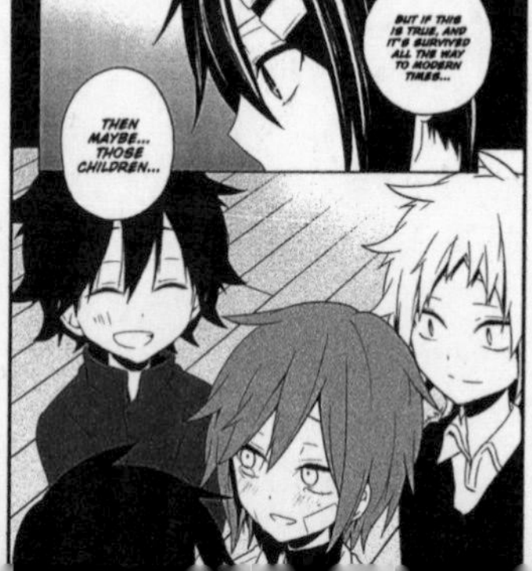
BUT IF THIS IS TRUE, AND IT'S SURVIVED ALL THE WAY TO MODERN TIMES...
THEN MAYBE... THOSE CHILDREN...

After awakening to their skills, Kido, Kano, and Seto spent their early years at a juvenile home. Ayaka, a researcher studying the Medusa myths of the past, decided to adopt the three of them, making them siblings to her own daughter, Ayano. So began a new family—and a new tragedy...

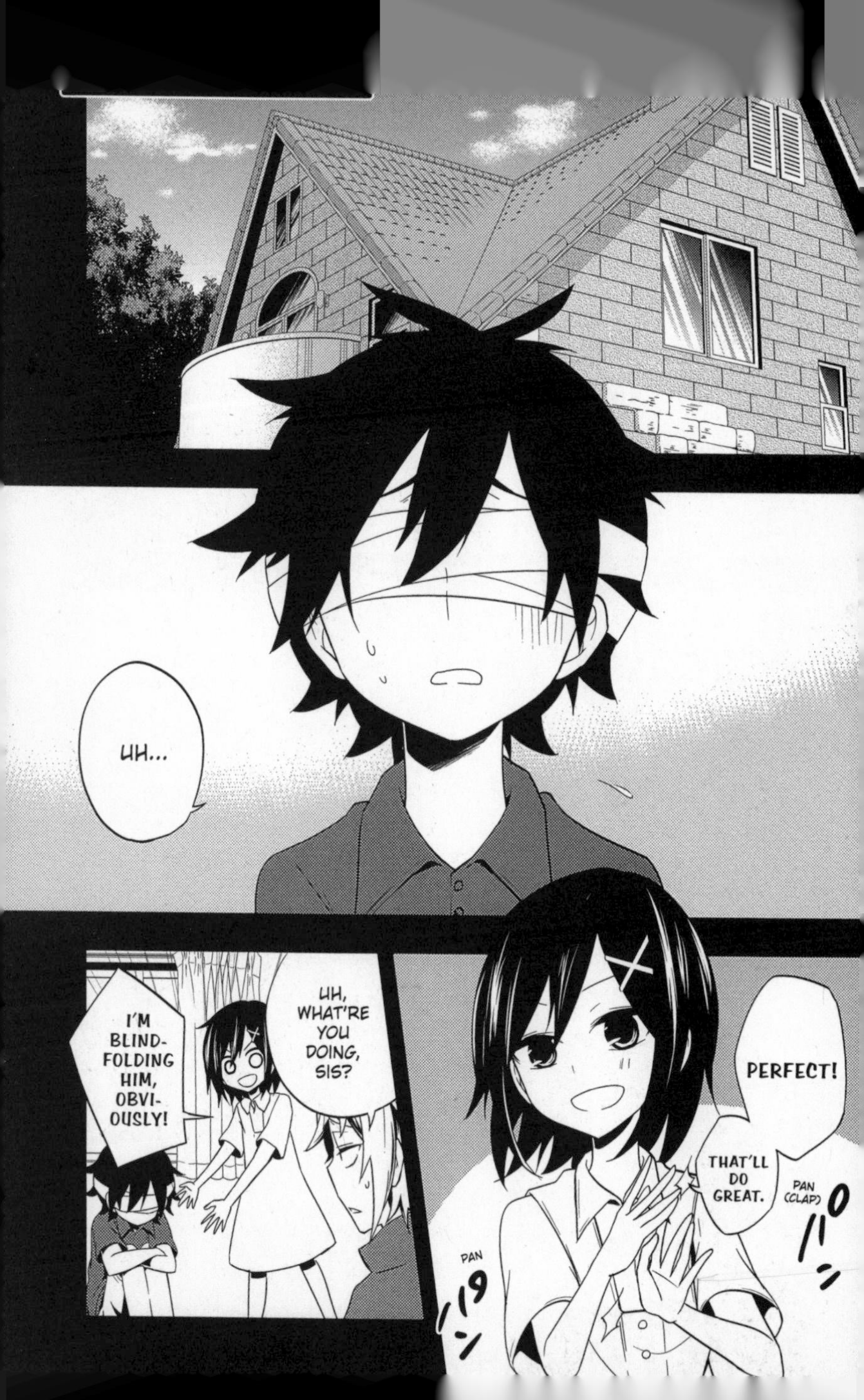
UH...
PERFECT!
THAT'LL DO GREAT.
PAN (CLAP)
PAN
UH, WHAT'RE YOU DOING, SIS?
I'M BLIND-FOLDING HIM, OBVI-OUSLY!

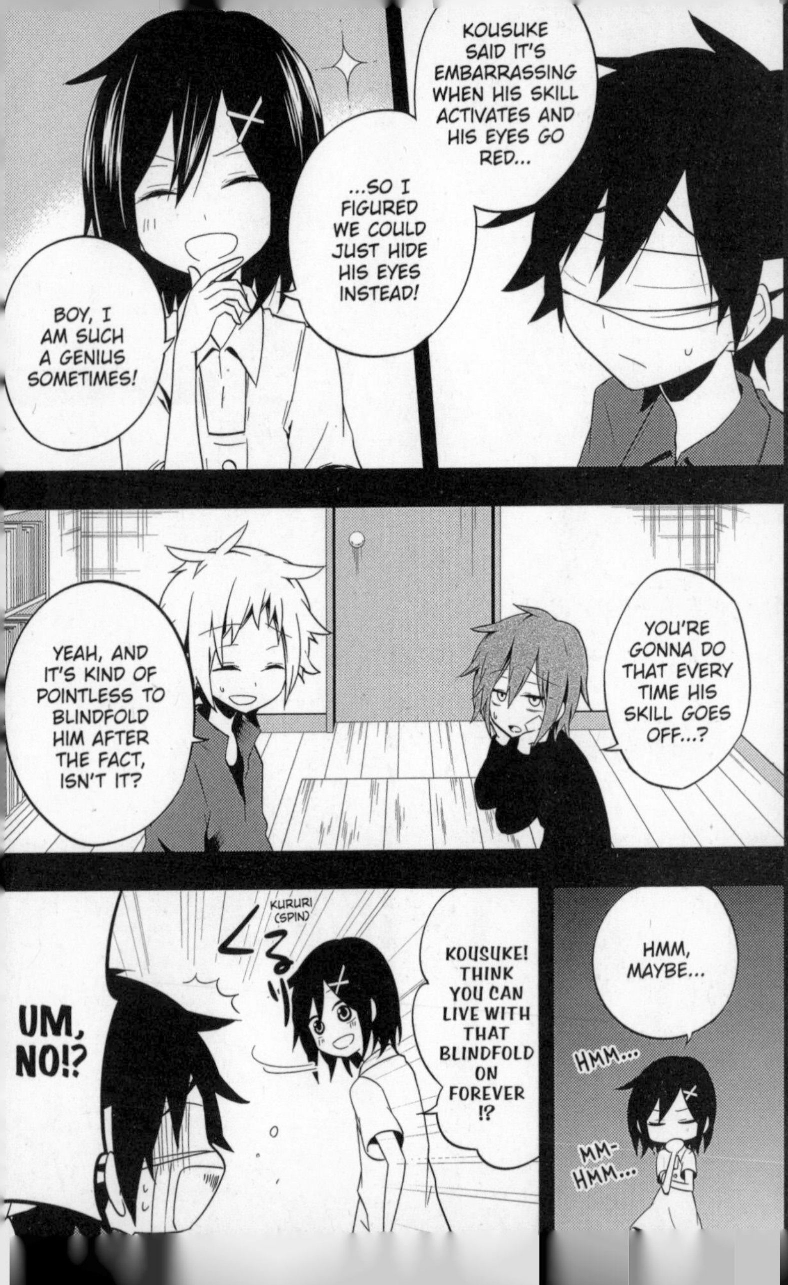
KOUSUKE SAID IT'S EMBARRASSING WHEN HIS SKILL ACTIVATES AND HIS EYES GO RED...
...SO I FIGURED WE COULD JUST HIDE HIS EYES INSTEAD!
BOY, I AM SUCH A GENIUS SOMETIMES!
YOU'RE GONNA DO THAT EVERY TIME HIS SKILL GOES OFF...?
YEAH, AND IT'S KIND OF POINTLESS TO BLINDFOLD HIM AFTER THE FACT, ISN'T IT?
HMM, MAYBE...
HMM...
MM-HMM...
KURURI (SPIN)
KOUSUKE! THINK YOU CAN LIVE WITH THAT BLINDFOLD ON FOREVER!?
UM, NO!?

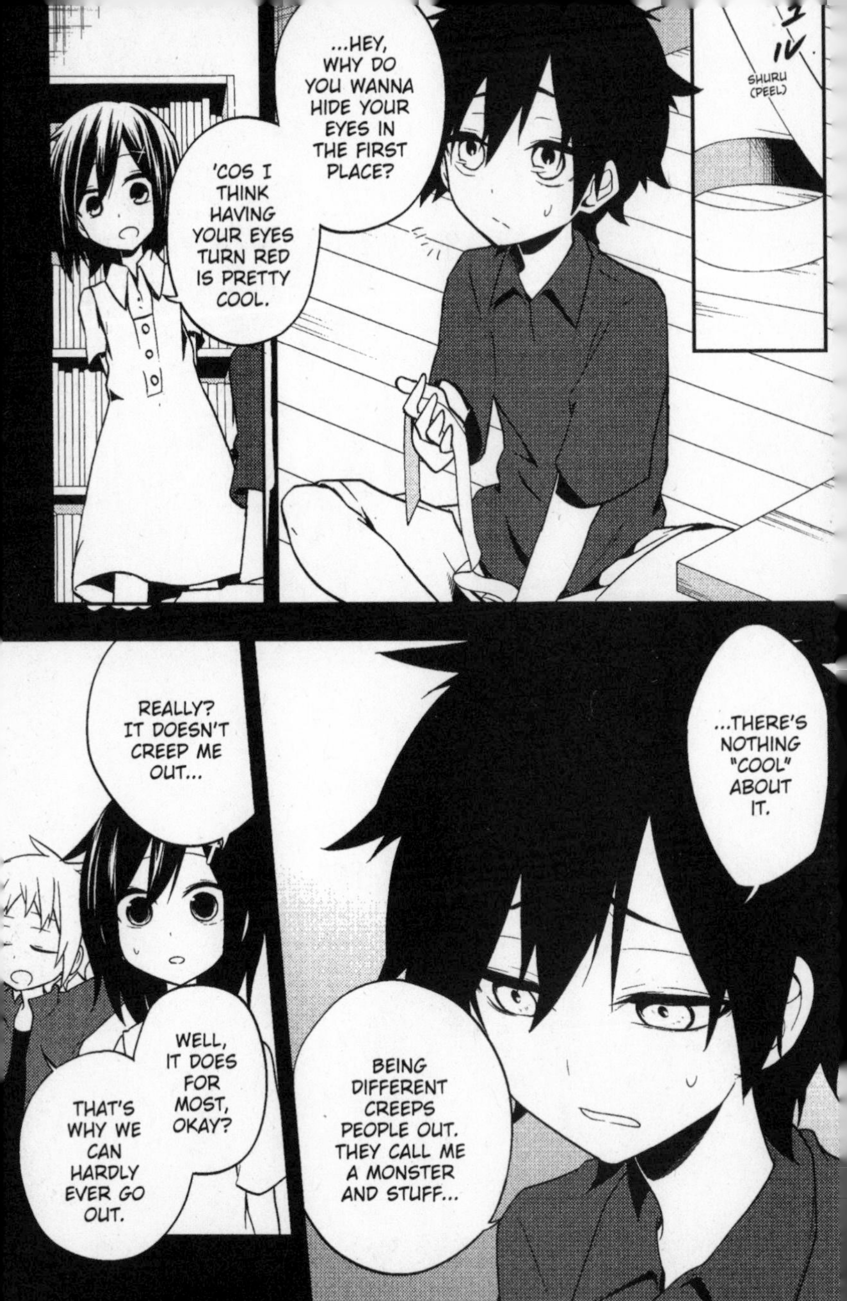
SHURU (PEEL)
...HEY, WHY DO YOU WANNA HIDE YOUR EYES IN THE FIRST PLACE?
'COS I THINK HAVING YOUR EYES TURN RED IS PRETTY COOL.
...THERE'S NOTHING "COOL" ABOUT IT.
BEING DIFFERENT CREEPS PEOPLE OUT. THEY CALL ME A MONSTER AND STUFF...
REALLY? IT DOESN'T CREEP ME OUT...
WELL, IT DOES FOR MOST, OKAY?
THAT'S WHY WE CAN HARDLY EVER GO OUT.

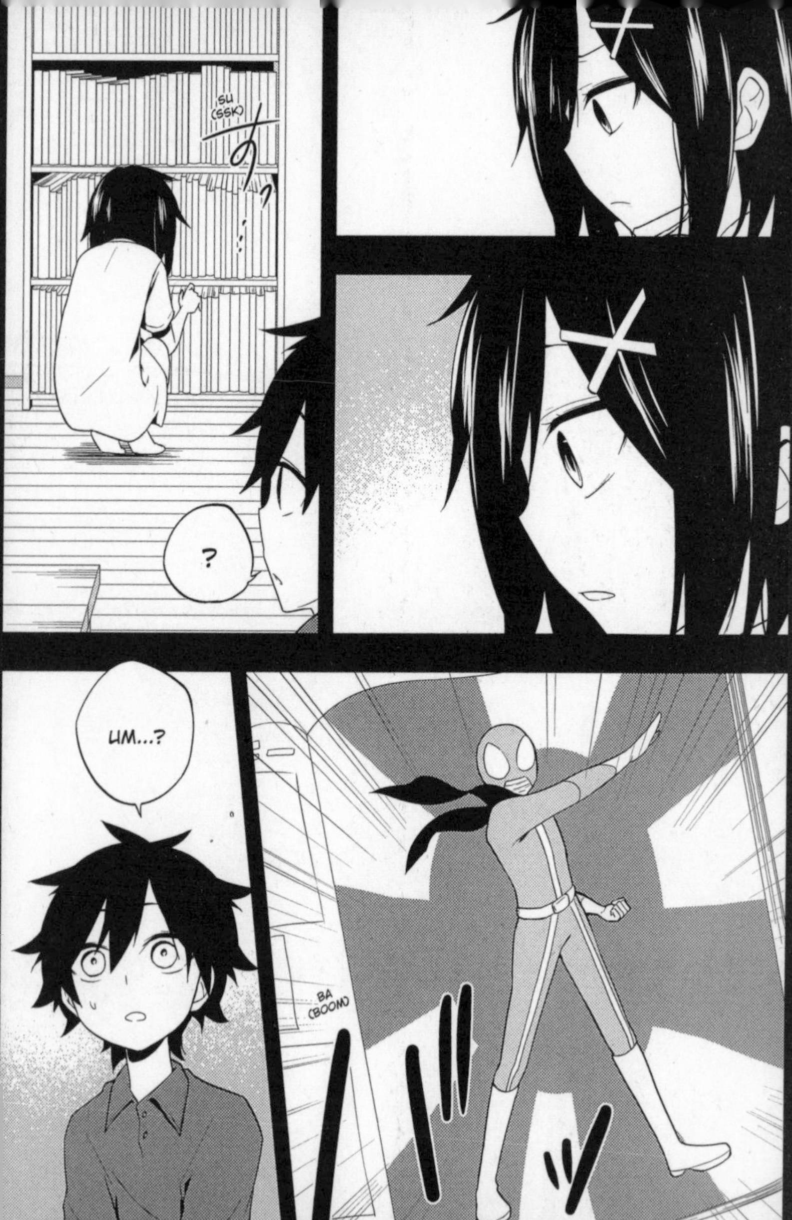
SU (SSK)
?
BA (BOOM)
UM...?

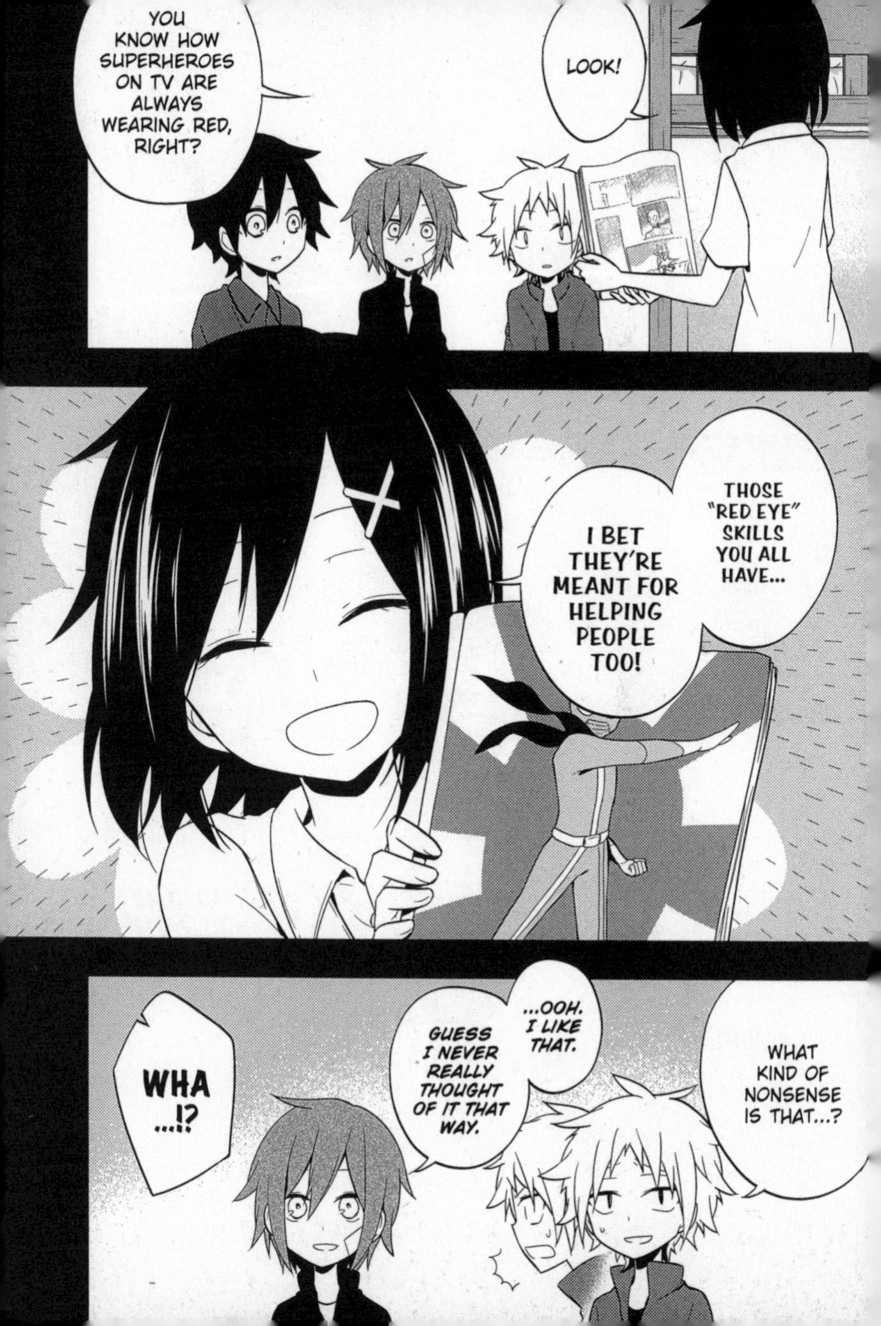
LOOK!
YOU KNOW HOW SUPERHEROES ON TV ARE ALWAYS WEARING RED, RIGHT?
THOSE "RED EYE" SKILLS YOU ALL HAVE...
I BET THEY'RE MEANT FOR HELPING PEOPLE TOO!
WHAT KIND OF NONSENSE IS THAT...?
...OOH. I LIKE THAT.
GUESS I NEVER REALLY THOUGHT OF IT THAT WAY.
WHA ...!?

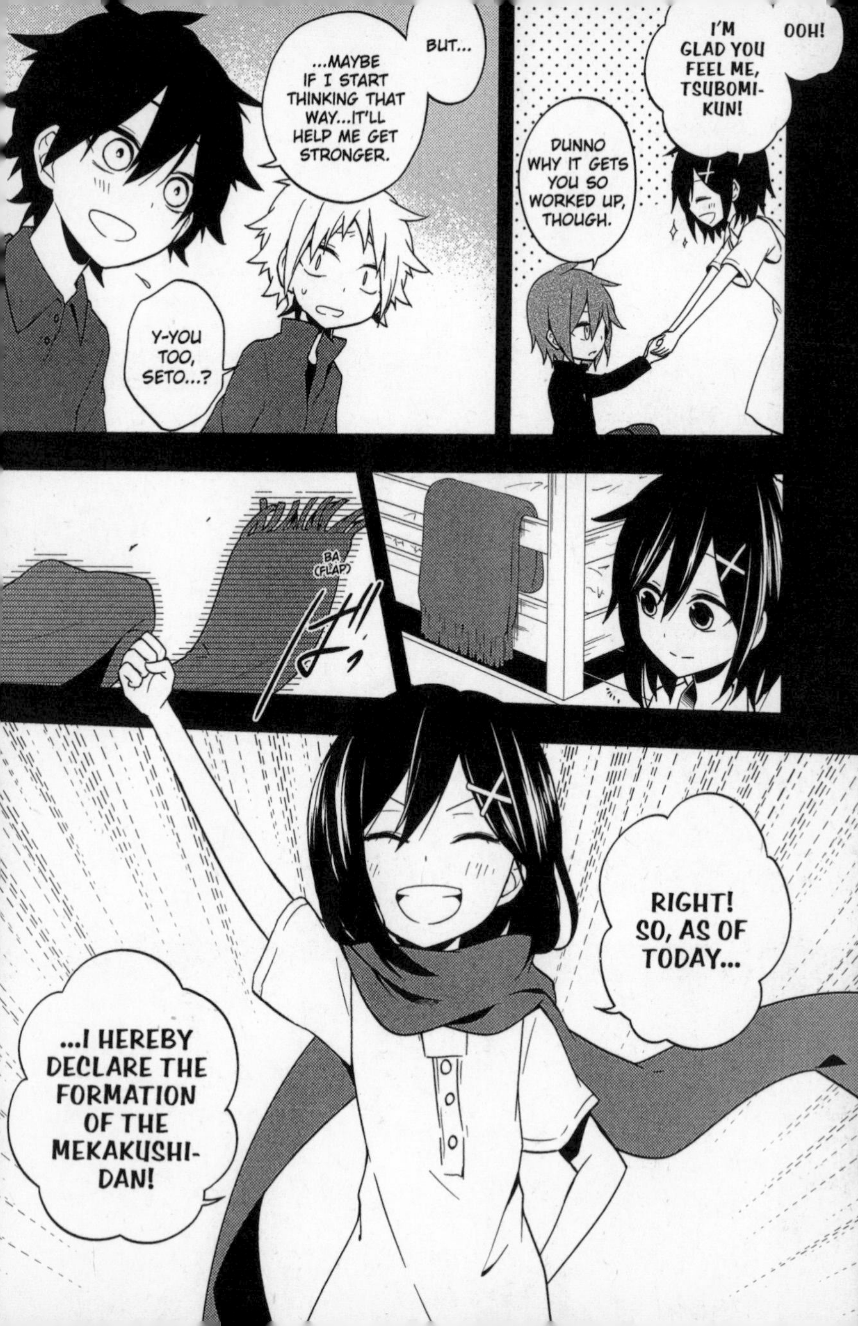
OOH!
I'M GLAD YOU FEEL ME, TSUBOMI-KUN!
DUNNO WHY IT GETS YOU SO WORKED UP, THOUGH.
BUT...
...MAYBE IF I START THINKING THAT WAY...IT'LL HELP ME GET STRONGER.
Y-YOU TOO, SETO...?
BA (FLAP)
RIGHT! SO, AS OF TODAY...
...I HEREBY DECLARE THE FORMATION OF THE MEKAKUSHI-DAN!

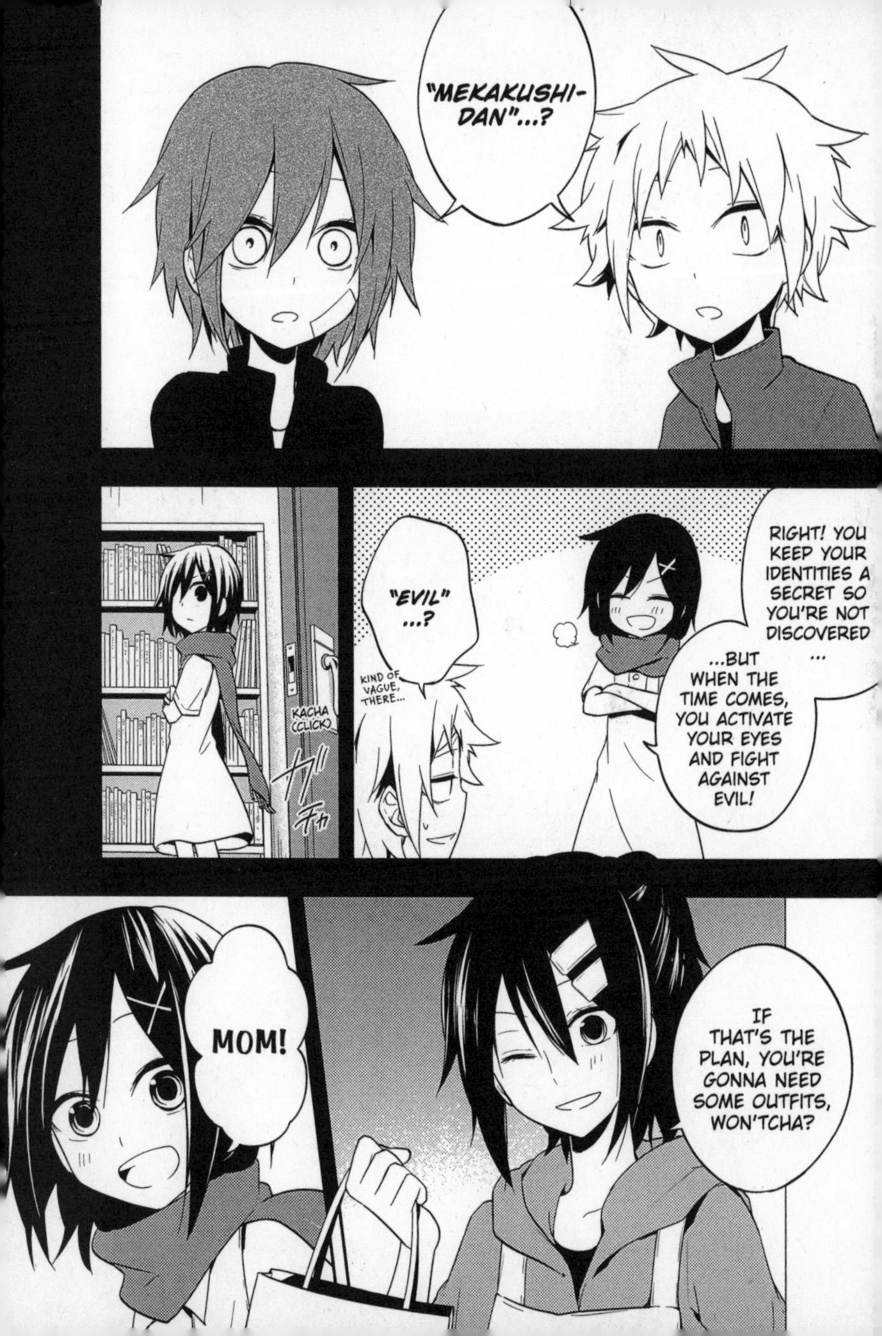
"MEKAKUSHI-DAN"...?
RIGHT! YOU KEEP YOUR IDENTITIES A SECRET SO YOU'RE NOT DISCOVERED...
...BUT WHEN THE TIME COMES, YOU ACTIVATE YOUR EYES AND FIGHT AGAINST EVIL!
"EVIL"...?
KIND OF VAGUE, THERE...
KACHA (CLICK)
IF THAT'S THE PLAN, YOU'RE GONNA NEED SOME OUTFITS, WON'TCHA?
MOM!

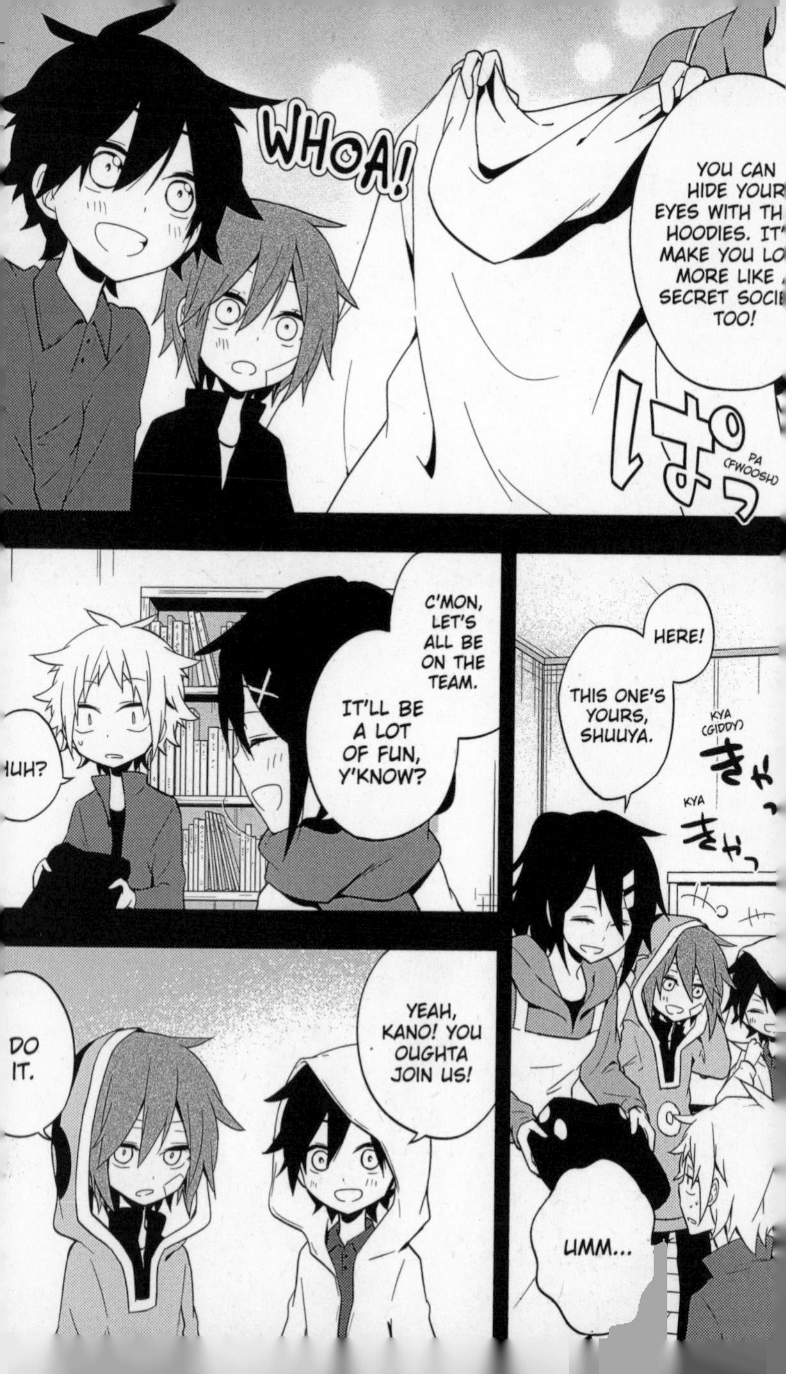
YOU CAN HIDE YOUR EYES WITH TH HOODIES. IT' MAKE YOU LO MORE LIKE SECRET SOCIE TOO!
ぱっ
PA (FWOOSH)
WHOA!
HERE!
THIS ONE'S YOURS, SHUUYA.
KYA (GIDDY)
きゃっ
KYA
きゃっ
UMM...
C'MON, LET'S ALL BE ON THE TEAM.
IT'LL BE A LOT OF FUN, Y'KNOW?
HUH?
YEAH, KANO! YOU OUGHTA JOIN US!
DO IT.

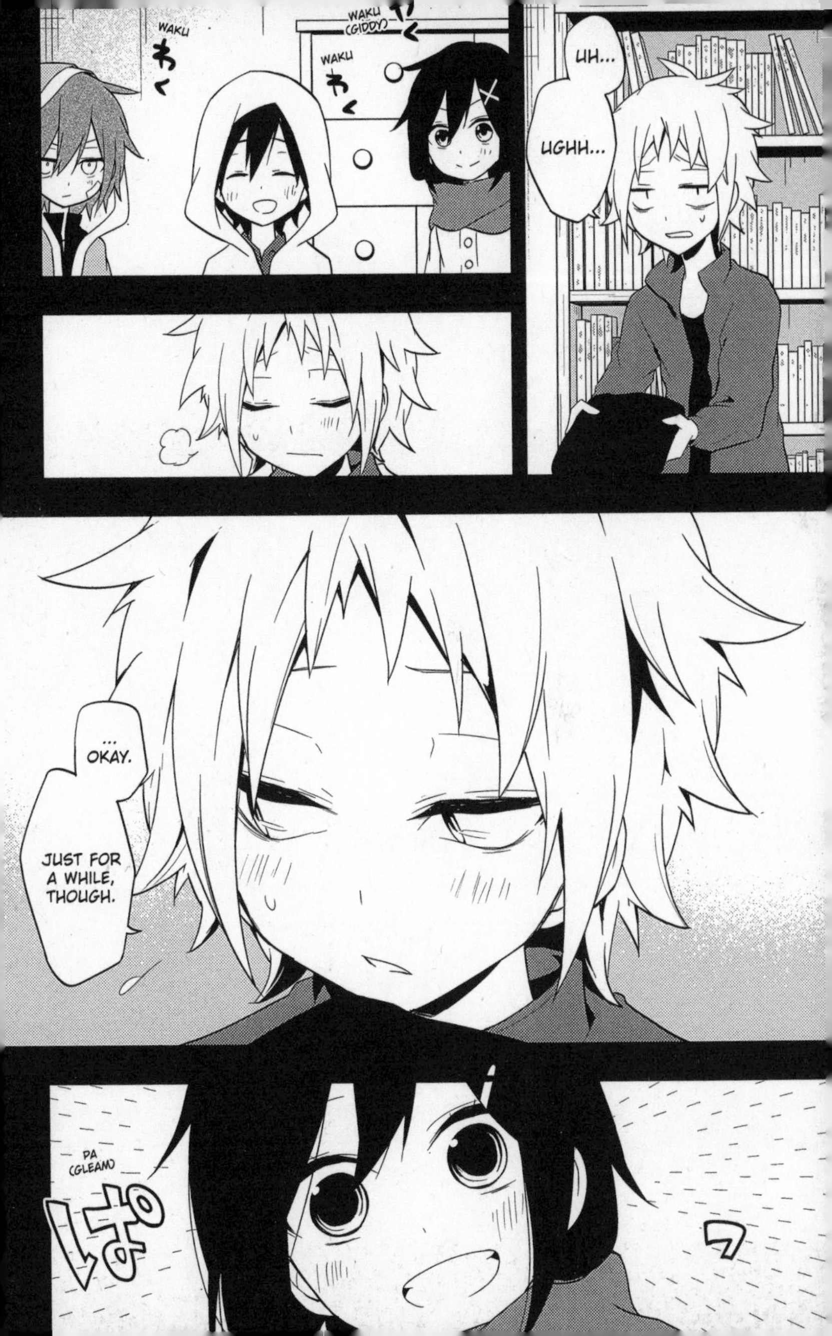
UH...
UGHH...
WAKU (GIDDY)
わく
WAKU
わく
WAKU
わく
... OKAY.
JUST FOR A WHILE, THOUGH.
PA (GLEAM)
ぱ

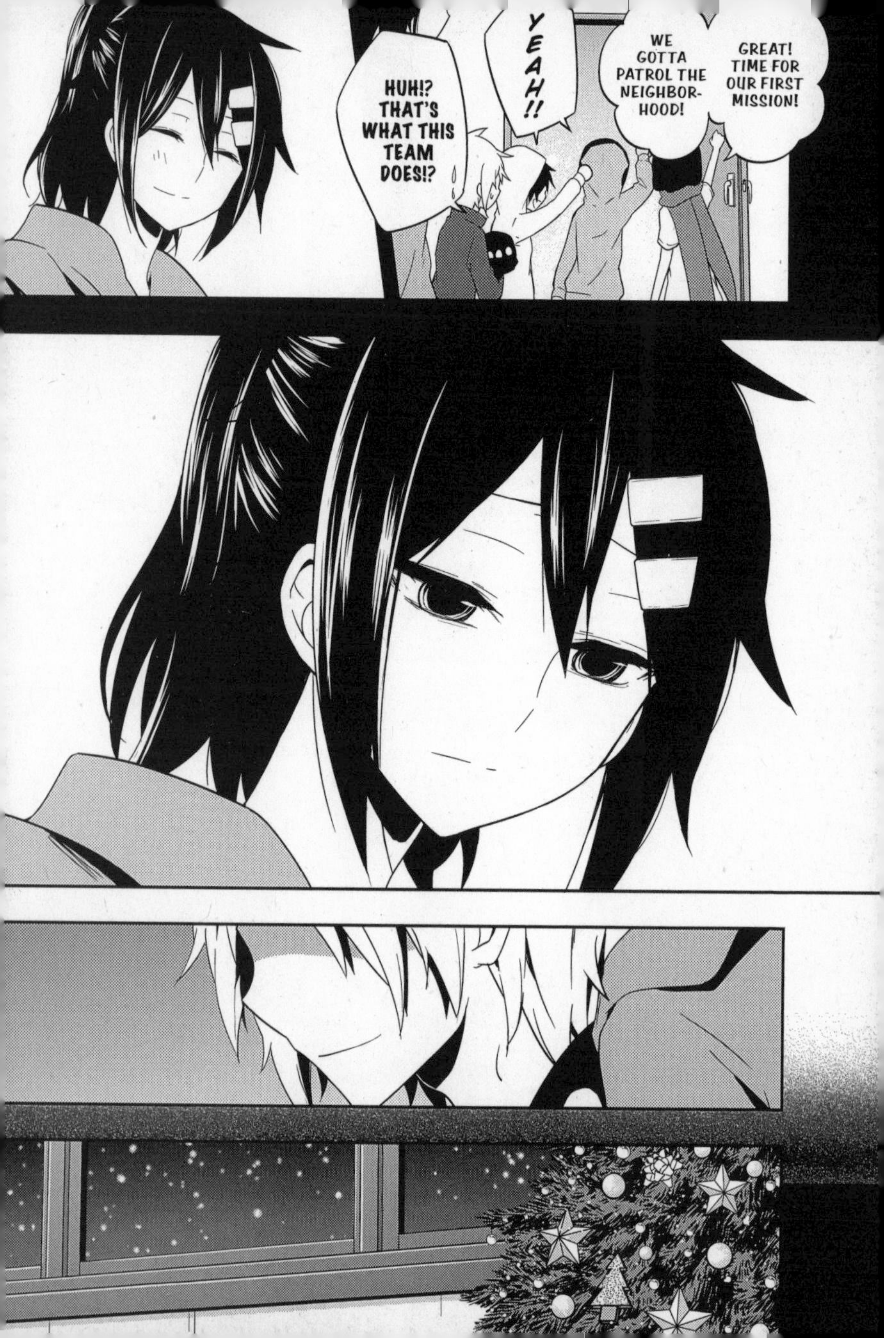
GREAT! TIME FOR OUR FIRST MISSION!
WE GOTTA PATROL THE NEIGHBOR-HOOD!
YEAH!!
HUH!? THAT'S WHAT THIS TEAM DOES!?

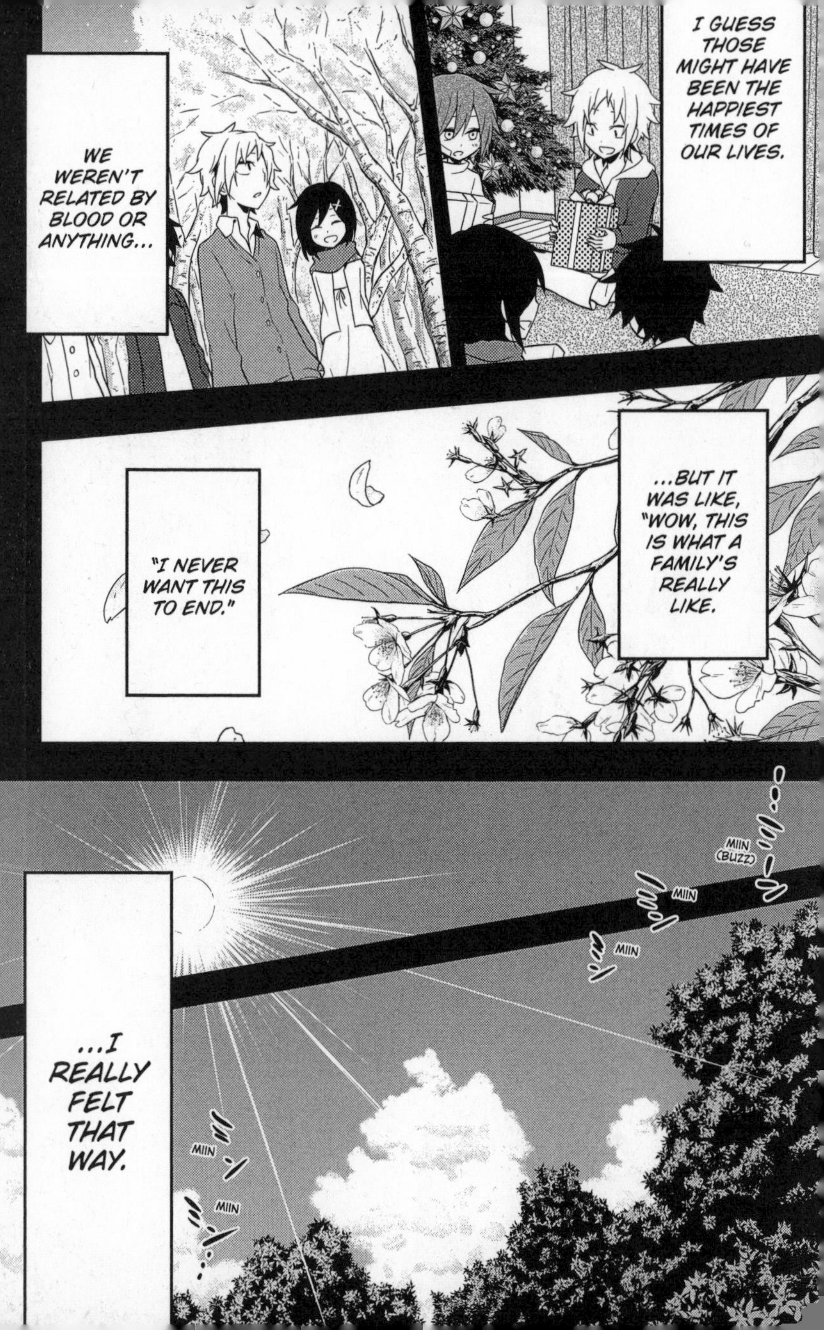
I GUESS THOSE MIGHT HAVE BEEN THE HAPPIEST TIMES OF OUR LIVES.
WE WEREN'T RELATED BY BLOOD OR ANYTHING...
...BUT IT WAS LIKE, "WOW, THIS IS WHAT A FAMILY'S REALLY LIKE.
"I NEVER WANT THIS TO END."
MIIN (BUZZ)
MIIN
MIIN
...I REALLY FELT THAT WAY.
MIIN
MIIN

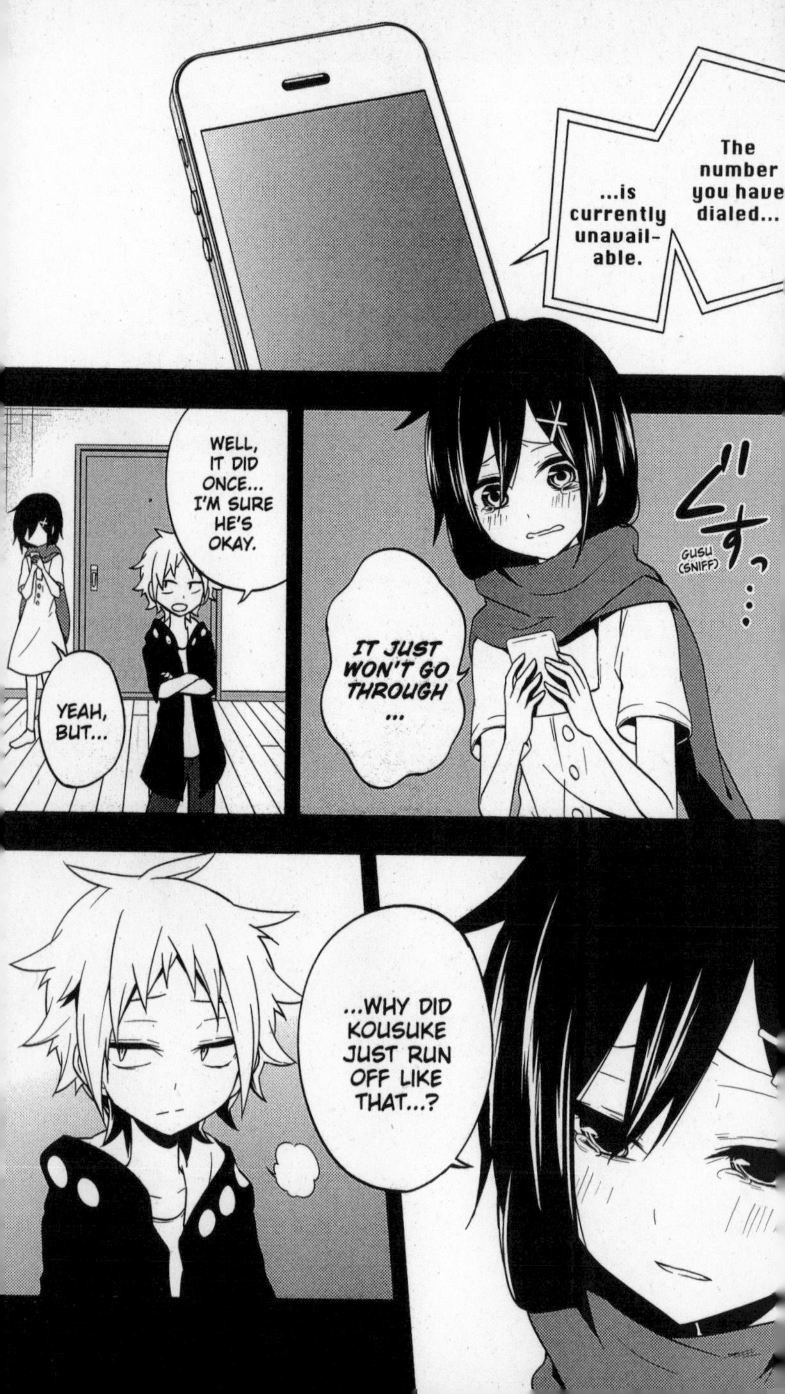
The number you have dialed...
...is currently unavail-able.
ぐすっ…
GUSU (SNIFF)
IT JUST WON'T GO THROUGH...
WELL, IT DID ONCE... I'M SURE HE'S OKAY.
YEAH, BUT...
...WHY DID KOUSUKE JUST RUN OFF LIKE THAT...?

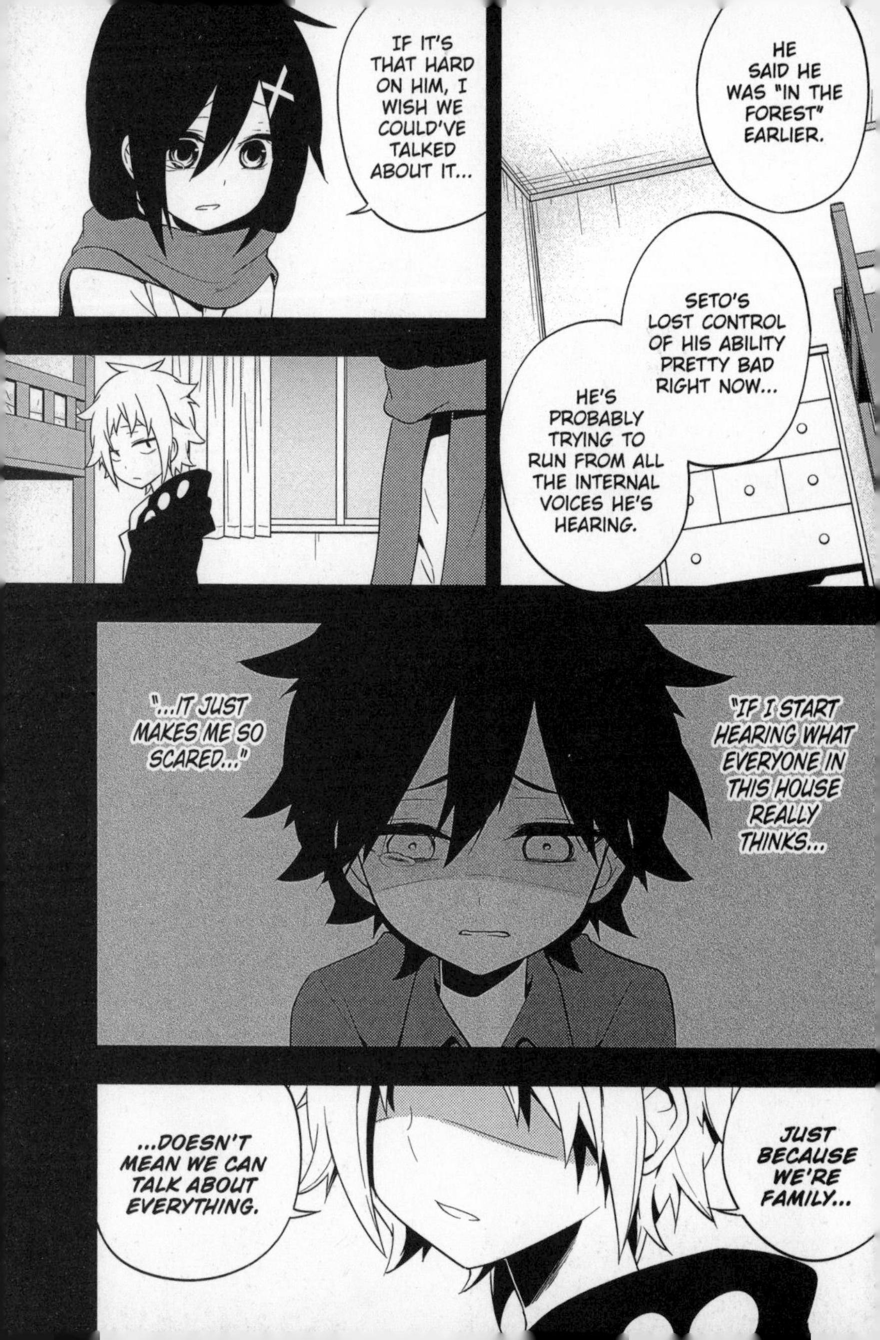
HE SAID HE WAS "IN THE FOREST" EARLIER.
SETO'S LOST CONTROL OF HIS ABILITY PRETTY BAD RIGHT NOW...
HE'S PROBABLY TRYING TO RUN FROM ALL THE INTERNAL VOICES HE'S HEARING.
IF IT'S THAT HARD ON HIM, I WISH WE COULD'VE TALKED ABOUT IT...
"IF I START HEARING WHAT EVERYONE IN THIS HOUSE REALLY THINKS...
"...IT JUST MAKES ME SO SCARED..."
JUST BECAUSE WE'RE FAMILY...
...DOESN'T MEAN WE CAN TALK ABOUT EVERYTHING.

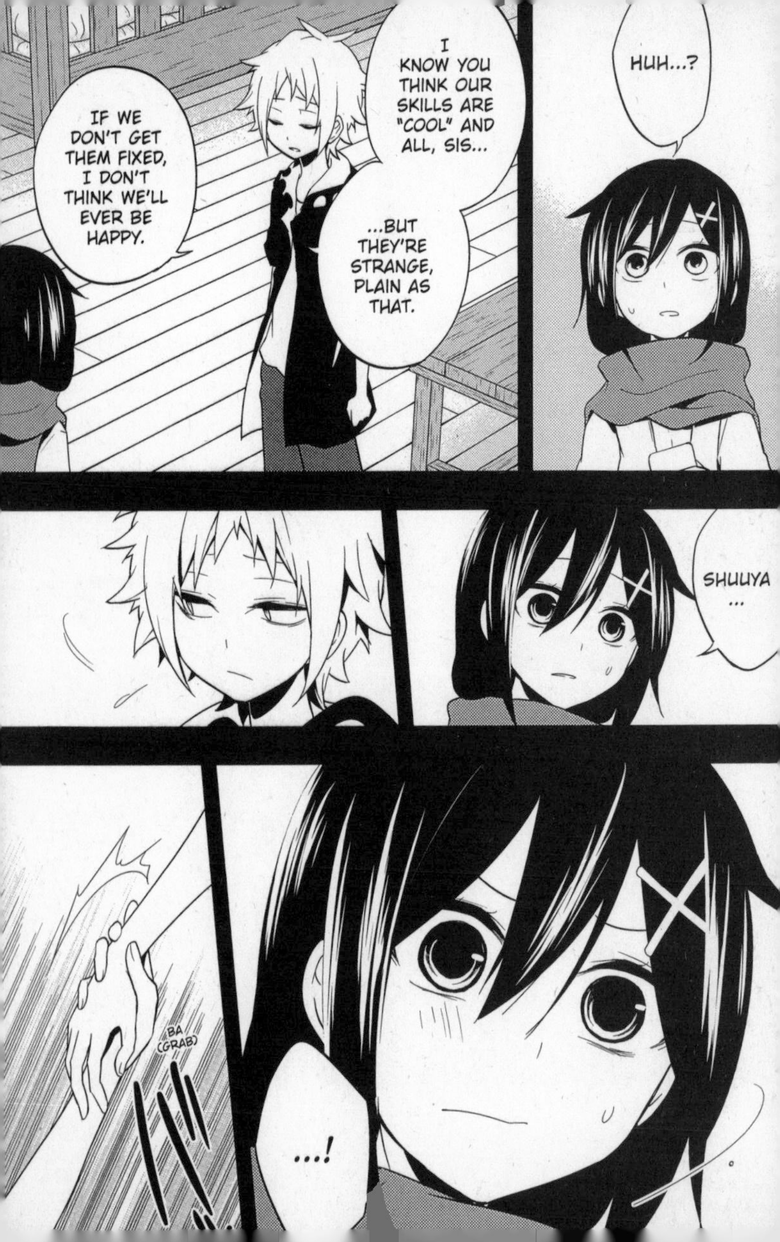
HUH...?
I KNOW YOU THINK OUR SKILLS ARE "COOL" AND ALL, SIS...
...BUT THEY'RE STRANGE, PLAIN AS THAT.
IF WE DON'T GET THEM FIXED, I DON'T THINK WE'LL EVER BE HAPPY.
SHUUYA ...
...!
BA (GRAB)

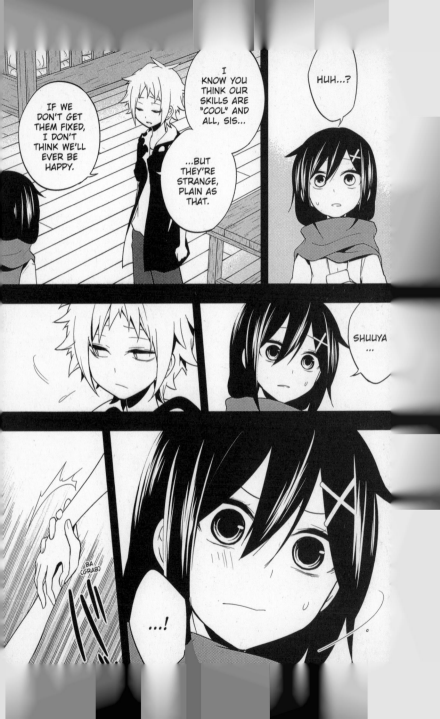

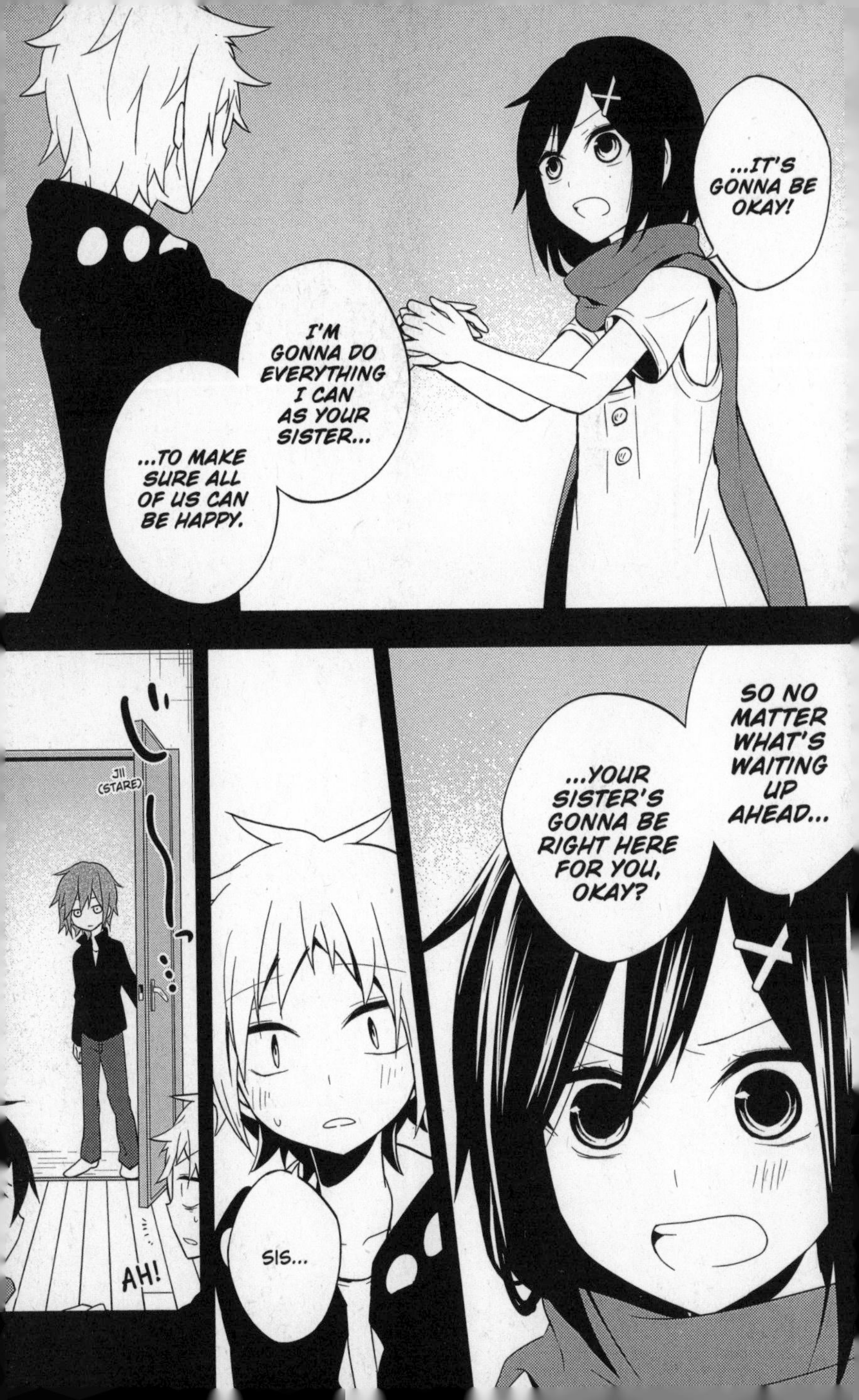
...IT'S GONNA BE OKAY!
I'M GONNA DO EVERYTHING I CAN AS YOUR SISTER...
...TO MAKE SURE ALL OF US CAN BE HAPPY.
SO NO MATTER WHAT'S WAITING UP AHEAD...
...YOUR SISTER'S GONNA BE RIGHT HERE FOR YOU, OKAY?
SIS...
JII (STARE)
AH!

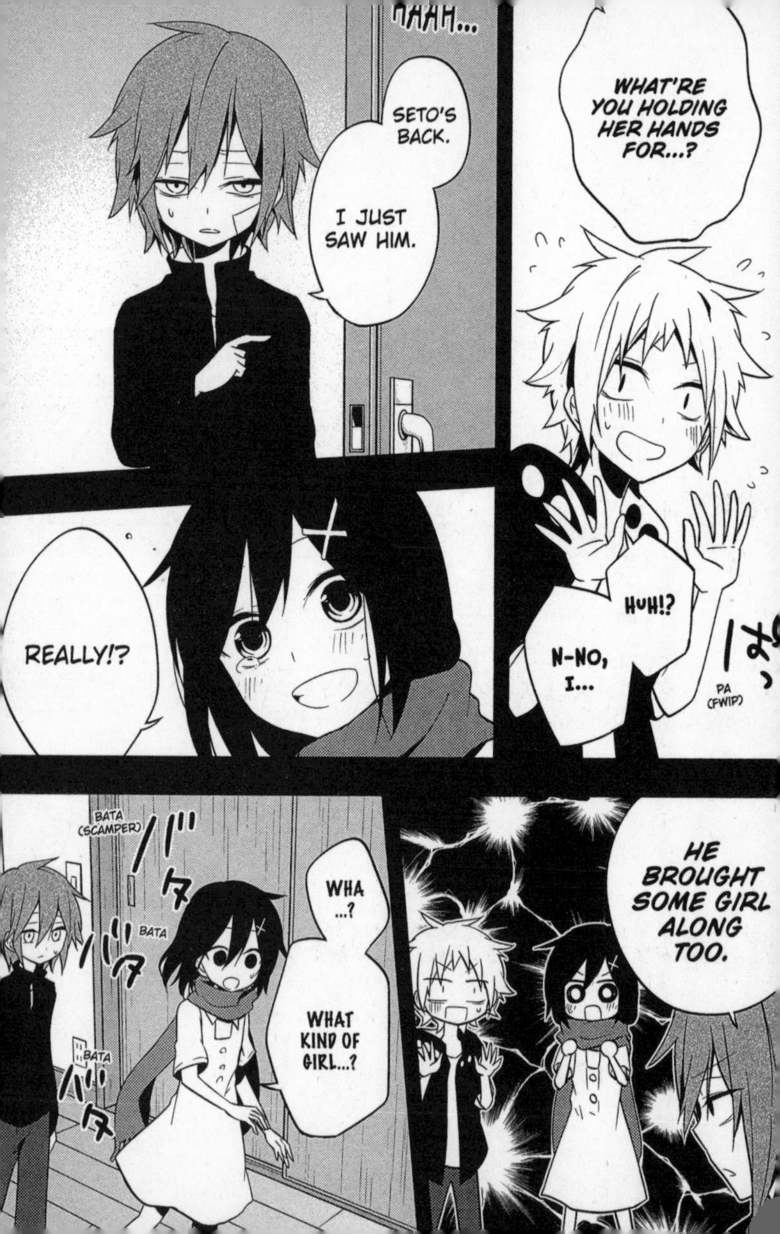
WHAT'RE YOU HOLDING HER HANDS FOR...?
HUH!?
N-NO, I...
PA (FWIP)
HAAH...
SETO'S BACK.
I JUST SAW HIM.
REALLY!?
HE BROUGHT SOME GIRL ALONG TOO.
WHA ...?
WHAT KIND OF GIRL...?
BATA (SCAMPER)
BATA
BATA

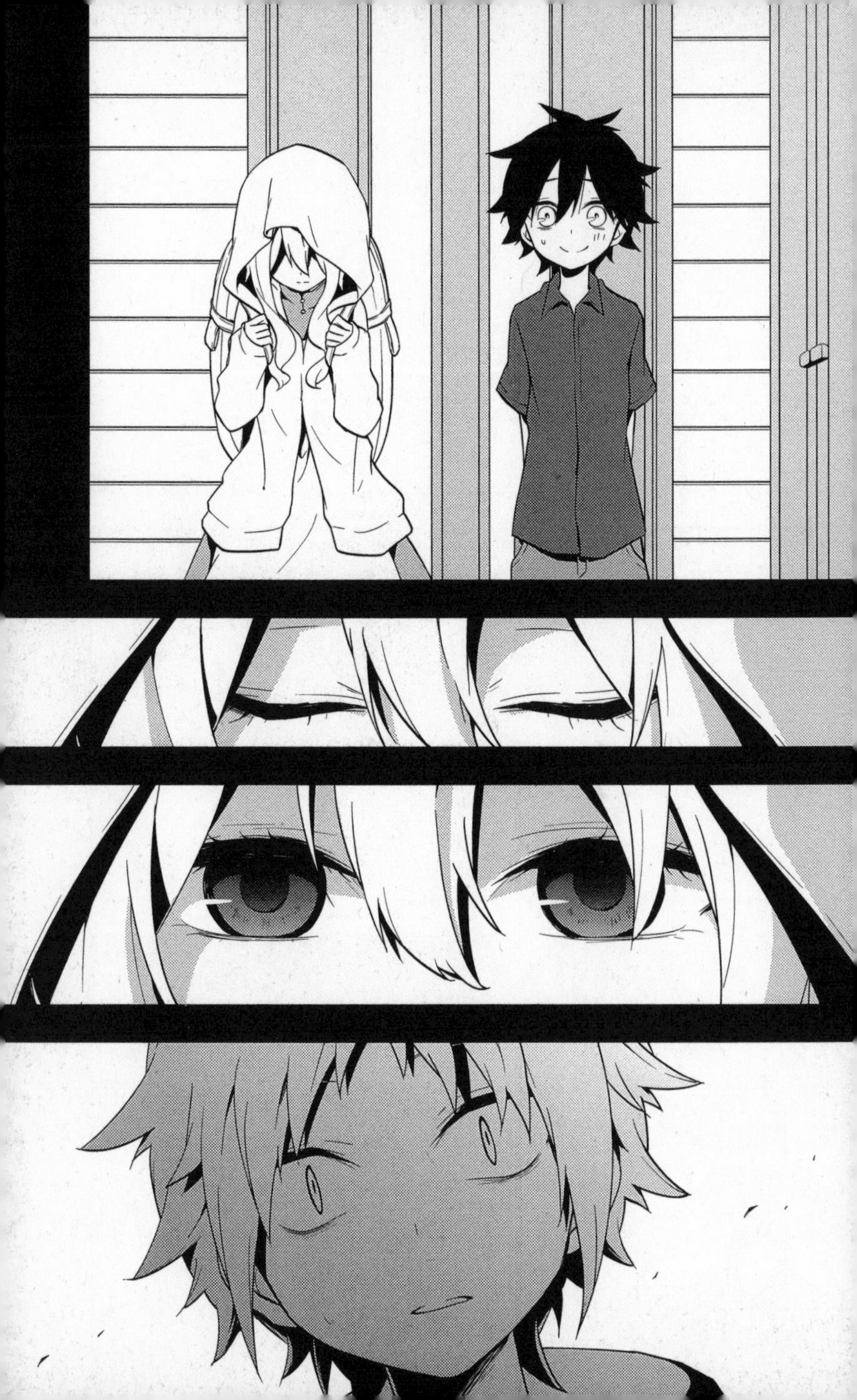

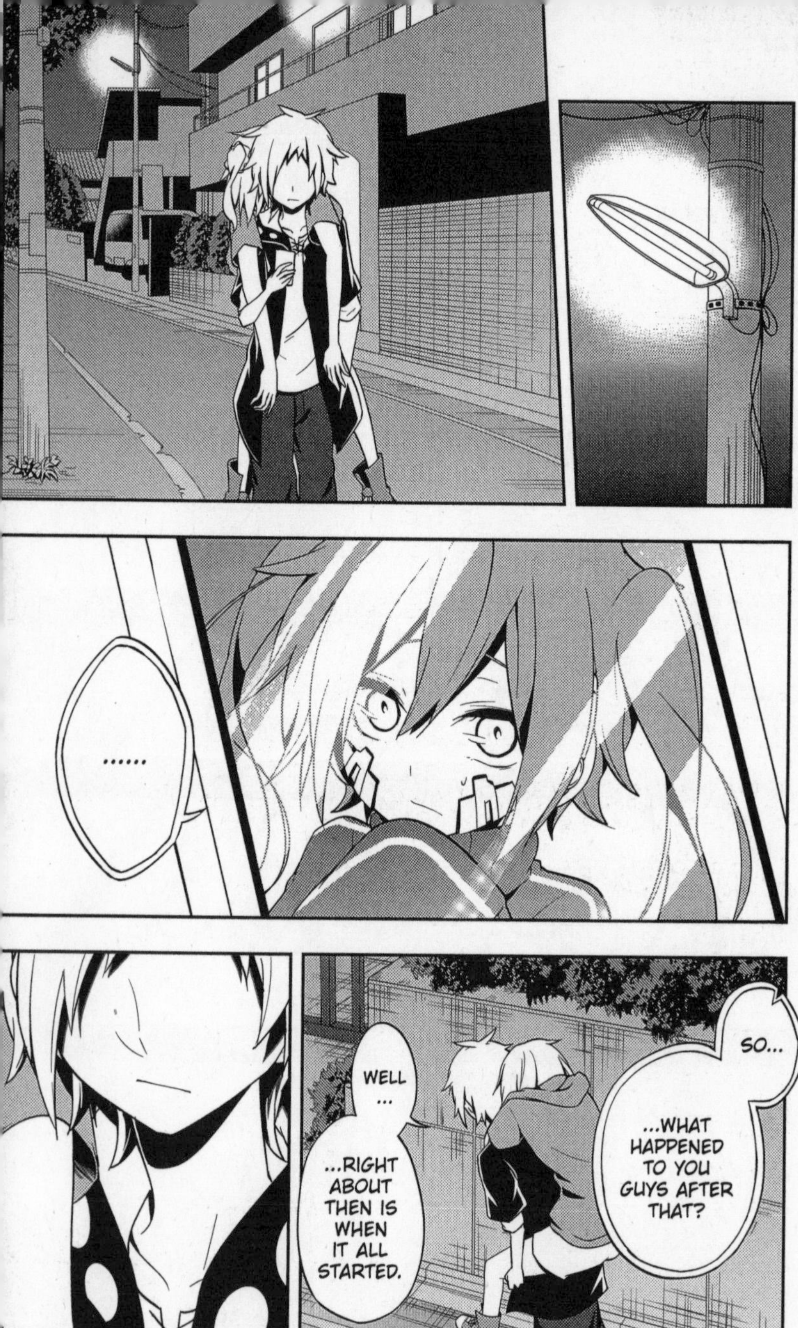

......
SO...
...WHAT HAPPENED TO YOU GUYS AFTER THAT?
WELL...
...RIGHT ABOUT THEN IS WHEN IT ALL STARTED.

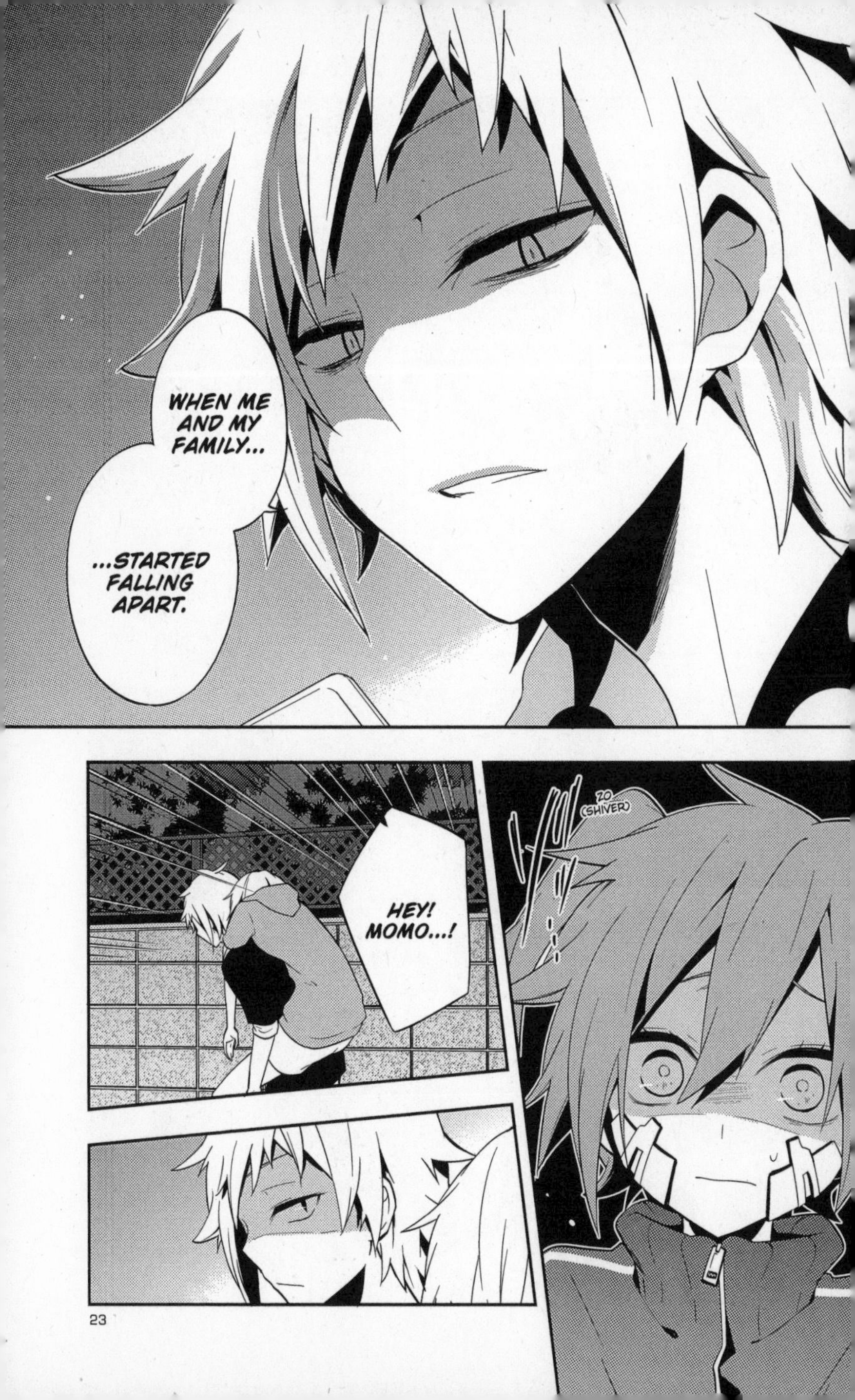
WHEN ME AND MY FAMILY...
...STARTED FALLING APART.
ZO (SHIVER)
HEY! MOMO...!

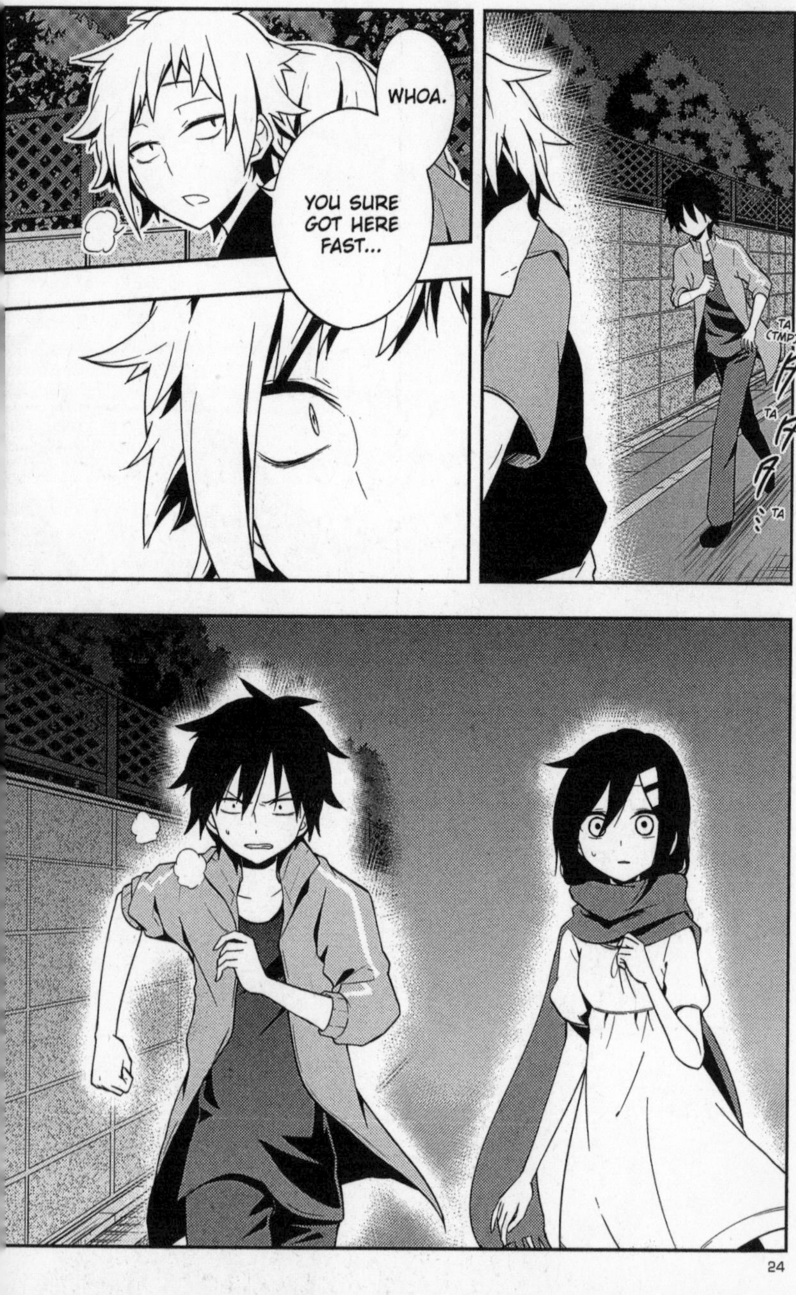
TA (TMP)
TA
TA
WHOA.
YOU SURE GOT HERE FAST...

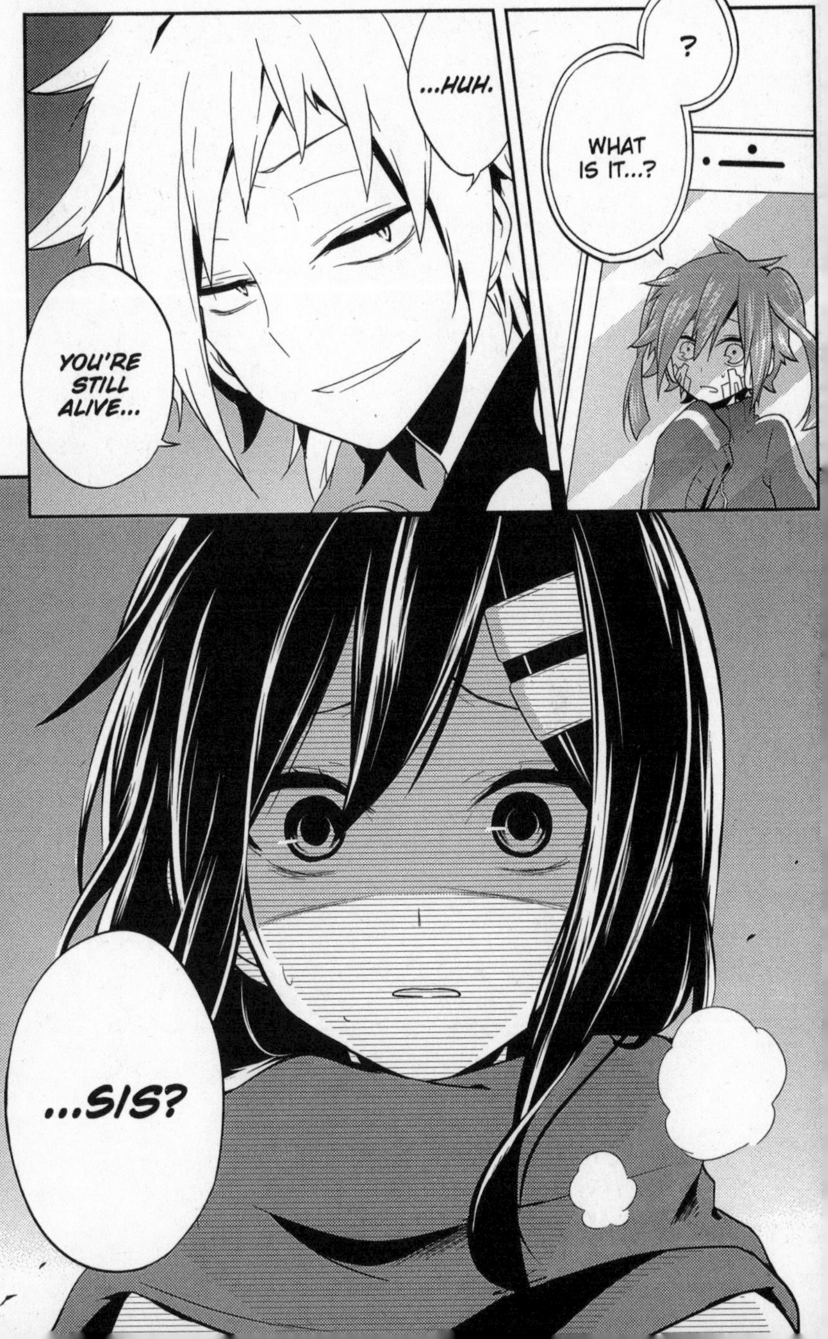
?
WHAT IS IT...?
...HUH.
YOU'RE STILL ALIVE...
...SIS?

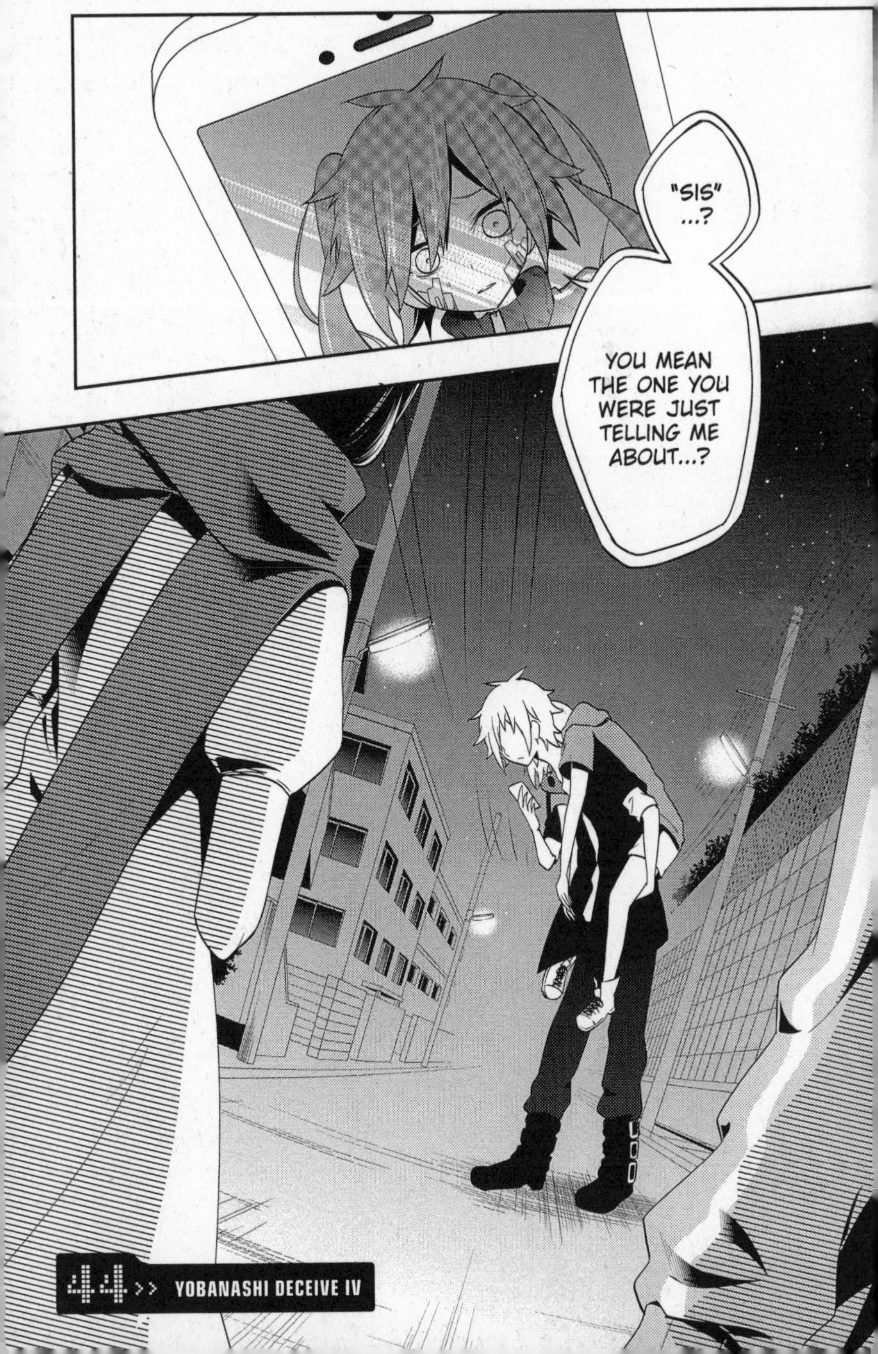
"SIS" ...?
YOU MEAN THE ONE YOU WERE JUST TELLING ME ABOUT...?

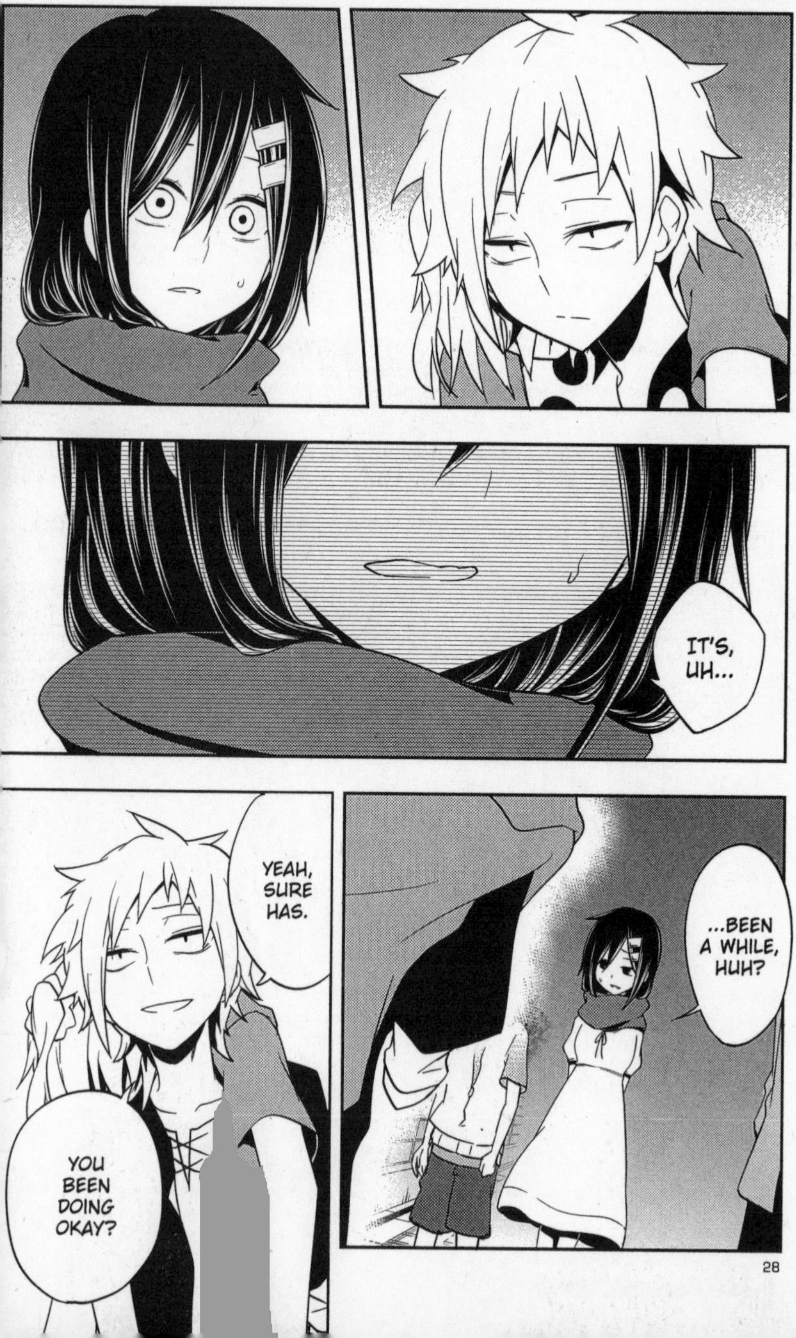
IT'S, UH...
...BEEN A WHILE, HUH?
YEAH, SURE HAS.
YOU BEEN DOING OKAY?

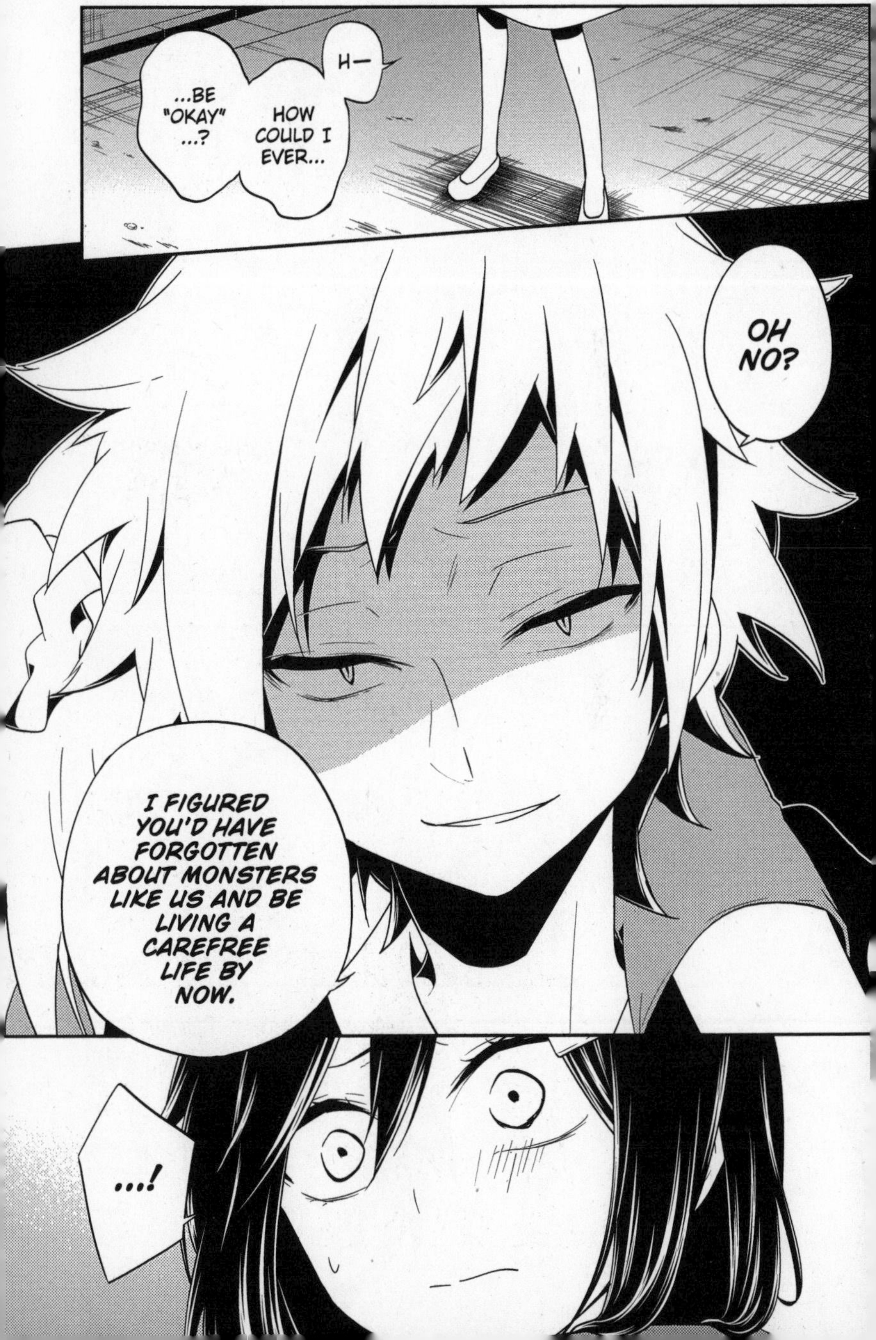
H—
HOW COULD I EVER...
...BE "OKAY" ...?
OH NO?
I FIGURED YOU'D HAVE FORGOTTEN ABOUT MONSTERS LIKE US AND BE LIVING A CAREFREE LIFE BY NOW.
...!

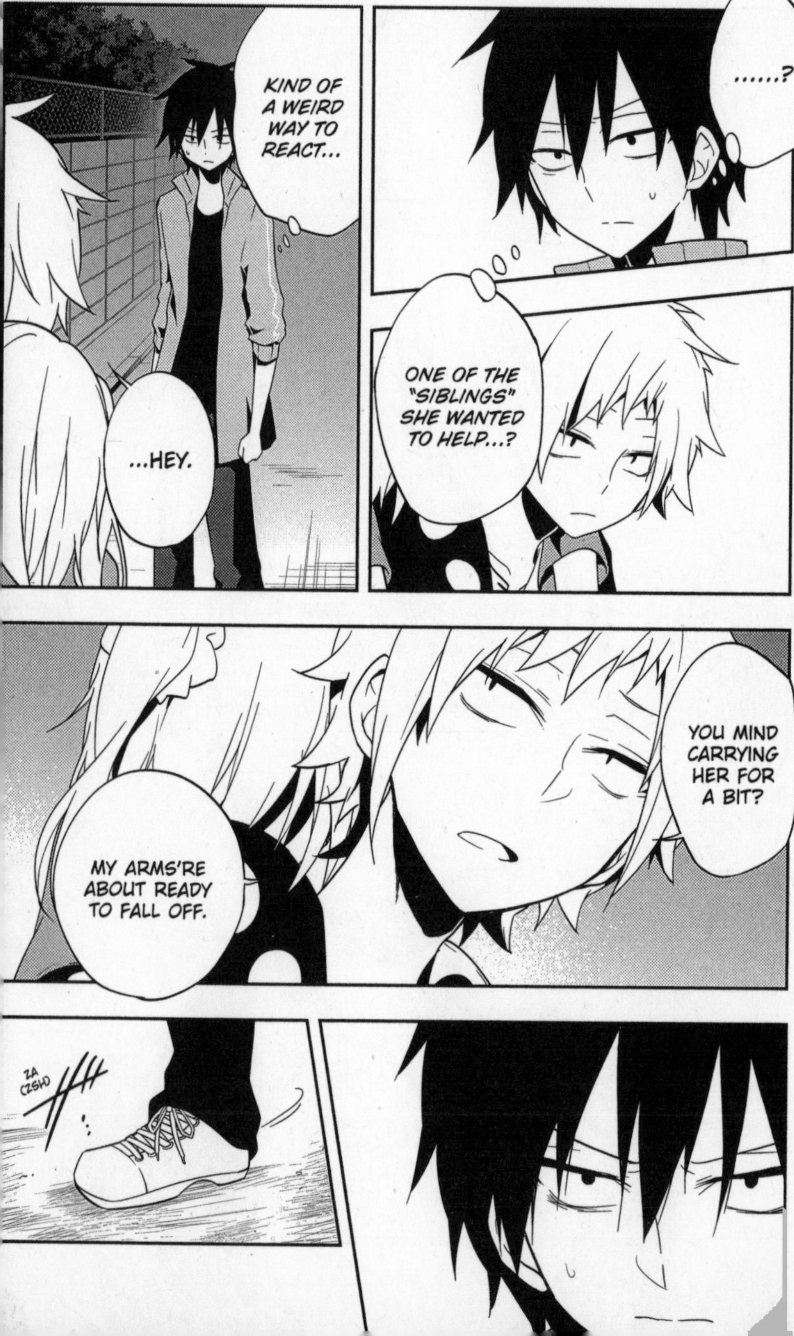
......?
ONE OF THE "SIBLINGS" SHE WANTED TO HELP...?
KIND OF A WEIRD WAY TO REACT...
...HEY.
YOU MIND CARRYING HER FOR A BIT?
MY ARMS'RE ABOUT READY TO FALL OFF.
ZA CZSHD

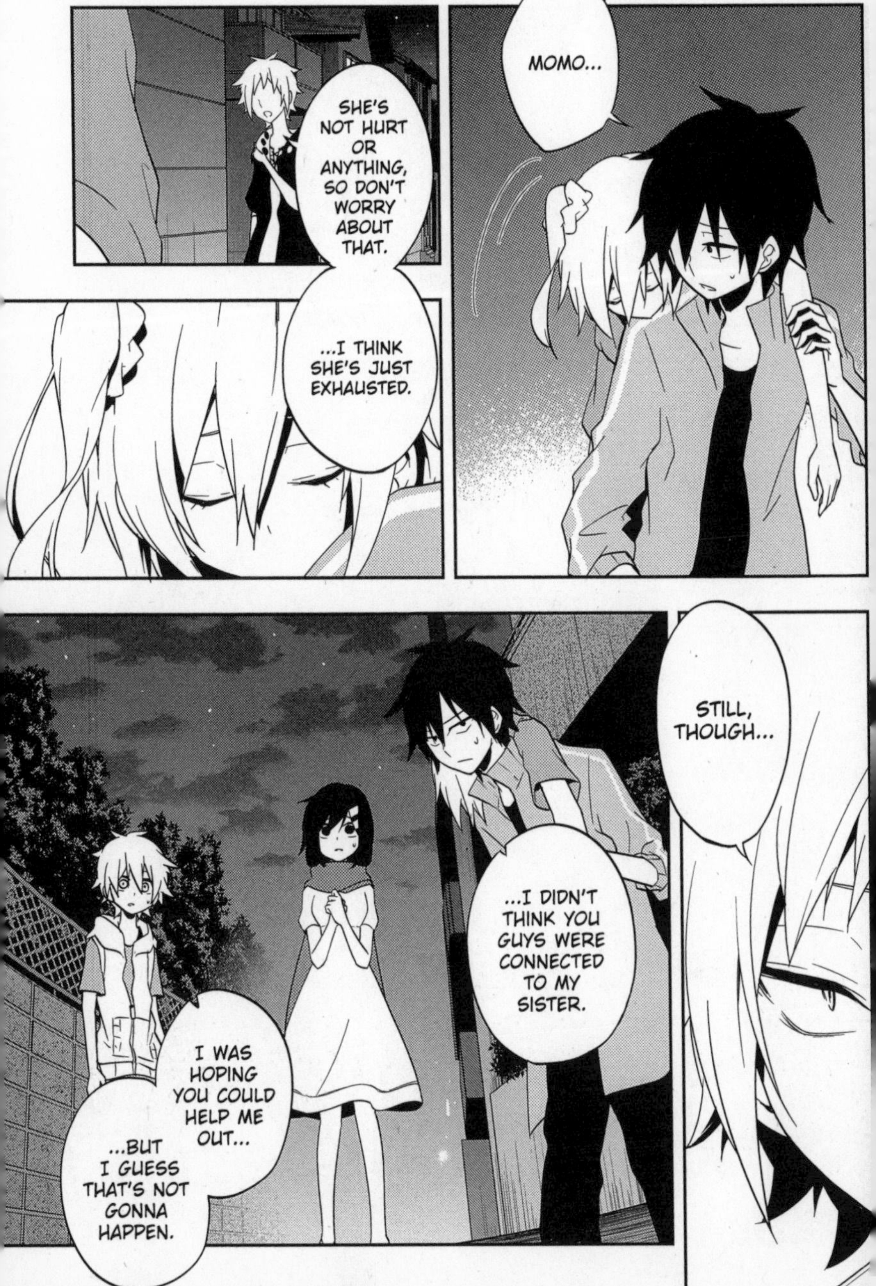
MOMO...
SHE'S NOT HURT OR ANYTHING, SO DON'T WORRY ABOUT THAT.
...I THINK SHE'S JUST EXHAUSTED.
STILL, THOUGH...
...I DIDN'T THINK YOU GUYS WERE CONNECTED TO MY SISTER.
I WAS HOPING YOU COULD HELP ME OUT...
...BUT I GUESS THAT'S NOT GONNA HAPPEN.

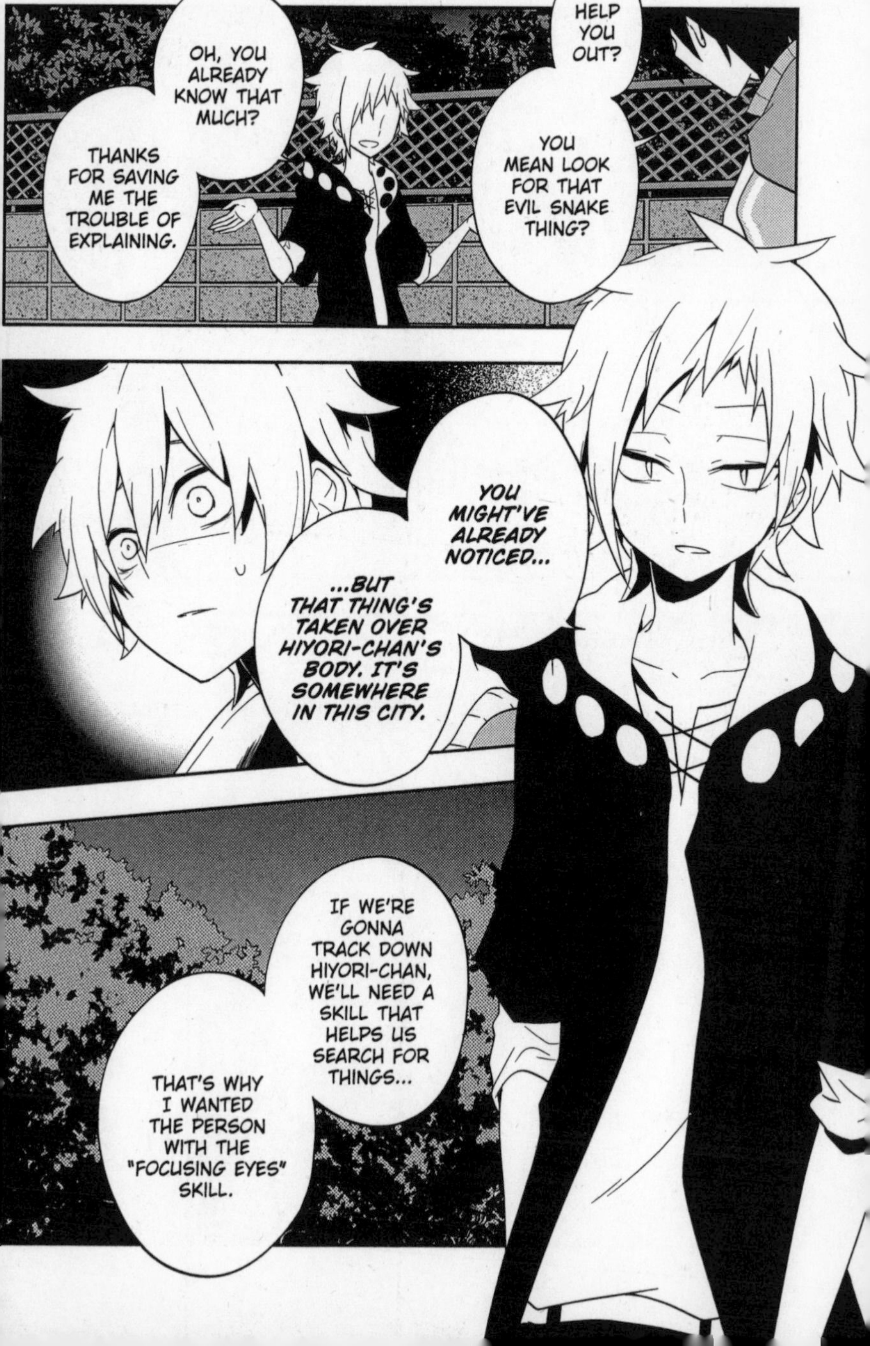
HELP YOU OUT?
YOU MEAN LOOK FOR THAT EVIL SNAKE THING?
OH, YOU ALREADY KNOW THAT MUCH?
THANKS FOR SAVING ME THE TROUBLE OF EXPLAINING.
YOU MIGHT'VE ALREADY NOTICED...
...BUT THAT THING'S TAKEN OVER HIYORI-CHAN'S BODY. IT'S SOMEWHERE IN THIS CITY.
IF WE'RE GONNA TRACK DOWN HIYORI-CHAN, WE'LL NEED A SKILL THAT HELPS US SEARCH FOR THINGS...
THAT'S WHY I WANTED THE PERSON WITH THE "FOCUSING EYES" SKILL.

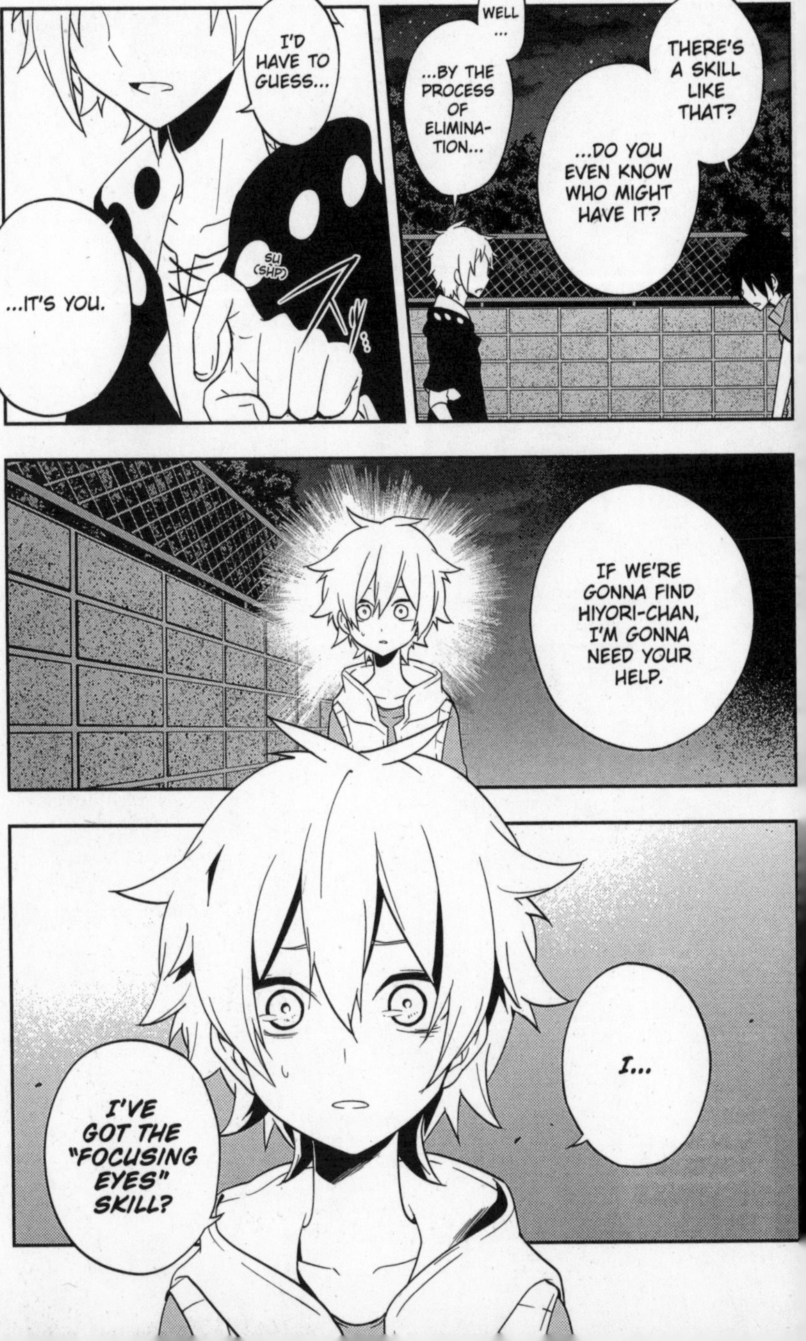
THERE'S A SKILL LIKE THAT?
...DO YOU EVEN KNOW WHO MIGHT HAVE IT?
WELL ...
...BY THE PROCESS OF ELIMINATION...
I'D HAVE TO GUESS...
SU (SHP)
...IT'S YOU.
IF WE'RE GONNA FIND HIYORI-CHAN, I'M GONNA NEED YOUR HELP.
I...
I'VE GOT THE "FOCUSING EYES" SKILL?

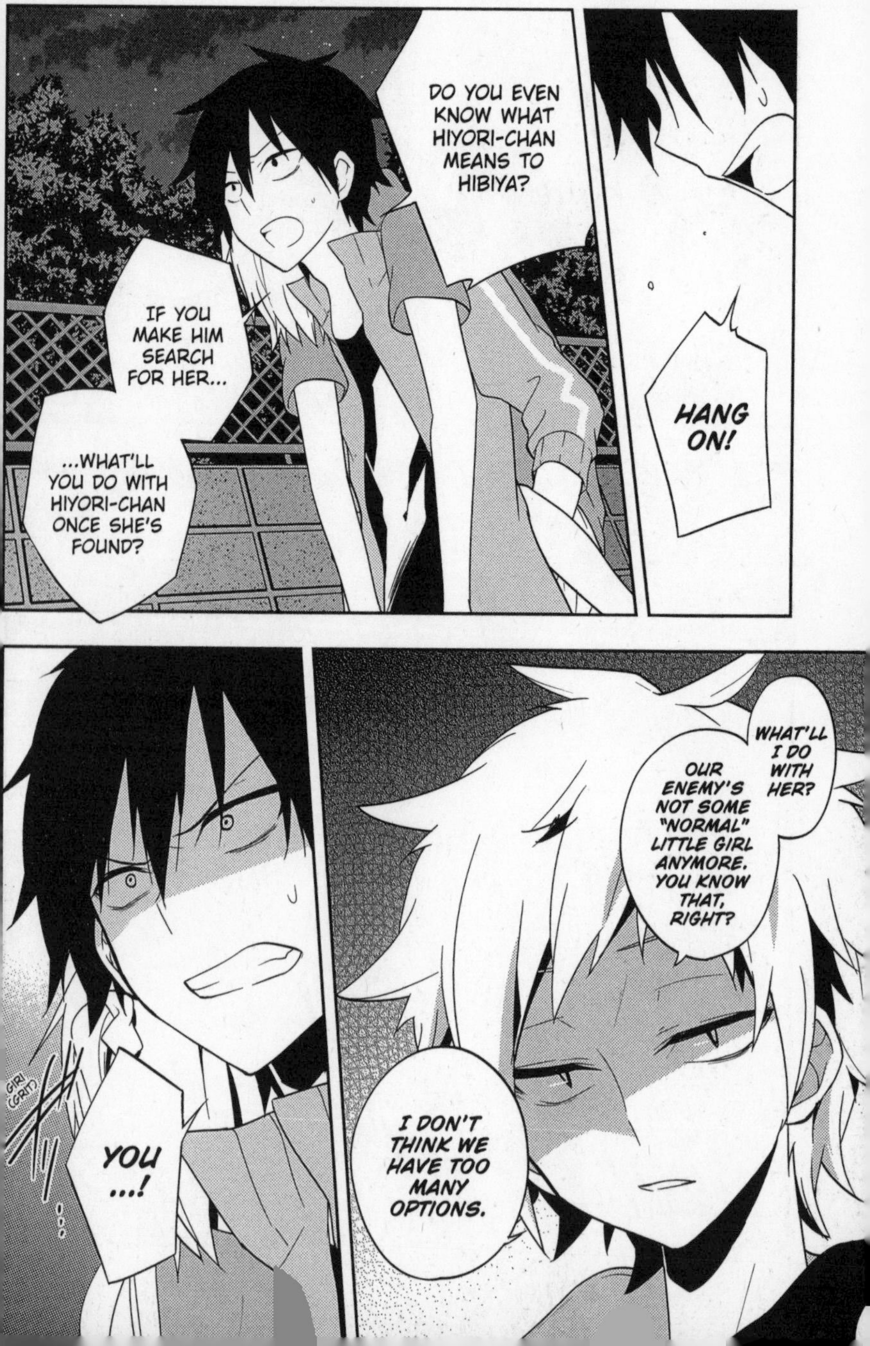
HANG ON!
DO YOU EVEN KNOW WHAT HIYORI-CHAN MEANS TO HIBIYA?
IF YOU MAKE HIM SEARCH FOR HER...
...WHAT'LL YOU DO WITH HIYORI-CHAN ONCE SHE'S FOUND?
WHAT'LL I DO WITH HER?
OUR ENEMY'S NOT SOME "NORMAL" LITTLE GIRL ANYMORE. YOU KNOW THAT, RIGHT?
I DON'T THINK WE HAVE TOO MANY OPTIONS.
GIRI (GRIT)
YOU...!

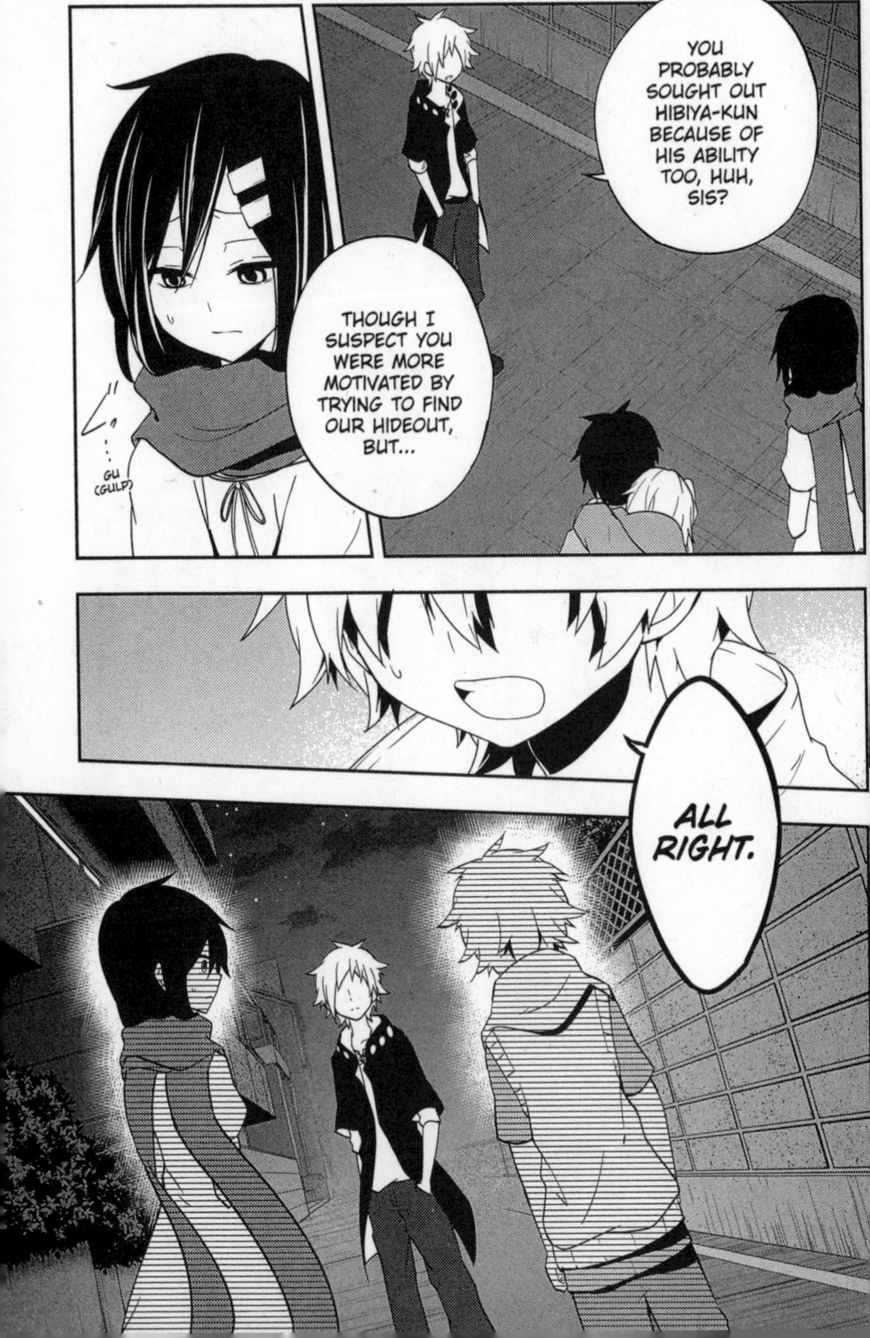
YOU PROBABLY SOUGHT OUT HIBIYA-KUN BECAUSE OF HIS ABILITY TOO, HUH, SIS?
THOUGH I SUSPECT YOU WERE MORE MOTIVATED BY TRYING TO FIND OUR HIDEOUT, BUT...
GU (GULP)
ALL RIGHT.

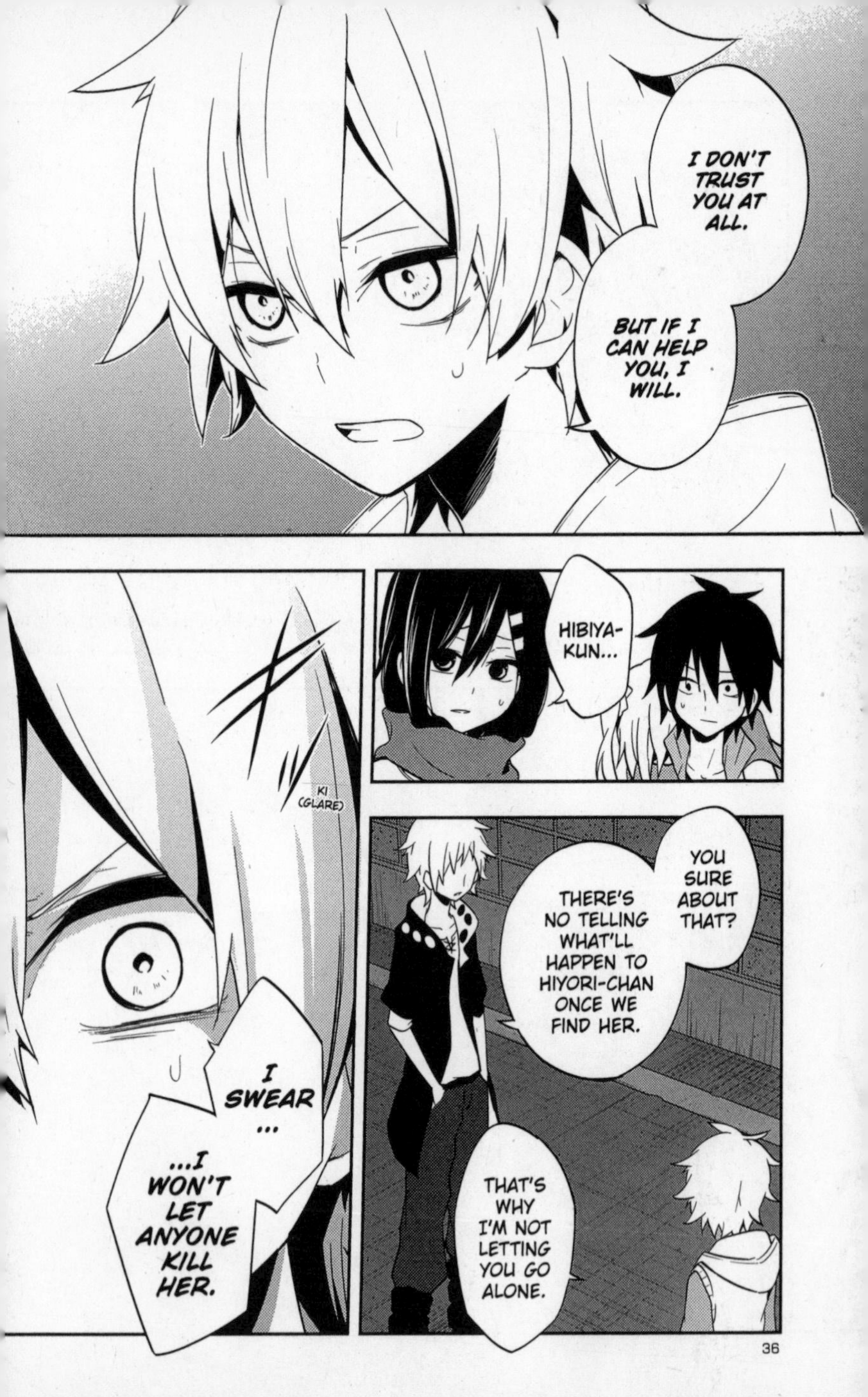
I DON'T TRUST YOU AT ALL.
BUT IF I CAN HELP YOU, I WILL.
HIBIYA-KUN...
YOU SURE ABOUT THAT?
THERE'S NO TELLING WHAT'LL HAPPEN TO HIYORI-CHAN ONCE WE FIND HER.
THAT'S WHY I'M NOT LETTING YOU GO ALONE.
KI (GLARE)
I SWEAR...
...I WON'T LET ANYONE KILL HER.

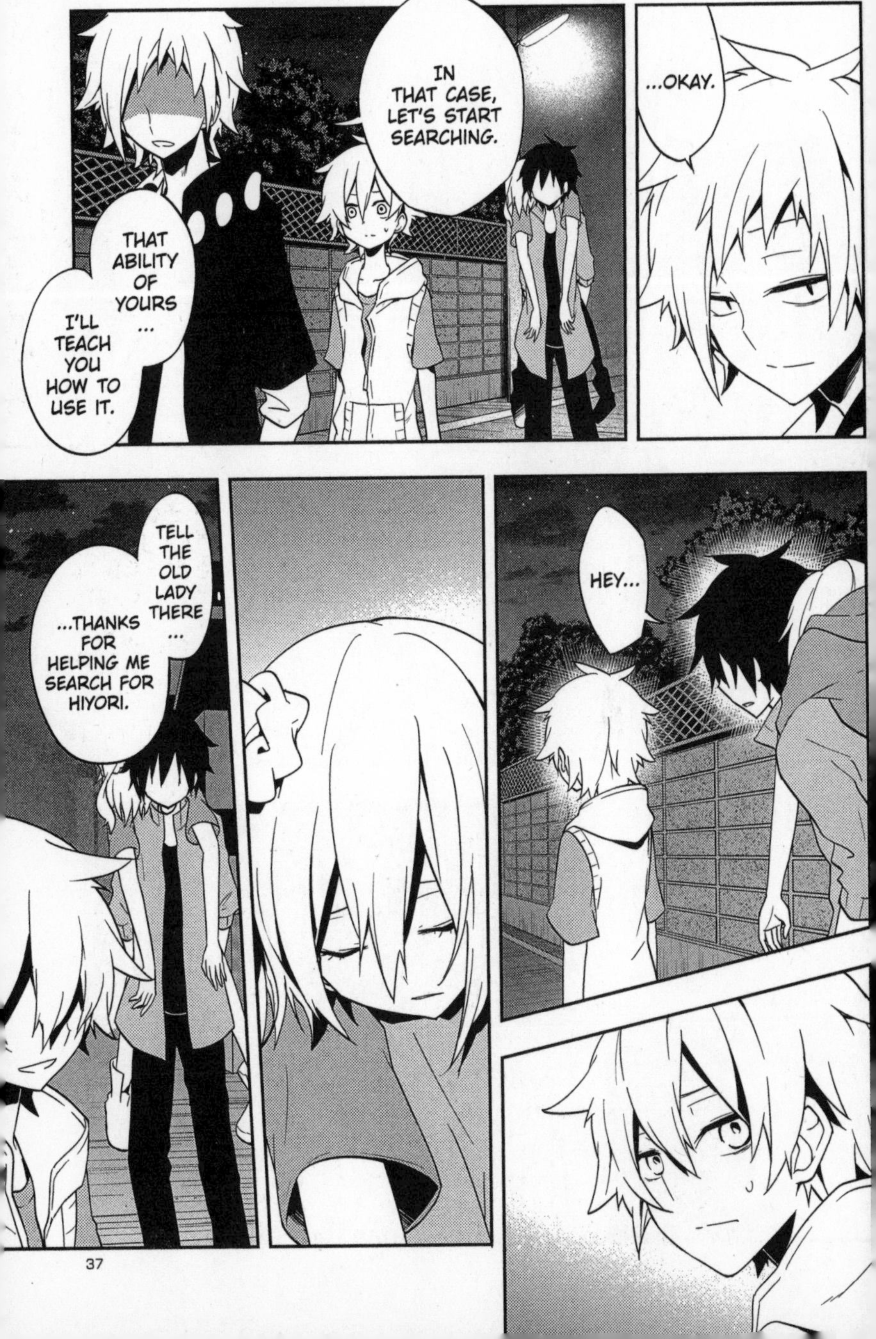
...OKAY.
IN THAT CASE, LET'S START SEARCHING.
THAT ABILITY OF YOURS ...
I'LL TEACH YOU HOW TO USE IT.
HEY...
TELL THE OLD LADY THERE ...
...THANKS FOR HELPING ME SEARCH FOR HIYORI.

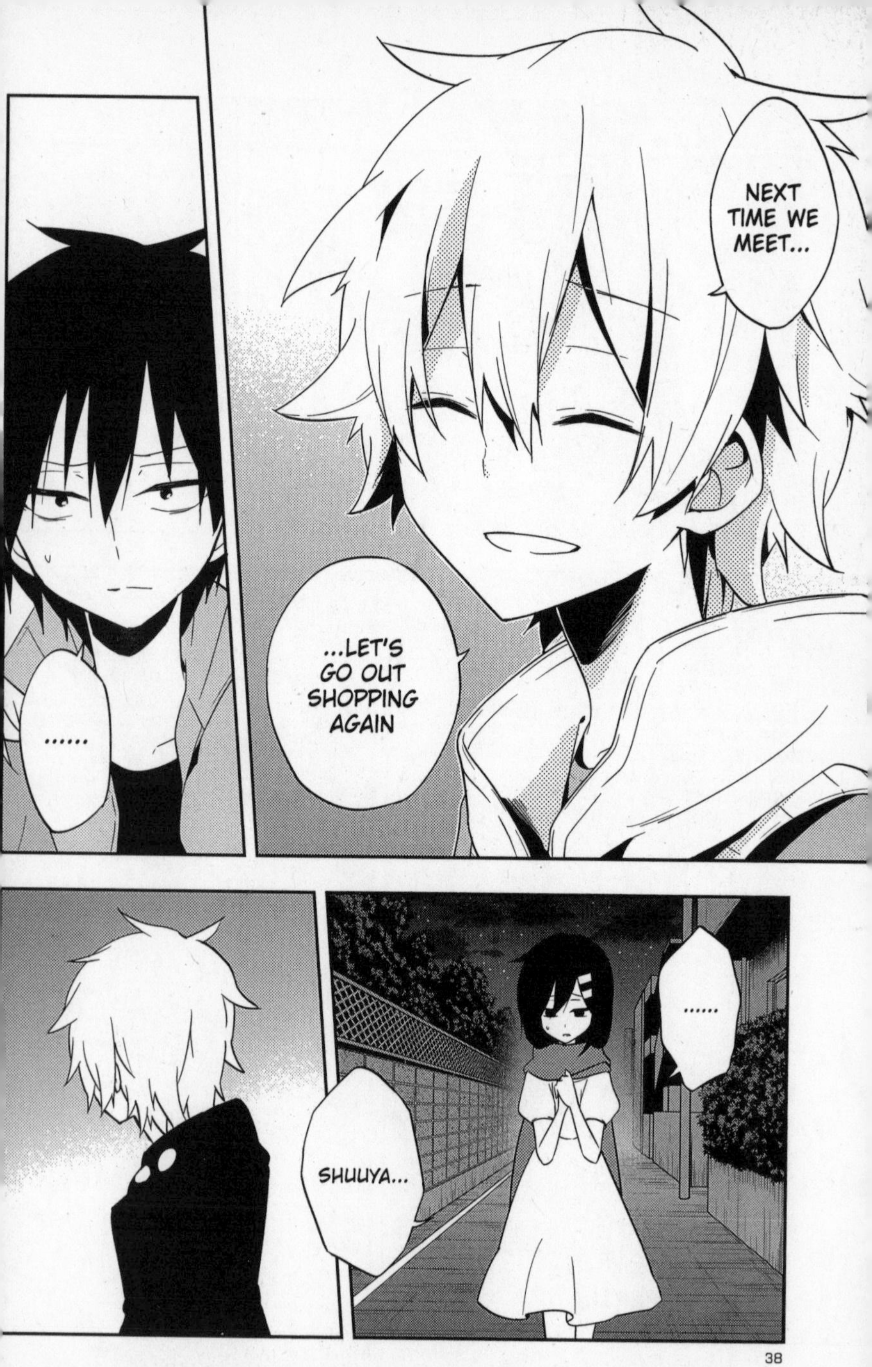
NEXT TIME WE MEET...
...LET'S GO OUT SHOPPING AGAIN
......
......
SHUUYA...

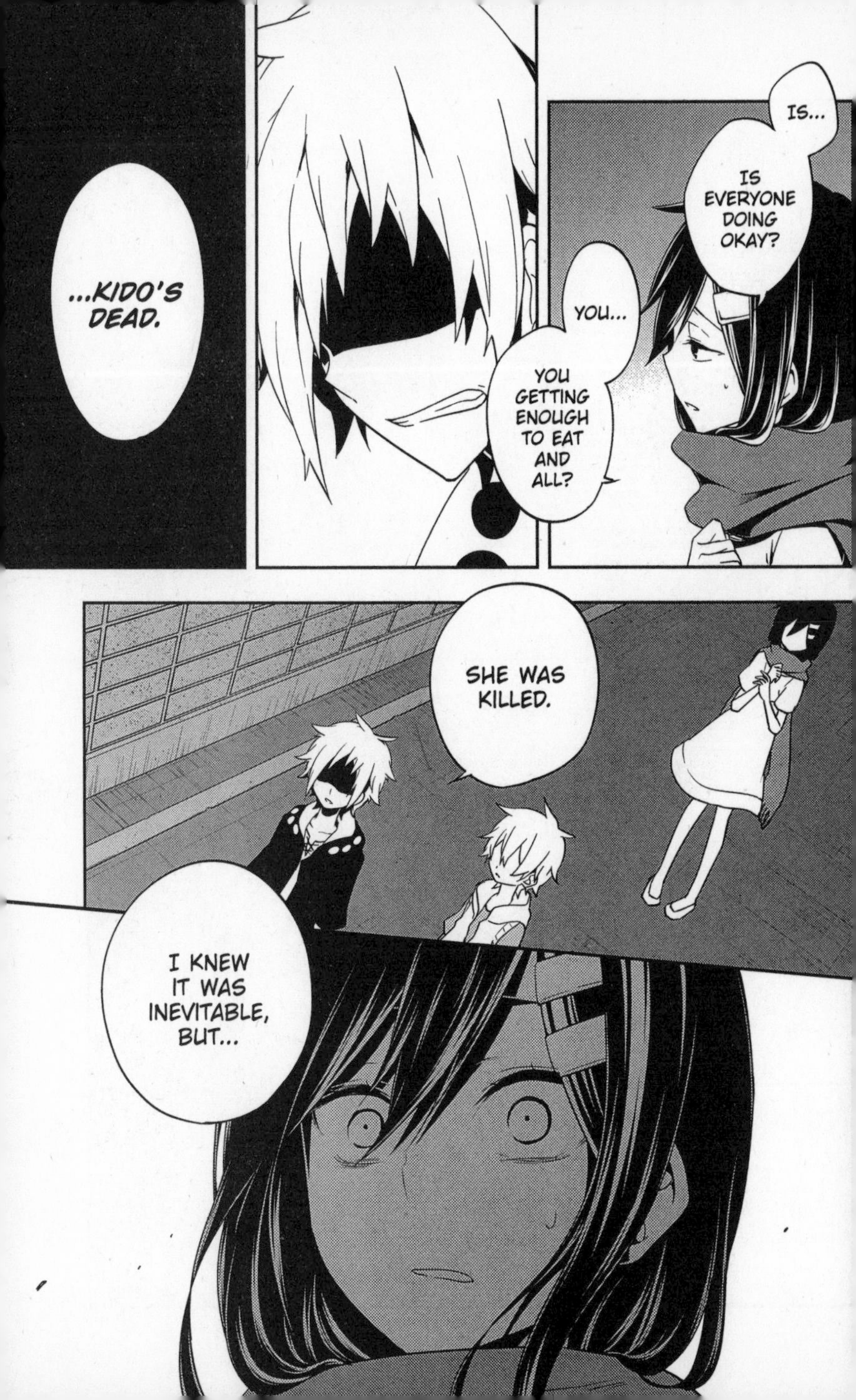
IS...
IS EVERYONE DOING OKAY?
YOU...
YOU GETTING ENOUGH TO EAT AND ALL?
...KIDO'S DEAD.
SHE WAS KILLED.
I KNEW IT WAS INEVITABLE, BUT...

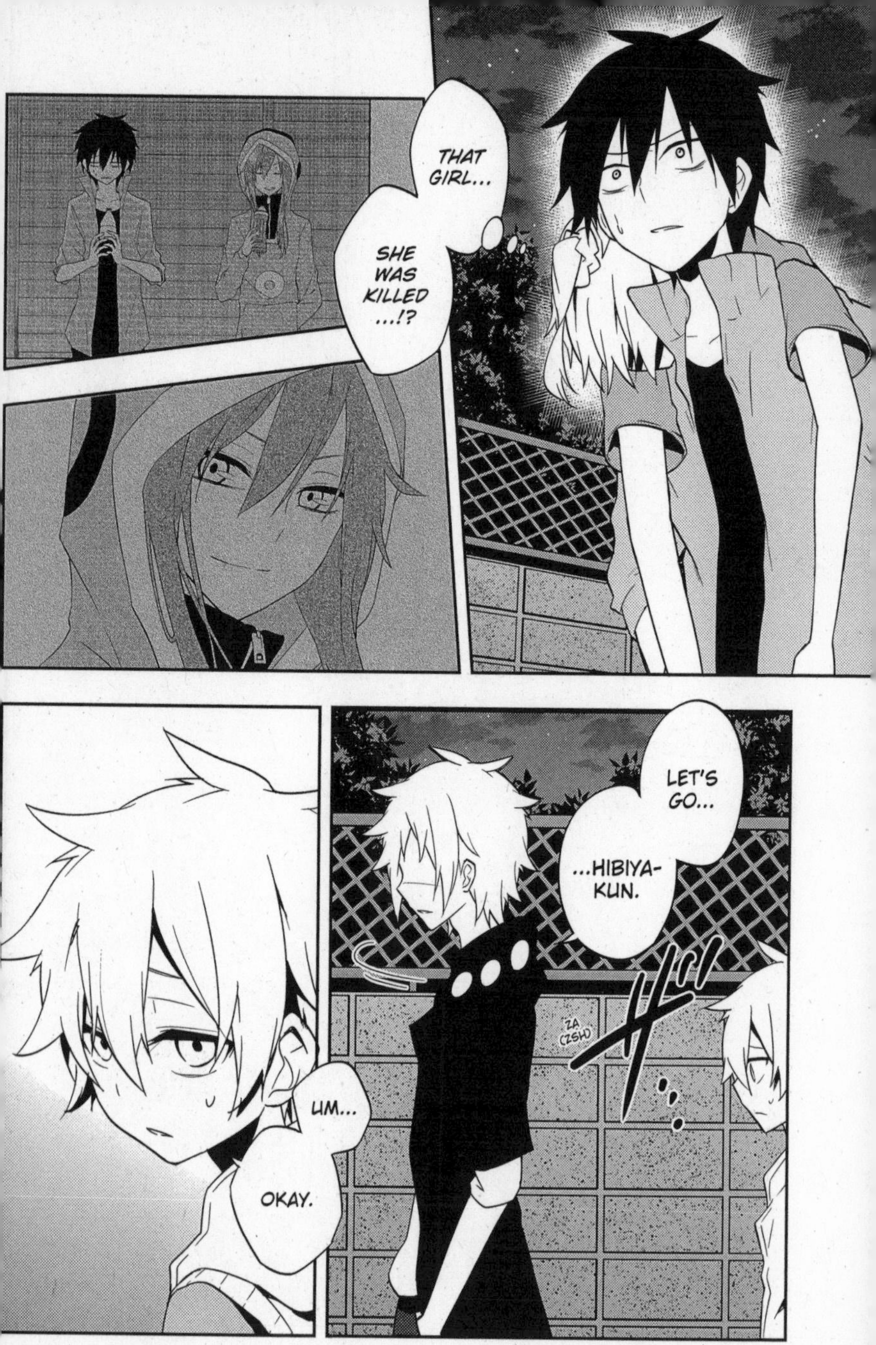
THAT GIRL...
SHE WAS KILLED ...!?
LET'S GO...
...HIBIYA-KUN.
ZA (ZSH)
UM...
OKAY.

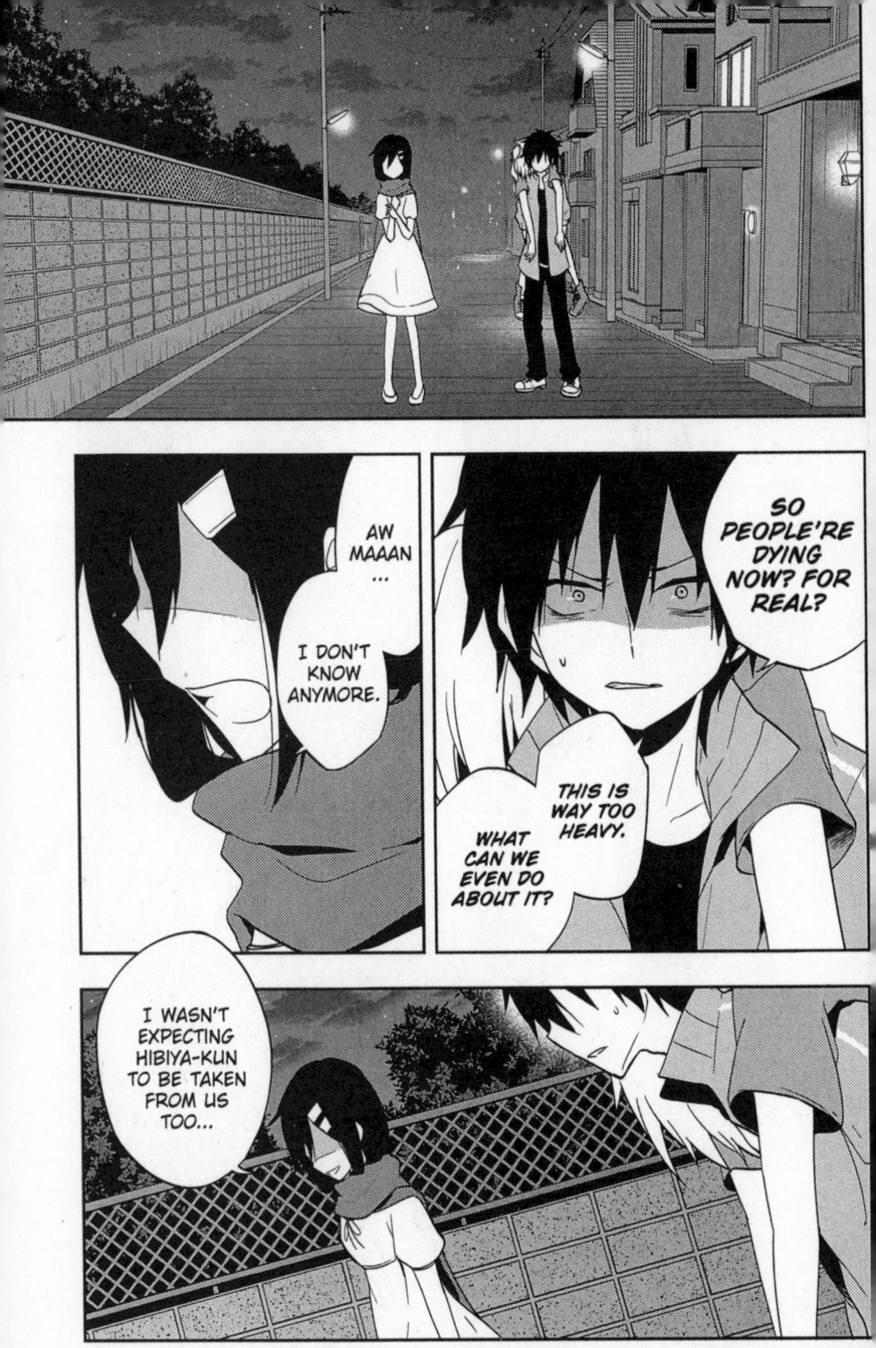
SO PEOPLE'RE DYING NOW? FOR REAL?
THIS IS WAY TOO HEAVY.
WHAT CAN WE EVEN DO ABOUT IT?
AW MAAAN ...
I DON'T KNOW ANYMORE.
I WASN'T EXPECTING HIBIYA-KUN TO BE TAKEN FROM US TOO...

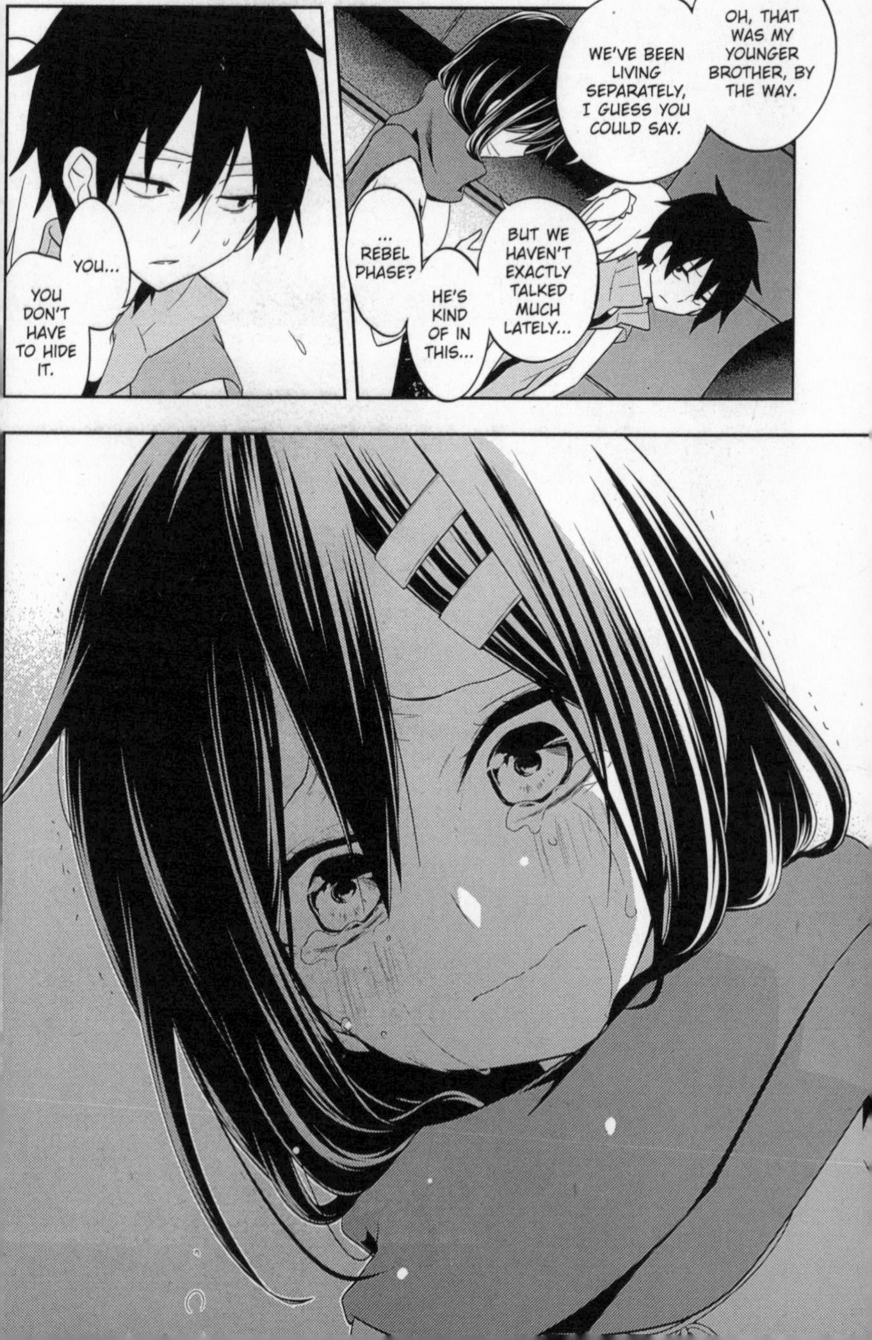
OH, THAT WAS MY YOUNGER BROTHER, BY THE WAY.
WE'VE BEEN LIVING SEPARATELY, I GUESS YOU COULD SAY.
BUT WE HAVEN'T EXACTLY TALKED MUCH LATELY...
HE'S KIND OF IN THIS...
... REBEL PHASE?
YOU...
YOU DON'T HAVE TO HIDE IT.

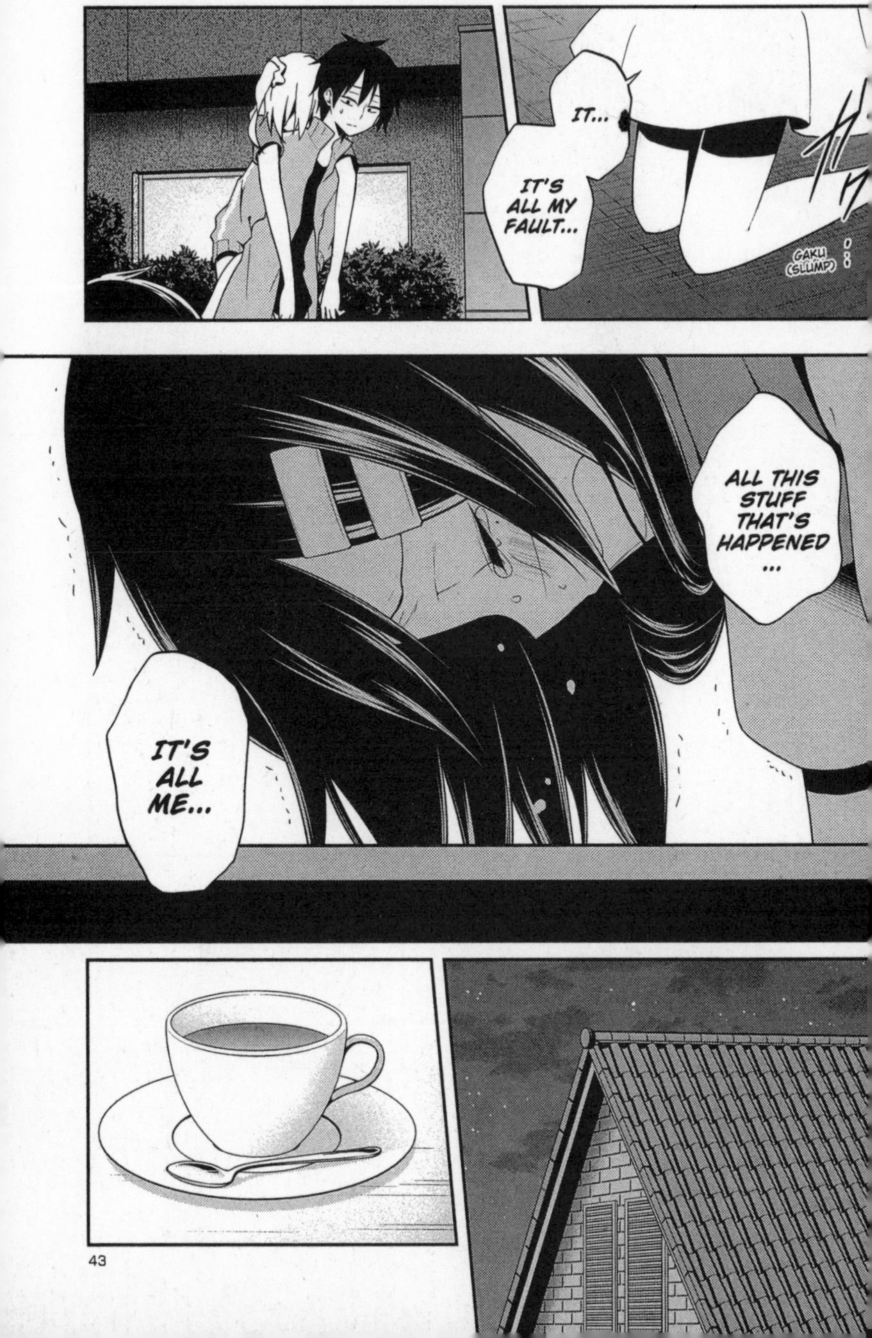
IT...
IT'S ALL MY FAULT...
GAKU (SLUMP)
ALL THIS STUFF THAT'S HAPPENED...
IT'S ALL ME...

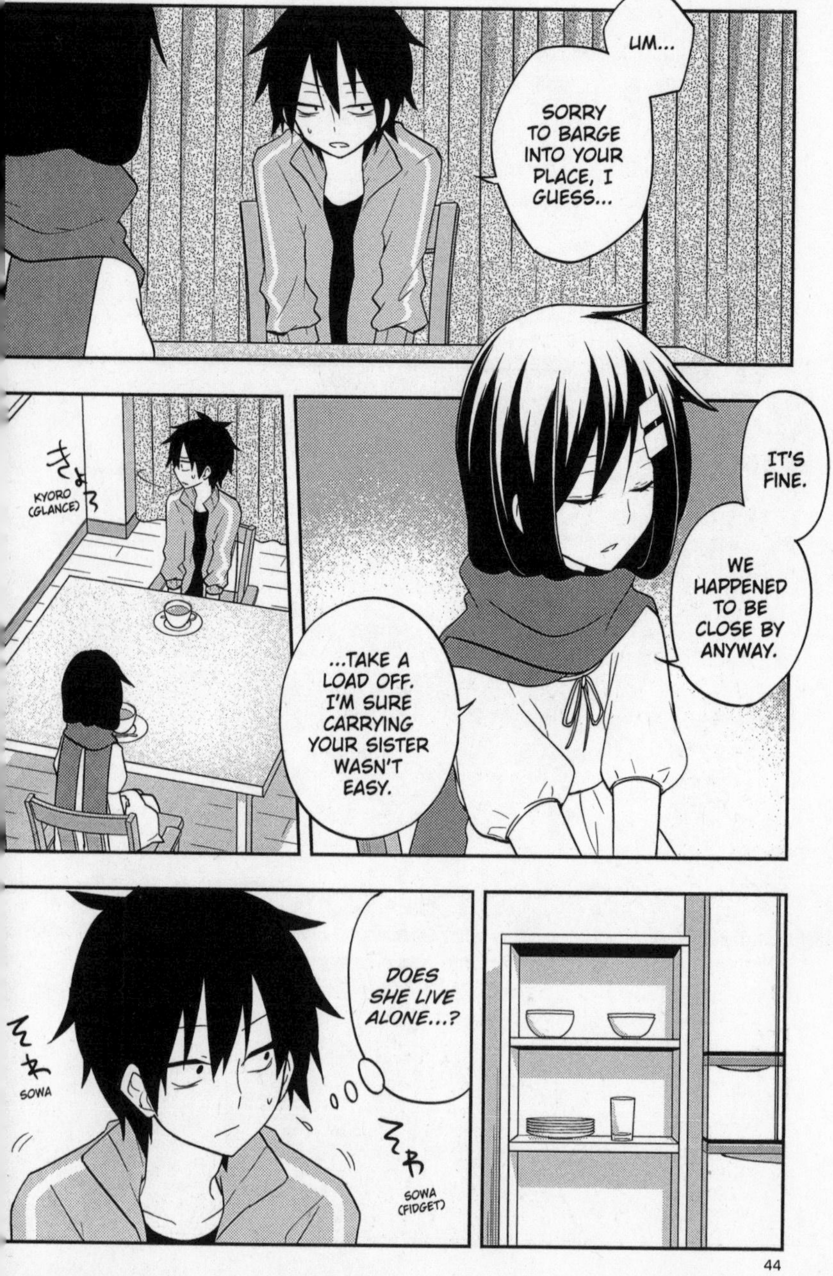
UM...
SORRY TO BARGE INTO YOUR PLACE, I GUESS...
IT'S FINE.
WE HAPPENED TO BE CLOSE BY ANYWAY.
...TAKE A LOAD OFF. I'M SURE CARRYING YOUR SISTER WASN'T EASY.
きょろ
KYORO (GLANCE)
DOES SHE LIVE ALONE...?
そわ
SOWA (FIDGET)
そわ
SOWA

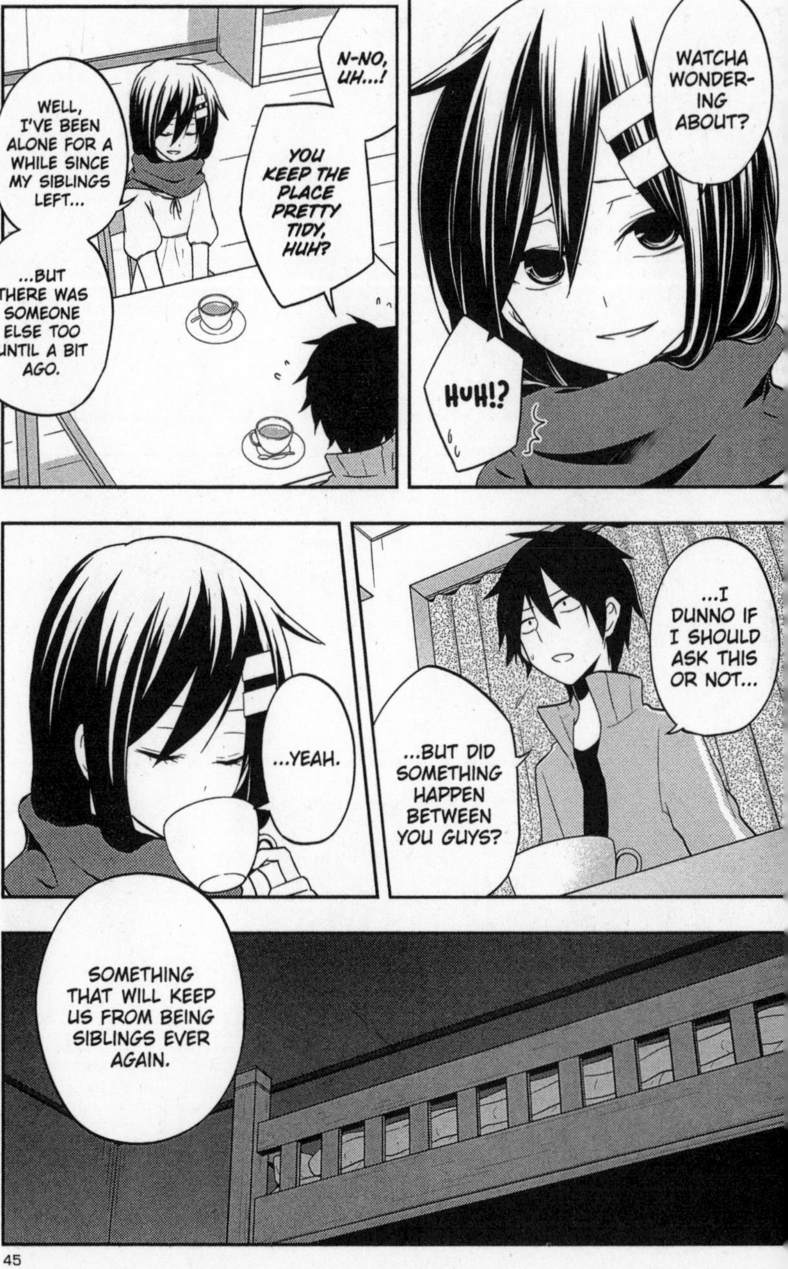
WATCHA WONDERING ABOUT?
HUH!?
N-NO, UH...!
YOU KEEP THE PLACE PRETTY TIDY, HUH?
WELL, I'VE BEEN ALONE FOR A WHILE SINCE MY SIBLINGS LEFT...
...BUT THERE WAS SOMEONE ELSE TOO UNTIL A BIT AGO.
...I DUNNO IF I SHOULD ASK THIS OR NOT...
...BUT DID SOMETHING HAPPEN BETWEEN YOU GUYS?
...YEAH.
SOMETHING THAT WILL KEEP US FROM BEING SIBLINGS EVER AGAIN.

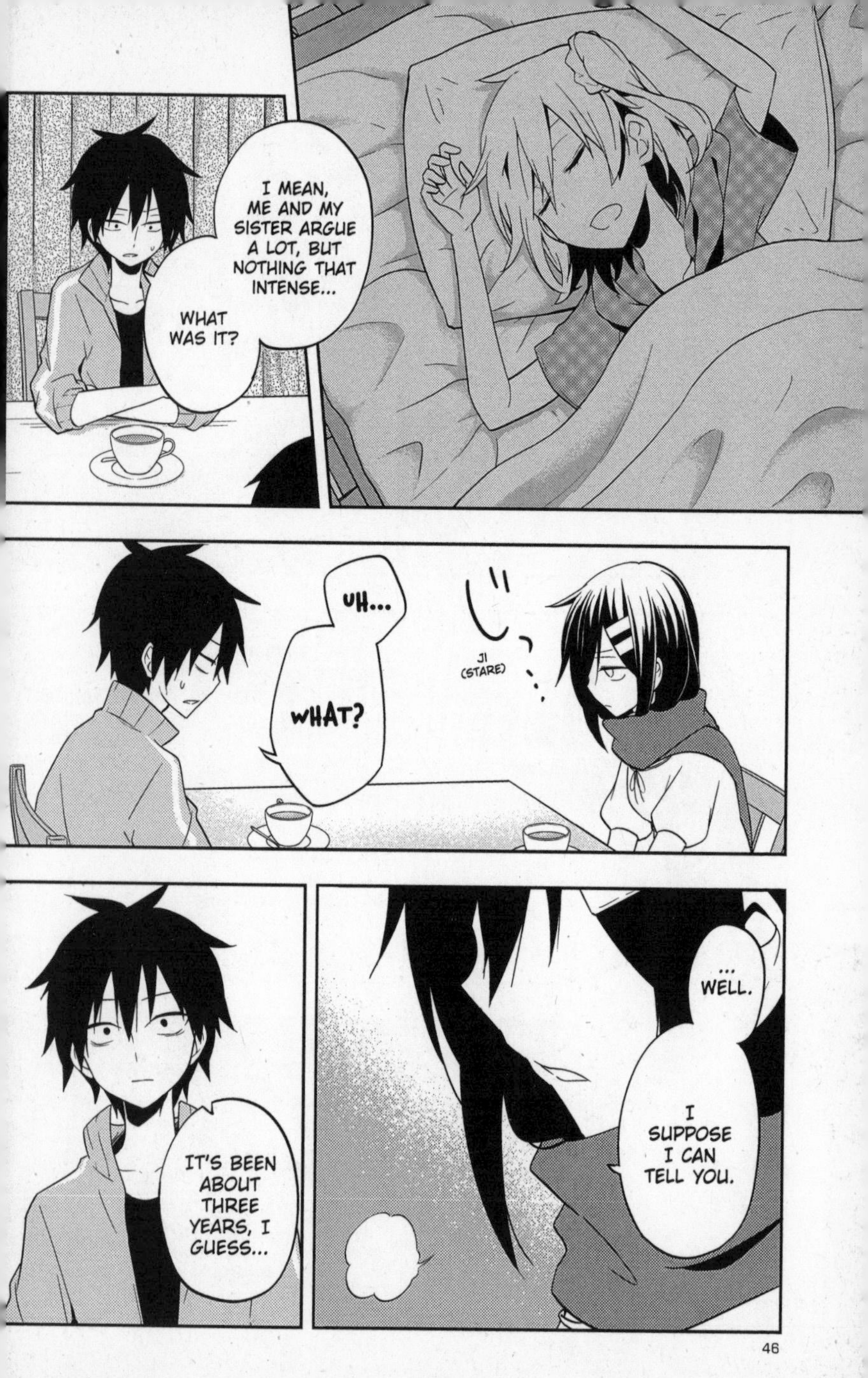
I MEAN, ME AND MY SISTER ARGUE A LOT, BUT NOTHING THAT INTENSE...
WHAT WAS IT?
JI (STARE)
UH...
WHAT?
... WELL.
I SUPPOSE I CAN TELL YOU.
IT'S BEEN ABOUT THREE YEARS, I GUESS...

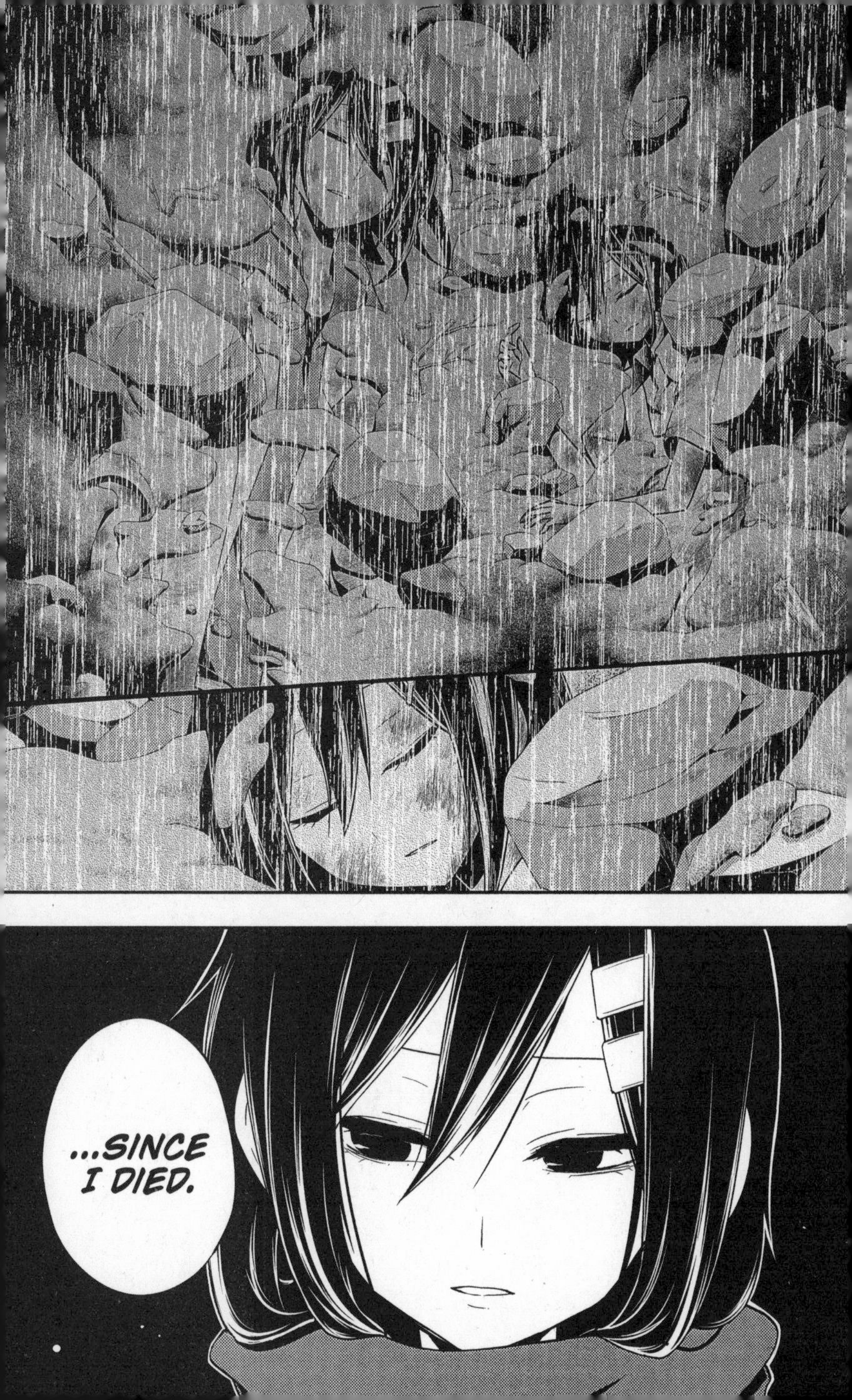
...SINCE I DIED.

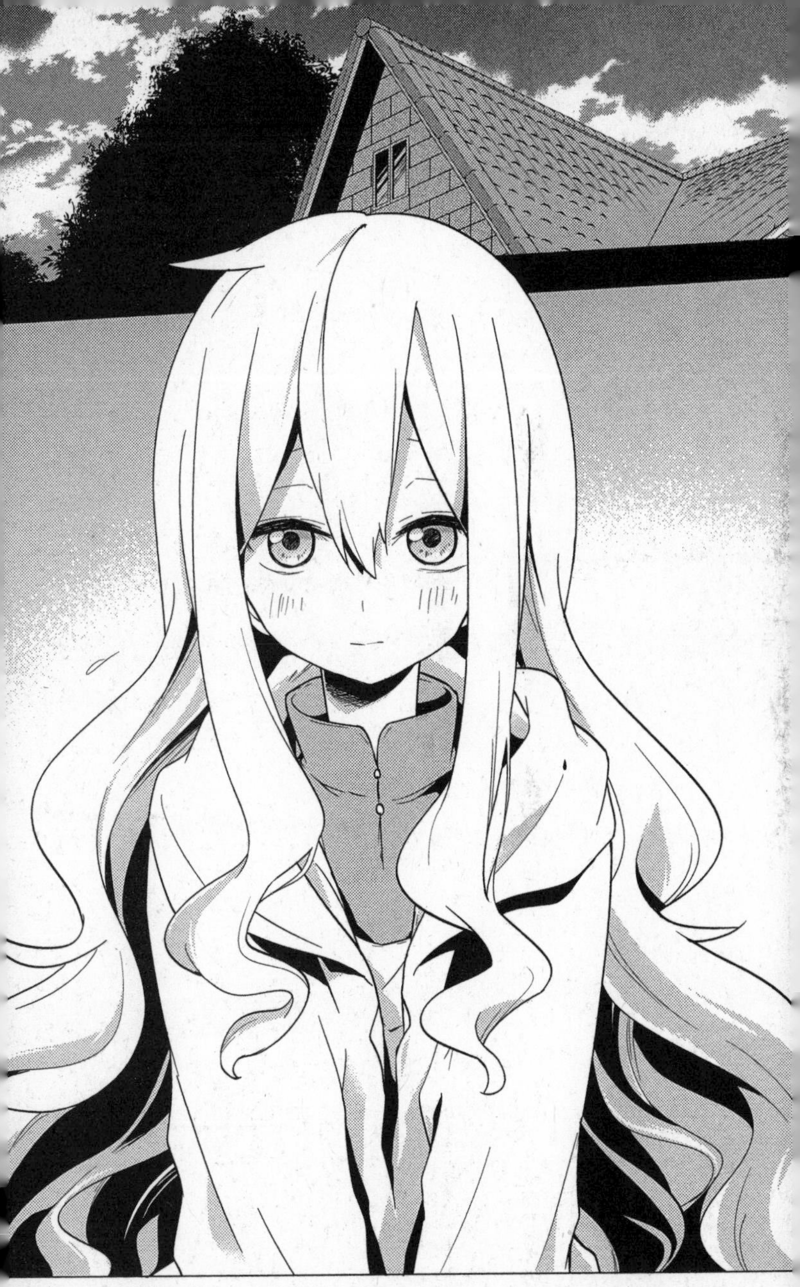

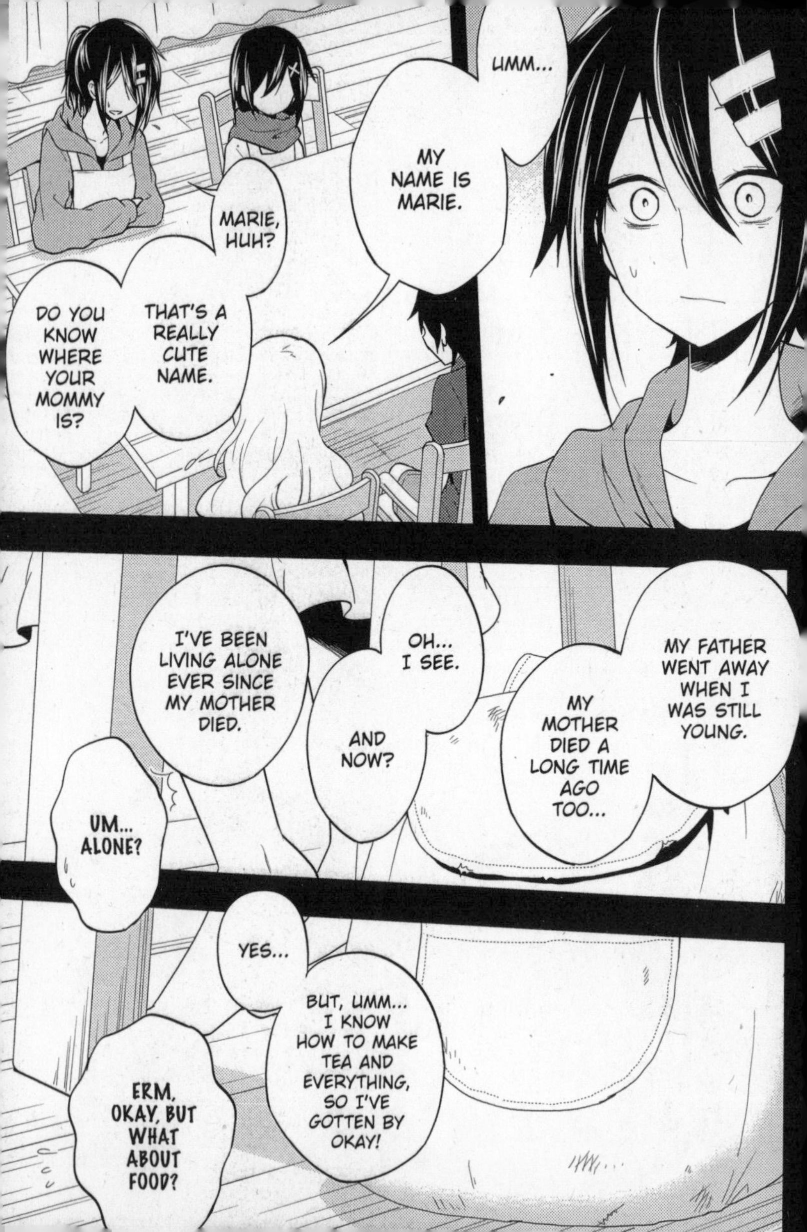
UMM...
MY NAME IS MARIE.
MARIE, HUH?
THAT'S A REALLY CUTE NAME.
DO YOU KNOW WHERE YOUR MOMMY IS?
MY FATHER WENT AWAY WHEN I WAS STILL YOUNG.
MY MOTHER DIED A LONG TIME AGO TOO...
OH... I SEE.
AND NOW?
I'VE BEEN LIVING ALONE EVER SINCE MY MOTHER DIED.
UM... ALONE?
YES...
BUT, UMM... I KNOW HOW TO MAKE TEA AND EVERYTHING, SO I'VE GOTTEN BY OKAY!
ERM, OKAY, BUT WHAT ABOUT FOOD?

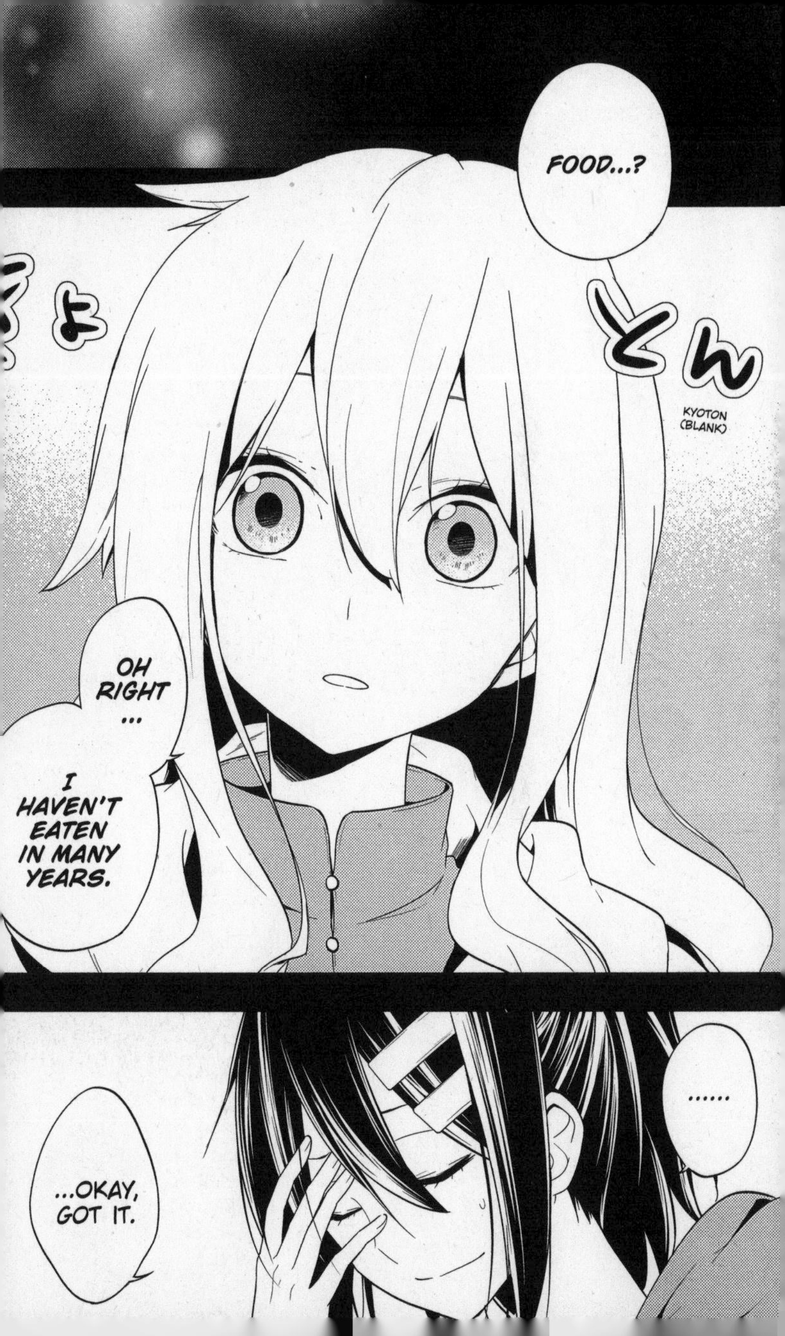
FOOD...?
KYOTON (BLANK)
OH RIGHT ...
I HAVEN'T EATEN IN MANY YEARS.
......
...OKAY, GOT IT.

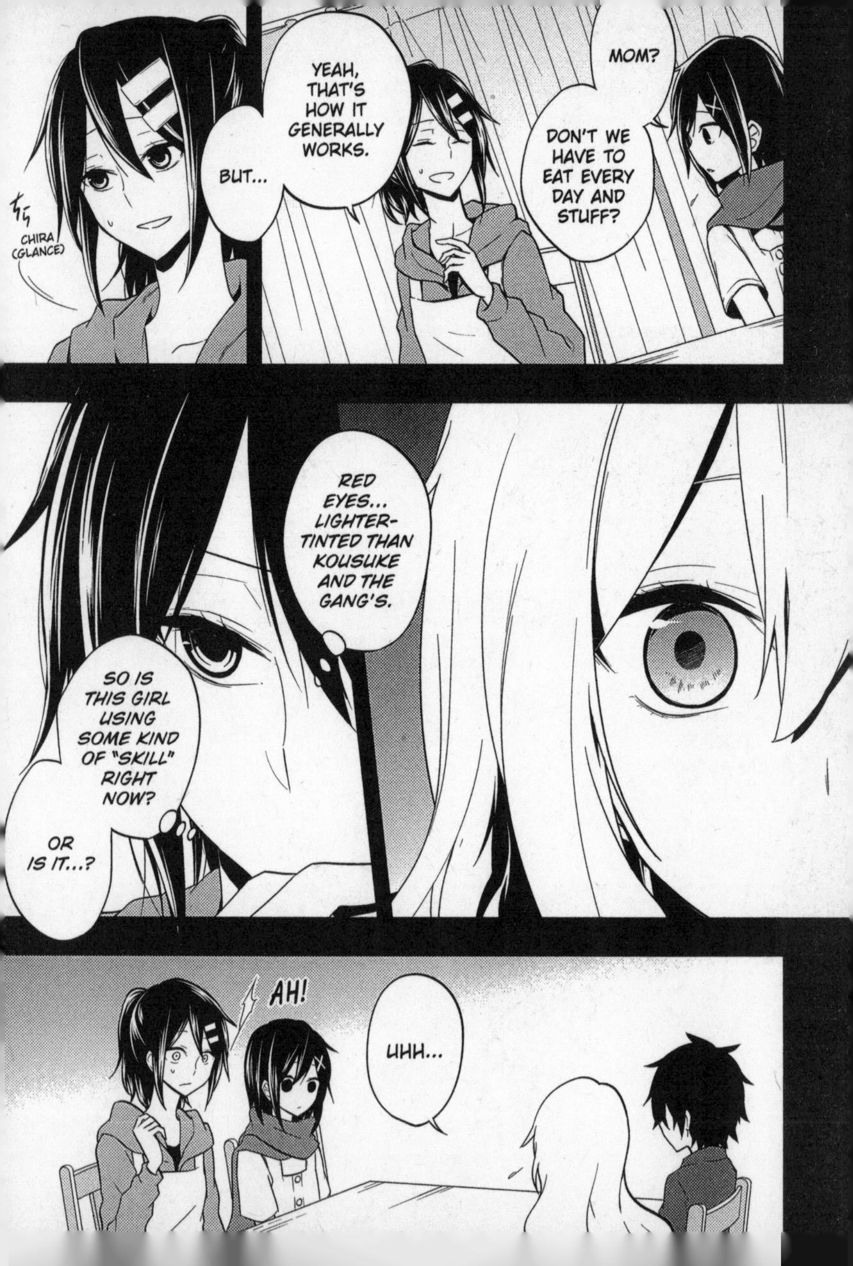
MOM?
DON'T WE HAVE TO EAT EVERY DAY AND STUFF?
YEAH, THAT'S HOW IT GENERALLY WORKS.
BUT...
ちら
CHIRA (GLANCE)
RED EYES... LIGHTER-TINTED THAN KOUSUKE AND THE GANG'S.
SO IS THIS GIRL USING SOME KIND OF "SKILL" RIGHT NOW?
OR IS IT...?
UHH...
AH!

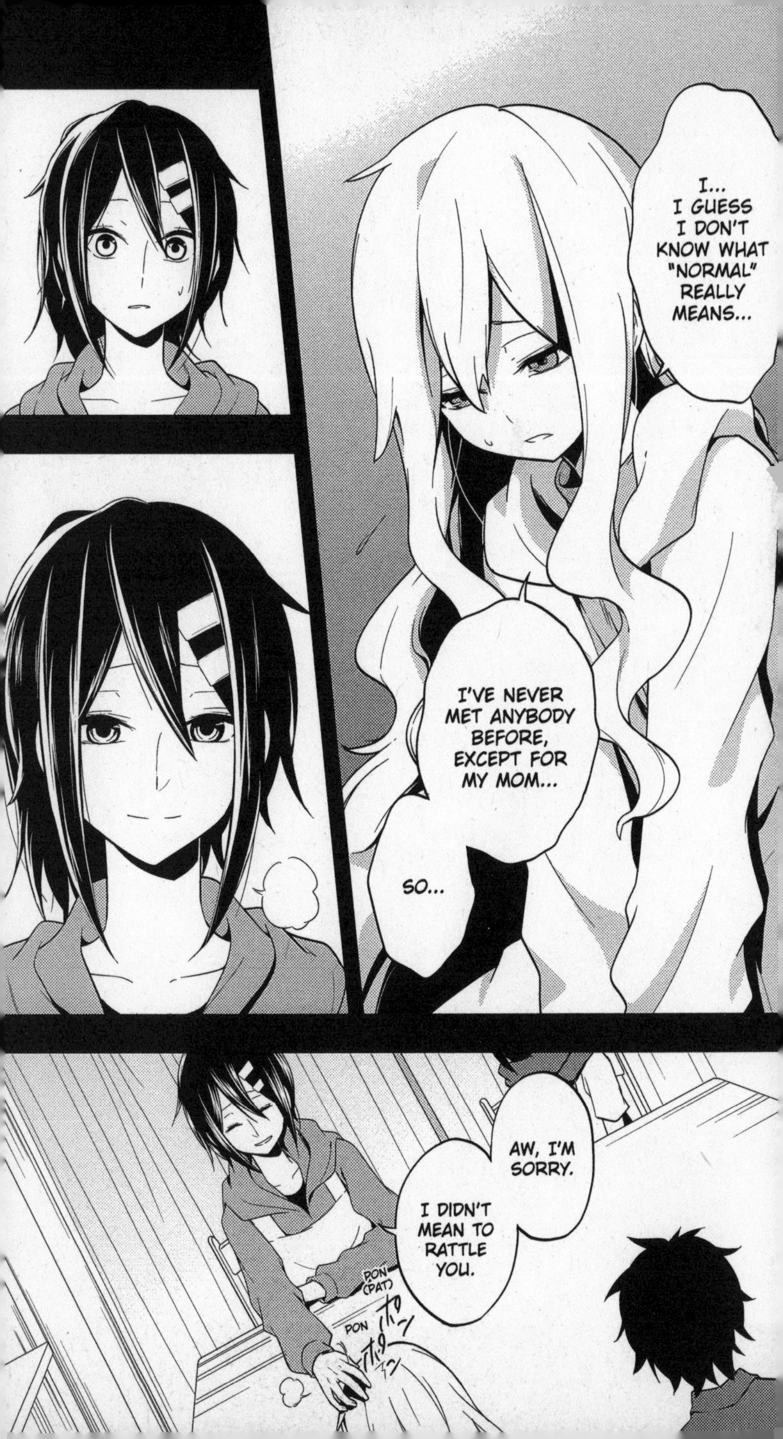
I... I GUESS I DON'T KNOW WHAT "NORMAL" REALLY MEANS...
I'VE NEVER MET ANYBODY BEFORE, EXCEPT FOR MY MOM...
SO...
AW, I'M SORRY.
I DIDN'T MEAN TO RATTLE YOU.
PON (PAT)
PON

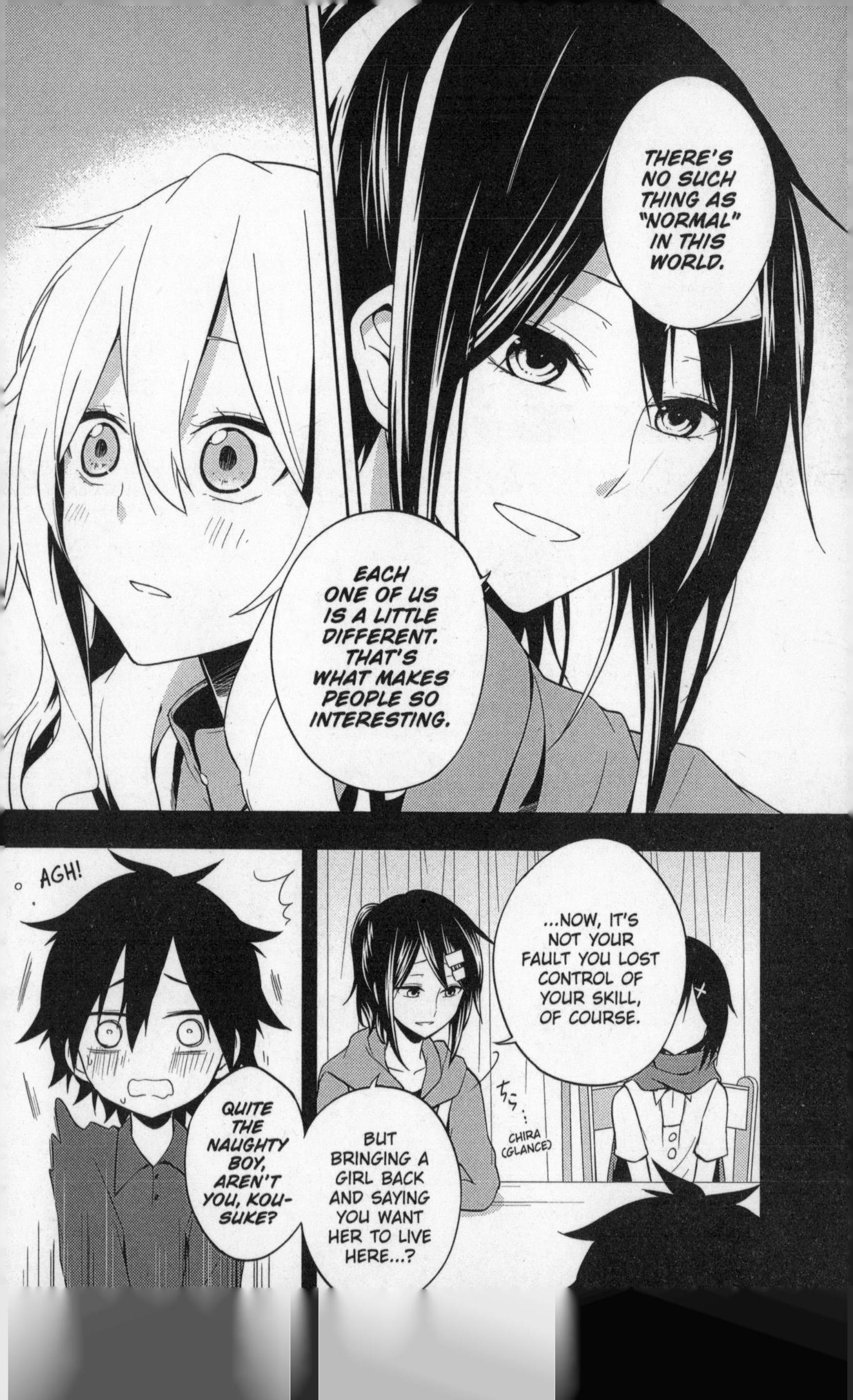
THERE'S NO SUCH THING AS "NORMAL" IN THIS WORLD.
EACH ONE OF US IS A LITTLE DIFFERENT. THAT'S WHAT MAKES PEOPLE SO INTERESTING.
...NOW, IT'S NOT YOUR FAULT YOU LOST CONTROL OF YOUR SKILL, OF COURSE.
ちら…
CHIRA (GLANCE)
BUT BRINGING A GIRL BACK AND SAYING YOU WANT HER TO LIVE HERE...?
QUITE THE NAUGHTY BOY, AREN'T YOU, KOU-SUKE?
AGH!

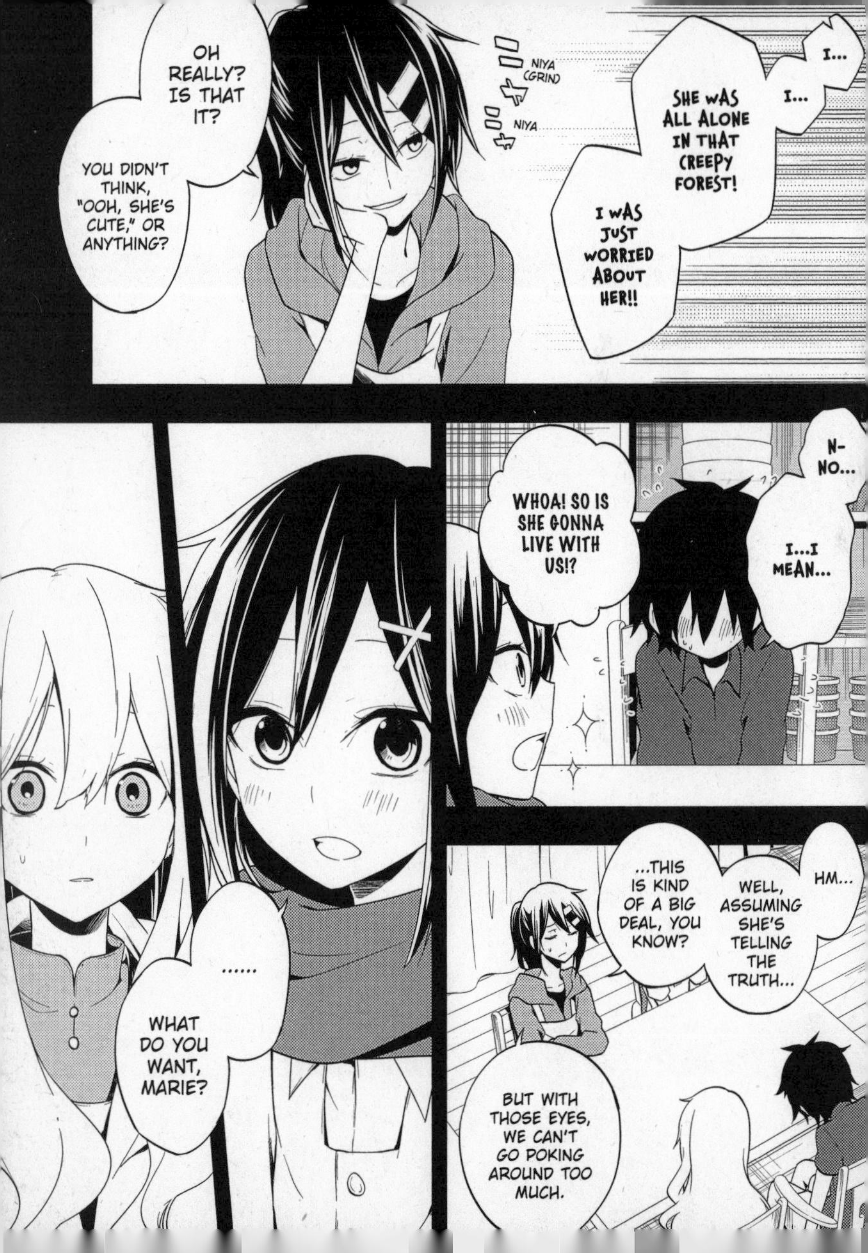
I...
I...
SHE WAS ALL ALONE IN THAT CREEPY FOREST!
I WAS JUST WORRIED ABOUT HER!!
NIYA (GRIN)
NIYA
OH REALLY? IS THAT IT?
YOU DIDN'T THINK, "OOH, SHE'S CUTE," OR ANYTHING?
N-NO...
I...I MEAN...
WHOA! SO IS SHE GONNA LIVE WITH US!?
HM...
WELL, ASSUMING SHE'S TELLING THE TRUTH...
...THIS IS KIND OF A BIG DEAL, YOU KNOW?
BUT WITH THOSE EYES, WE CAN'T GO POKING AROUND TOO MUCH.
......
WHAT DO YOU WANT, MARIE?

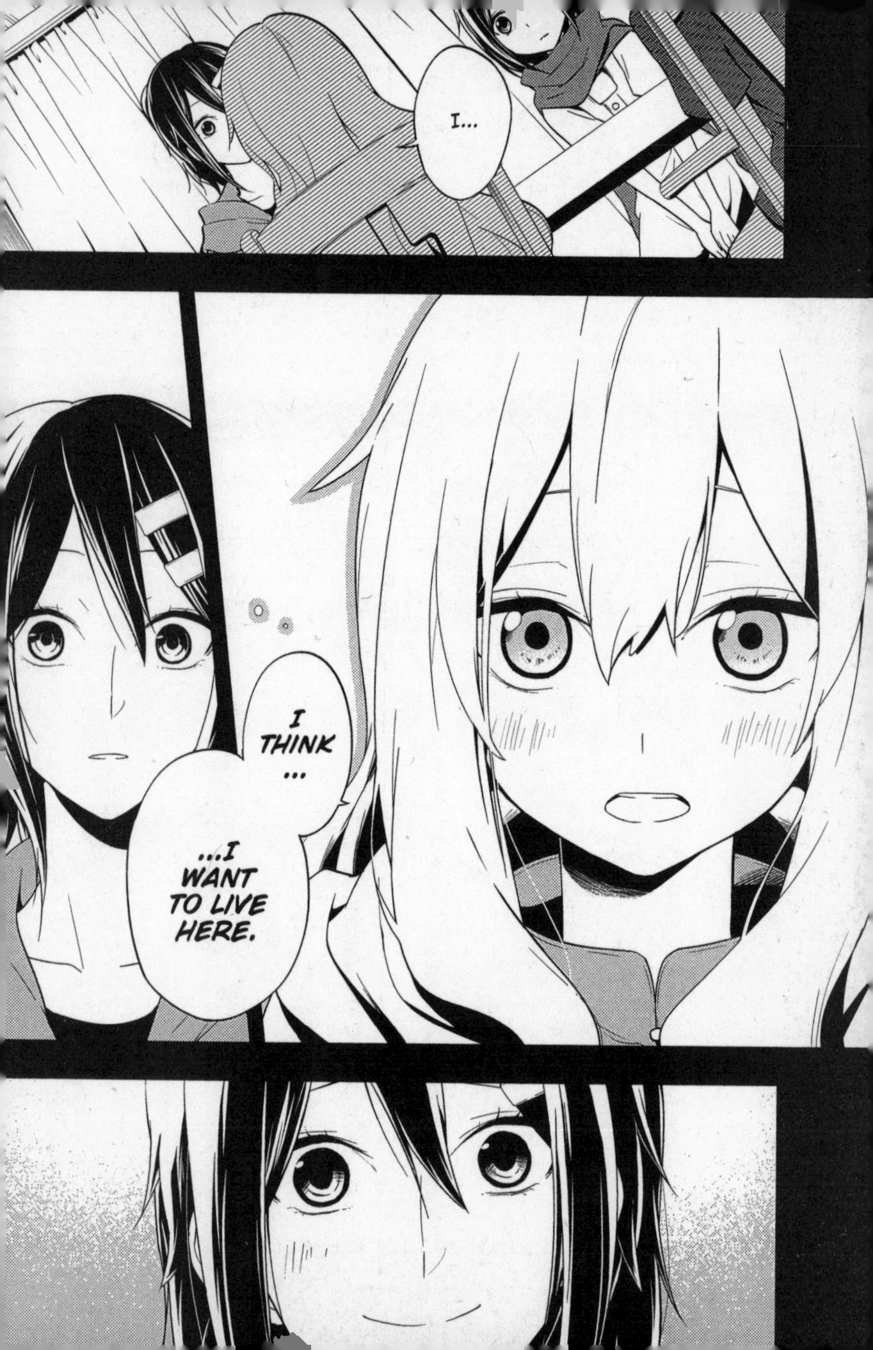
I...
I THINK ...
...I WANT TO LIVE HERE.

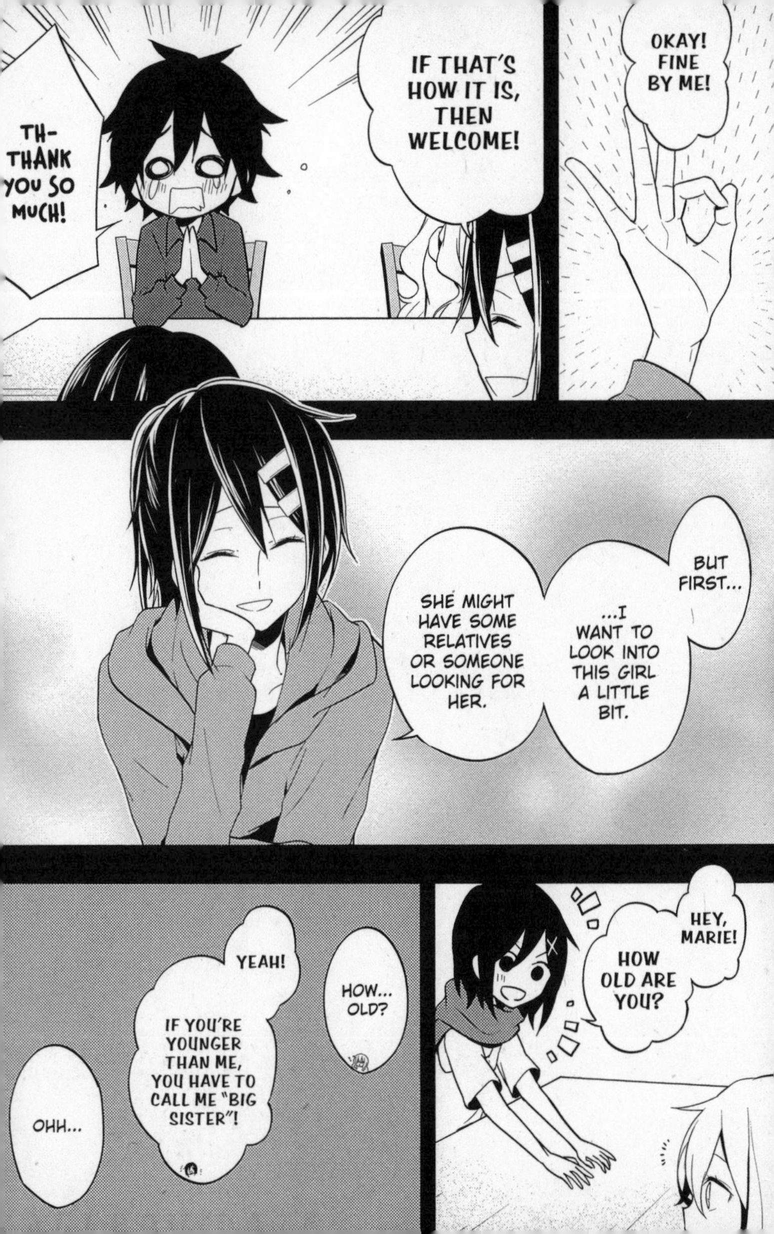
OKAY! FINE BY ME!
IF THAT'S HOW IT IS, THEN WELCOME!
TH-THANK YOU SO MUCH!
BUT FIRST...
...I WANT TO LOOK INTO THIS GIRL A LITTLE BIT.
SHE MIGHT HAVE SOME RELATIVES OR SOMEONE LOOKING FOR HER.
HEY, MARIE!
HOW OLD ARE YOU?
HOW... OLD?
YEAH!
IF YOU'RE YOUNGER THAN ME, YOU HAVE TO CALL ME "BIG SISTER"!
OHH...

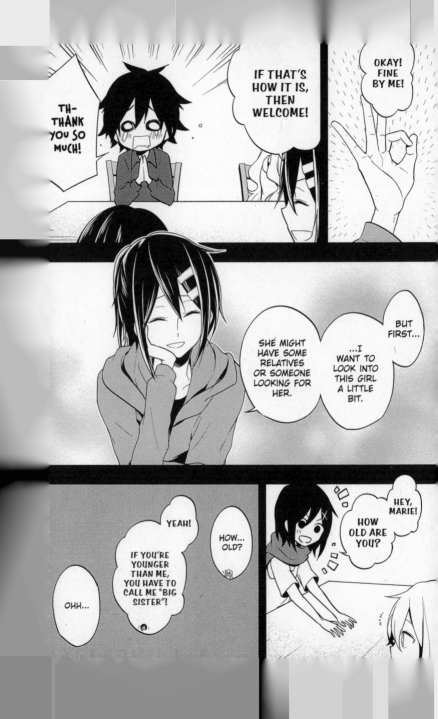

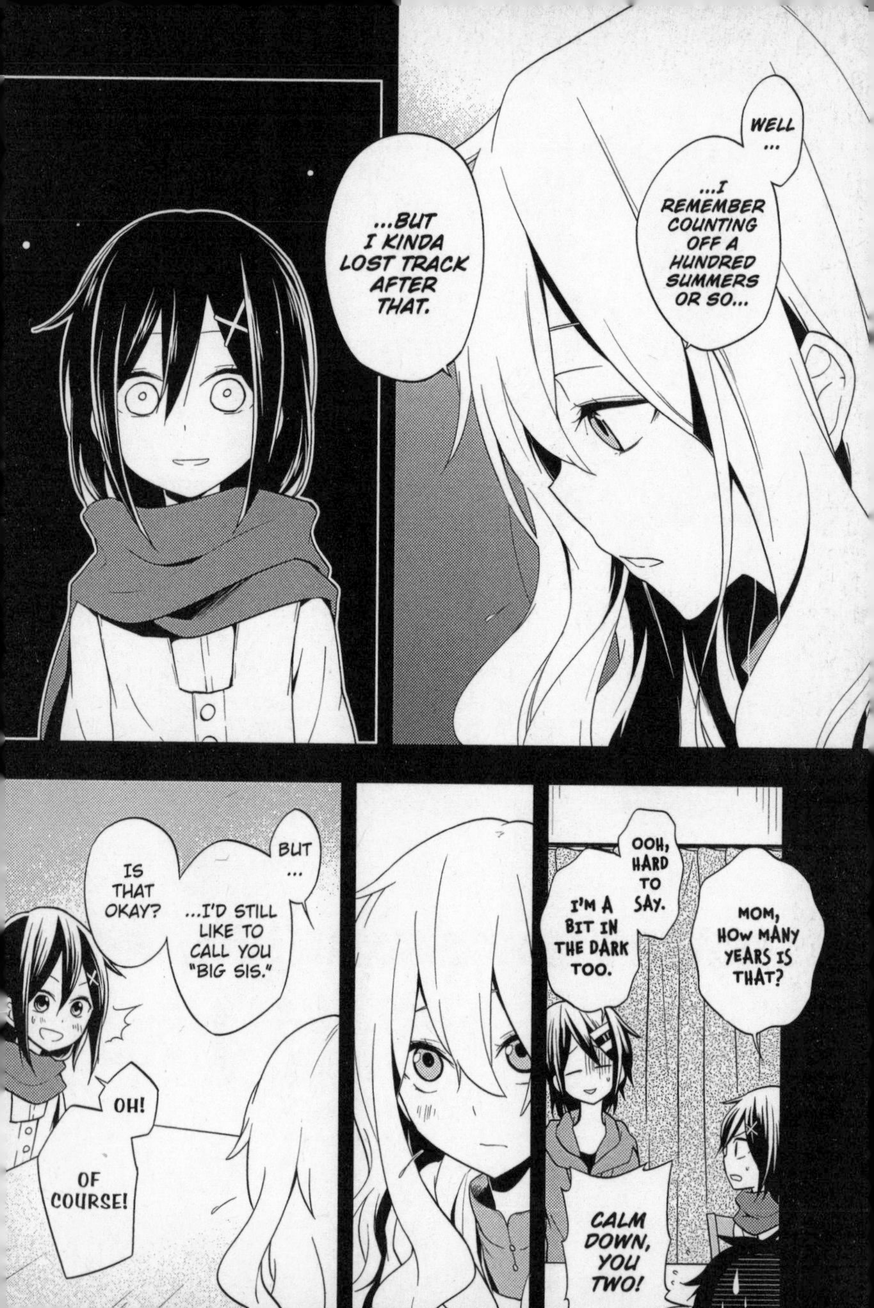
WELL...
...I REMEMBER COUNTING OFF A HUNDRED SUMMERS OR SO...
...BUT I KINDA LOST TRACK AFTER THAT.
MOM, HOW MANY YEARS IS THAT?
OOH, HARD TO SAY.
I'M A BIT IN THE DARK TOO.
CALM DOWN, YOU TWO!
BUT...
...I'D STILL LIKE TO CALL YOU "BIG SIS."
IS THAT OKAY?
OH!
OF COURSE!

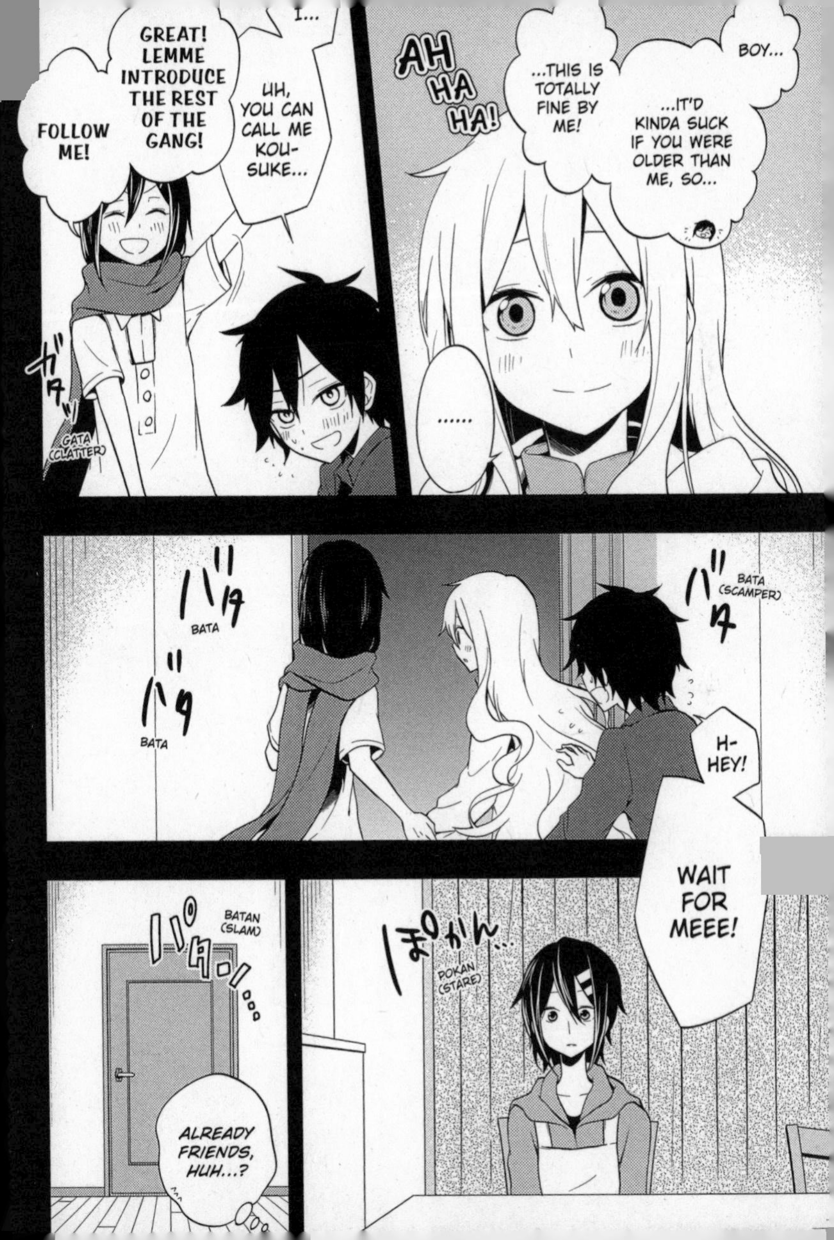
BOY...
...IT'D KINDA SUCK IF YOU WERE OLDER THAN ME, SO...
...THIS IS TOTALLY FINE BY ME!
AH HA HA!
......
I...
UH, YOU CAN CALL ME KOU-SUKE...
GREAT! LEMME INTRODUCE THE REST OF THE GANG!
FOLLOW ME!
GATA (CLATTER)
BATA (SCAMPER)
H-HEY!
BATA
BATA
WAIT FOR MEEE!
POKAN (STARE)
BATAN (SLAM)
ALREADY FRIENDS, HUH...?

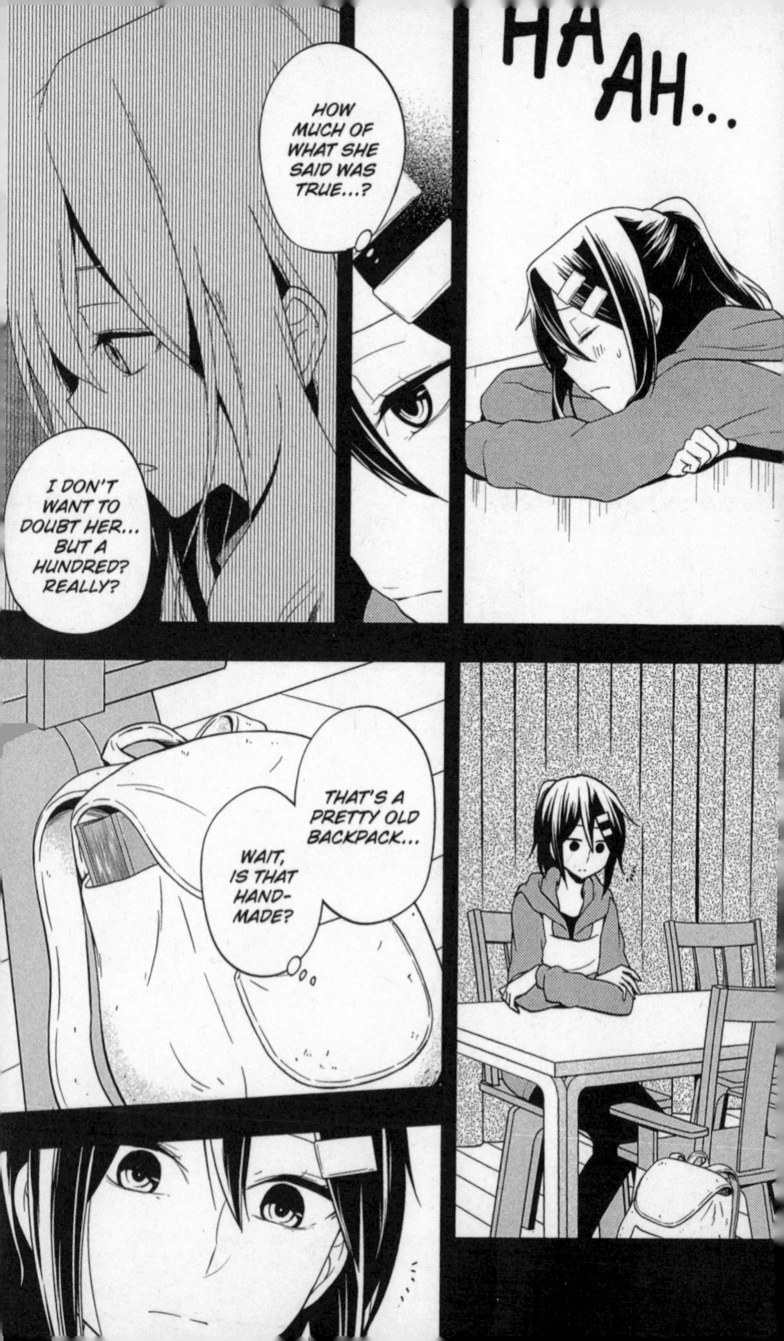
HAAH...
HOW MUCH OF WHAT SHE SAID WAS TRUE...?
I DON'T WANT TO DOUBT HER... BUT A HUNDRED? REALLY?
THAT'S A PRETTY OLD BACKPACK...
WAIT, IS THAT HAND-MADE?

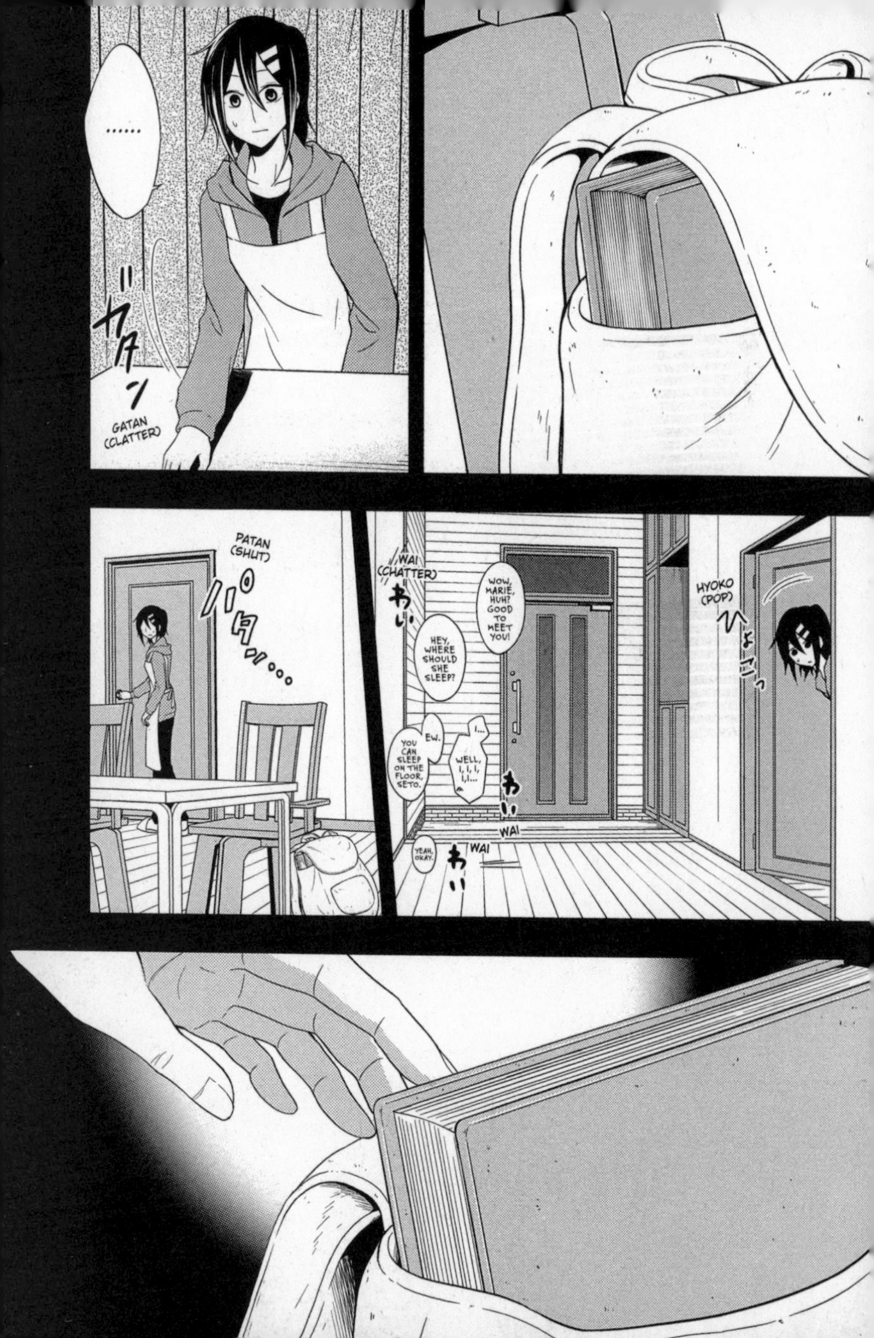
......
GATAN (CLATTER)
HYOKO (POP)
WAI (CHATTER)
WOW, MARIE, HUH? GOOD TO MEET YOU!
HEY, WHERE SHOULD SHE SLEEP?
I...
WELL, I, I, I, I, I...
EW.
YOU CAN SLEEP ON THE FLOOR, SETO.
WAI
WAI
YEAH, OKAY.
PATAN (SHUT)

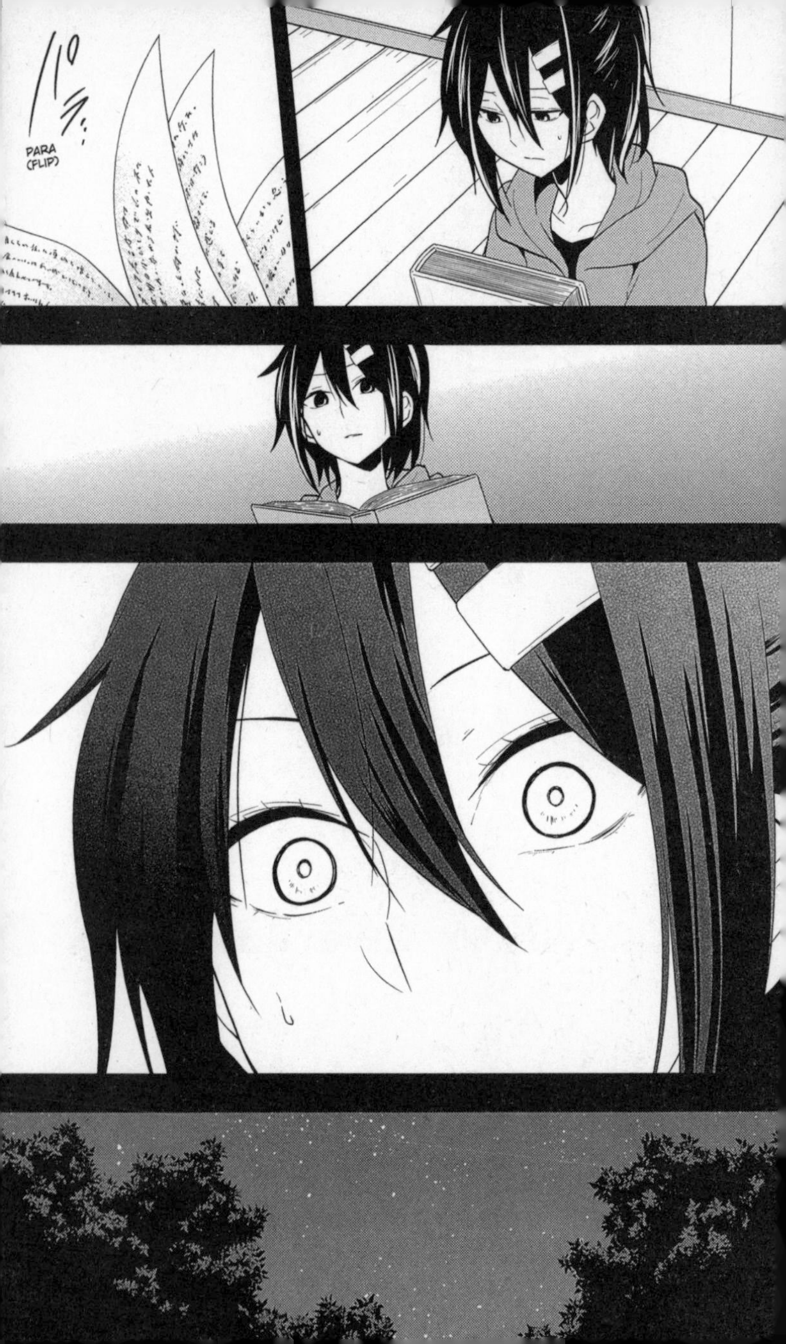
パラ
PARA (FLIP)

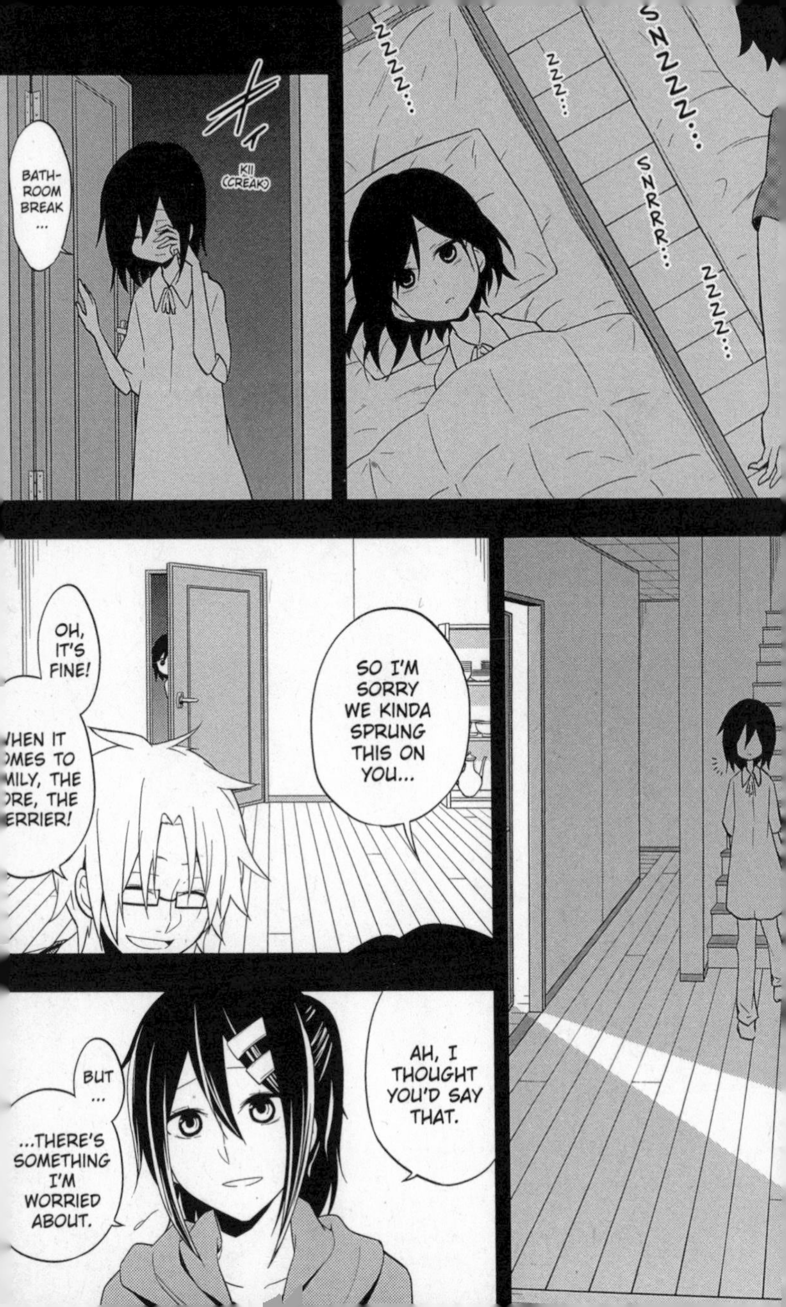
SNZZZZ...
ZZZ...
ZZZZ...
SNRRR...
ZZZZ...
KII (CREAK)
BATH-ROOM BREAK...
SO I'M SORRY WE KINDA SPRUNG THIS ON YOU...
OH, IT'S FINE!
WHEN IT OMES TO MILY, THE ORE, THE ERRIER!
AH, I THOUGHT YOU'D SAY THAT.
BUT...
...THERE'S SOMETHING I'M WORRIED ABOUT.

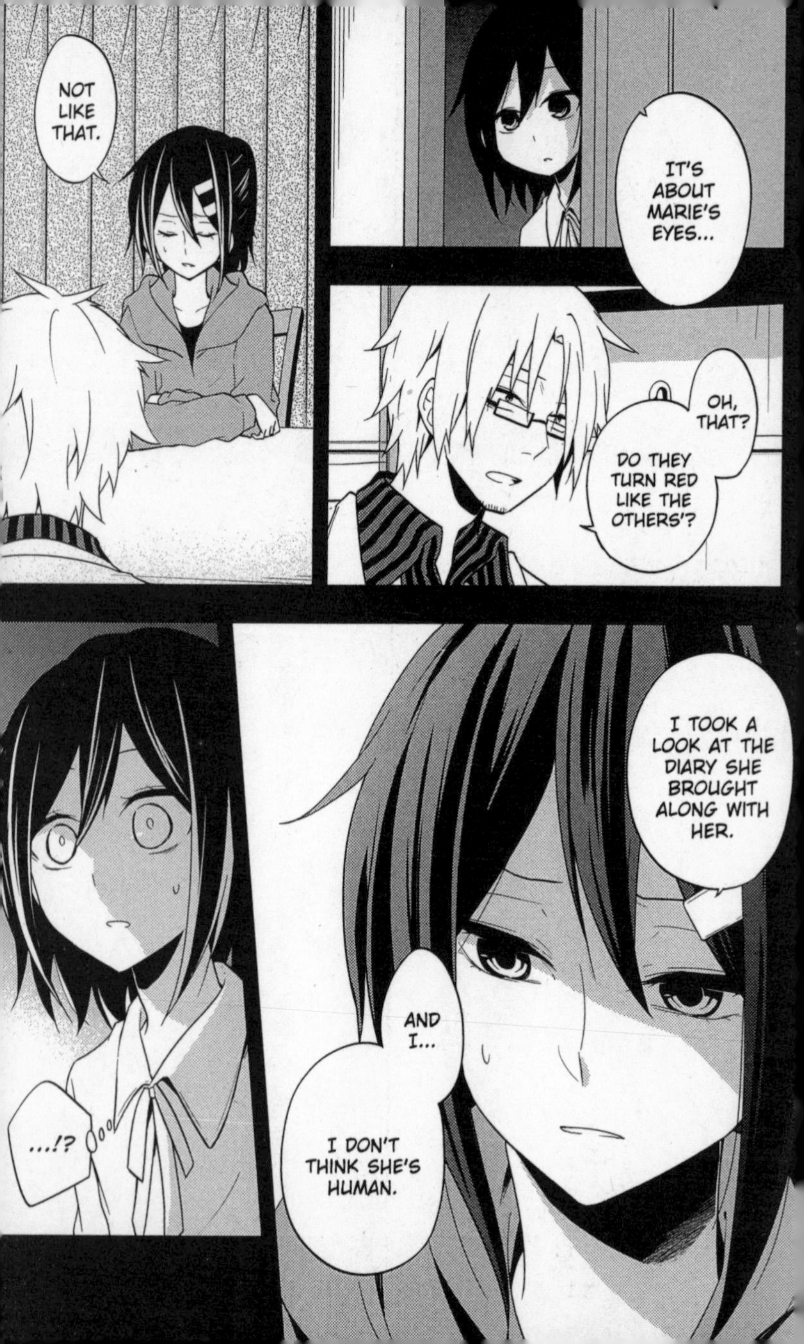

IT'S ABOUT MARIE'S EYES...
OH, THAT?
DO THEY TURN RED LIKE THE OTHERS'?
NOT LIKE THAT.
I TOOK A LOOK AT THE DIARY SHE BROUGHT ALONG WITH HER.
AND I...
I DON'T THINK SHE'S HUMAN.
...!?

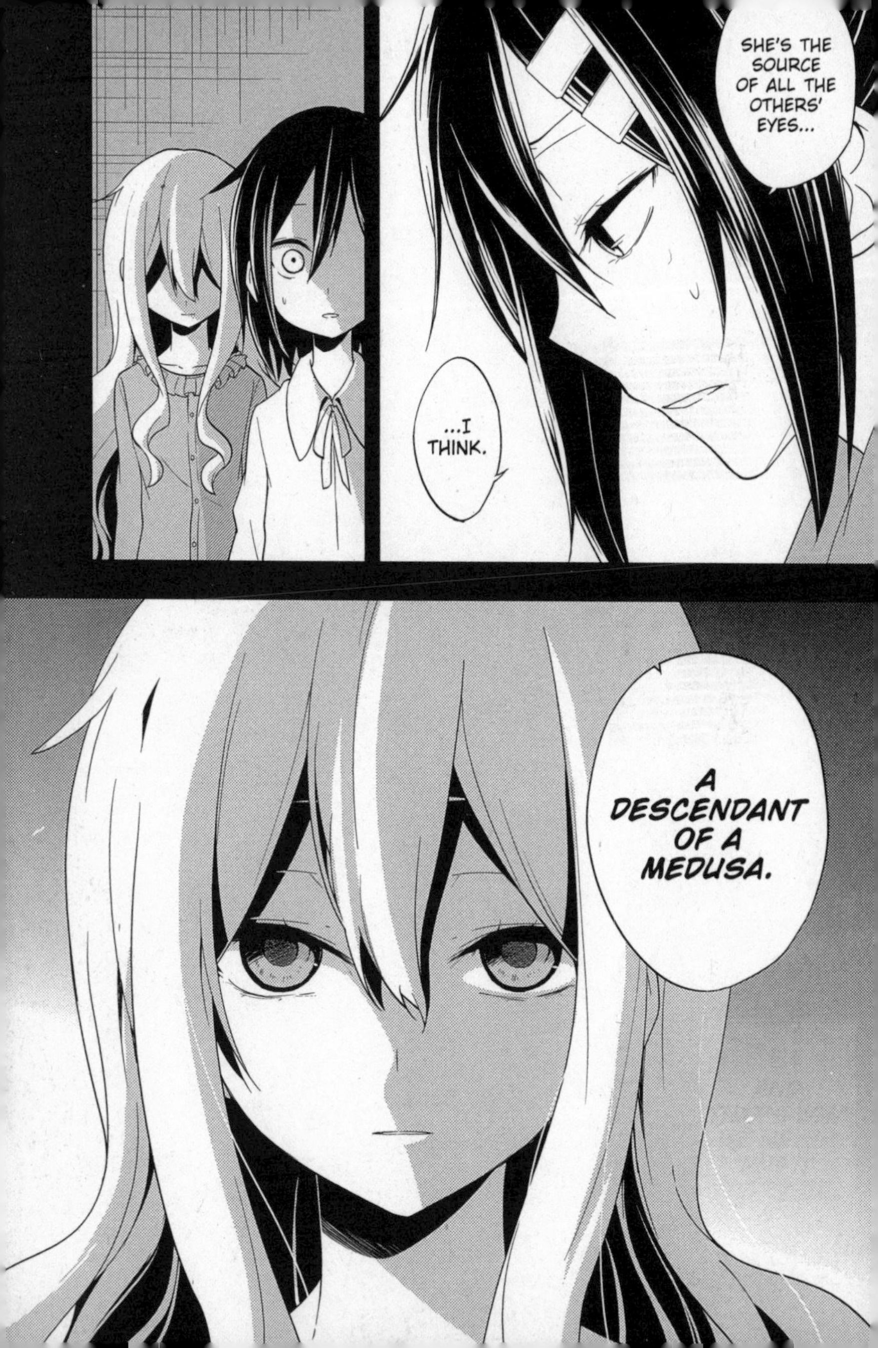
SHE'S THE SOURCE OF ALL THE OTHERS' EYES...
...I THINK.
A DESCENDANT OF A MEDUSA.

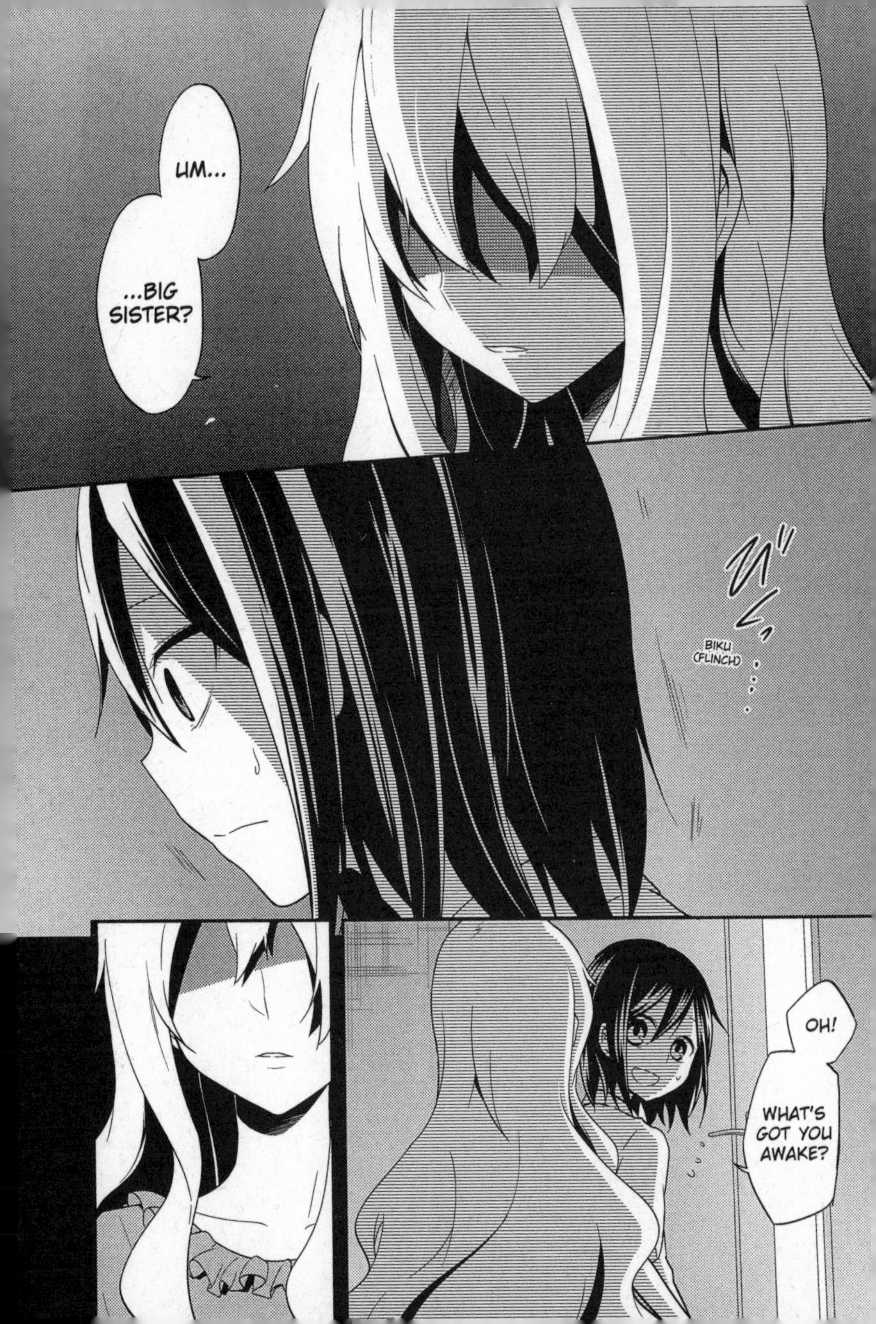
UM...
...BIG SISTER?
BIKU (FLINCH)
OH!
WHAT'S GOT YOU AWAKE?

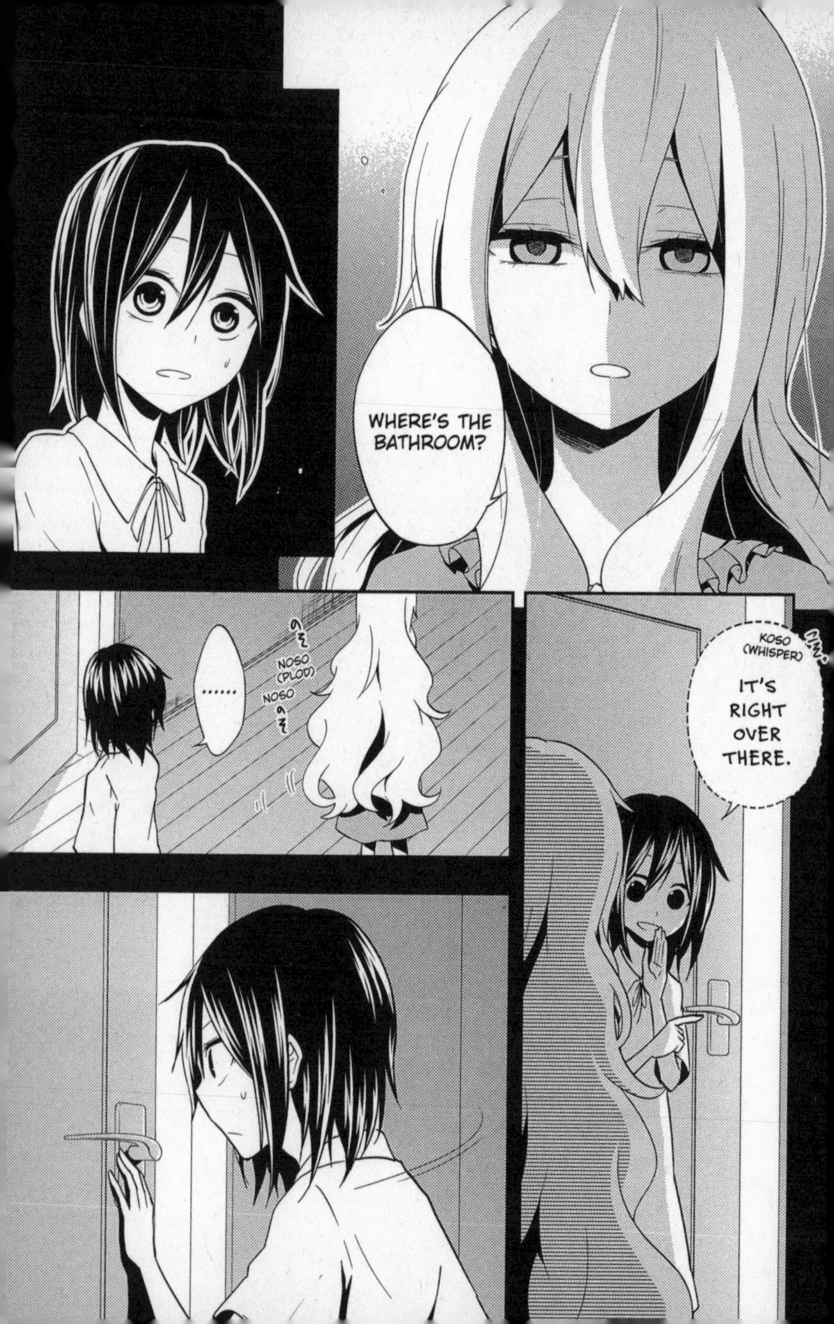
WHERE'S THE BATHROOM?
KOSO (WHISPER)
IT'S RIGHT OVER THERE.
......
NOSO (PLOD)
NOSO

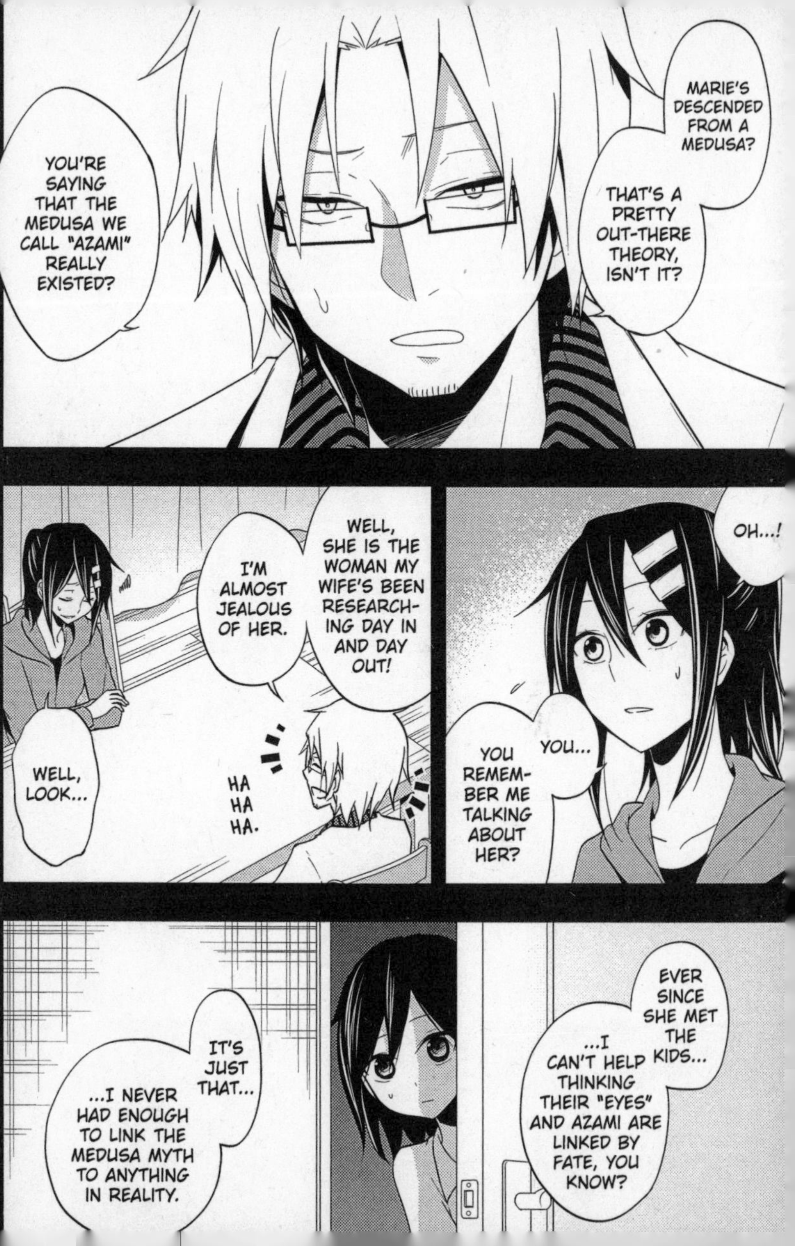
MARIE'S DESCENDED FROM A MEDUSA?
THAT'S A PRETTY OUT-THERE THEORY, ISN'T IT?
YOU'RE SAYING THAT THE MEDUSA WE CALL "AZAMI" REALLY EXISTED?
OH...!
YOU...
YOU REMEMBER ME TALKING ABOUT HER?
WELL, SHE IS THE WOMAN MY WIFE'S BEEN RESEARCHING DAY IN AND DAY OUT!
I'M ALMOST JEALOUS OF HER.
HA HA HA.
WELL, LOOK...
EVER SINCE SHE MET THE KIDS...
...I CAN'T HELP THINKING THEIR "EYES" AND AZAMI ARE LINKED BY FATE, YOU KNOW?
IT'S JUST THAT...
...I NEVER HAD ENOUGH TO LINK THE MEDUSA MYTH TO ANYTHING IN REALITY.

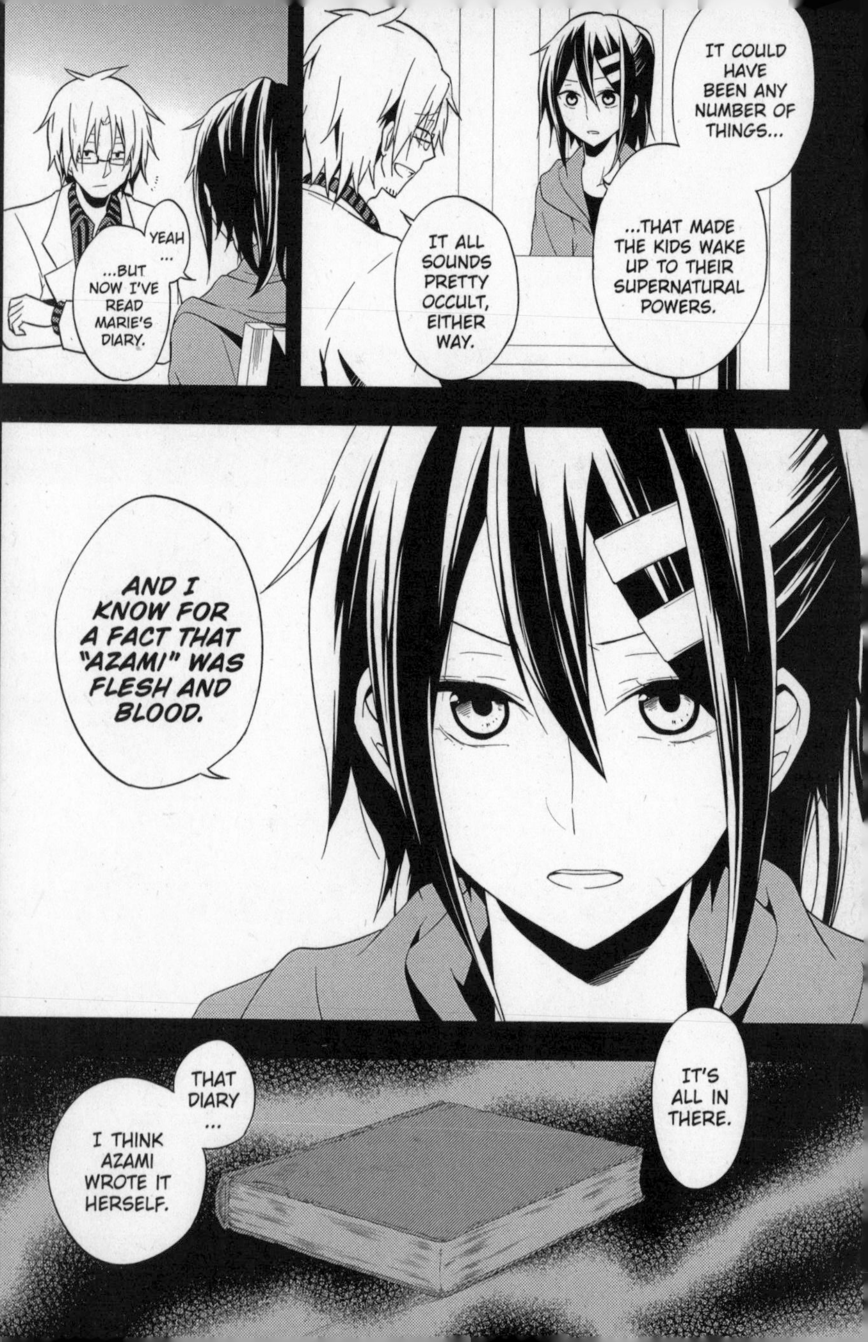
IT COULD HAVE BEEN ANY NUMBER OF THINGS...
...THAT MADE THE KIDS WAKE UP TO THEIR SUPERNATURAL POWERS.
IT ALL SOUNDS PRETTY OCCULT, EITHER WAY.
YEAH ...
...BUT NOW I'VE READ MARIE'S DIARY.
AND I KNOW FOR A FACT THAT "AZAMI" WAS FLESH AND BLOOD.
IT'S ALL IN THERE.
THAT DIARY ...
I THINK AZAMI WROTE IT HERSELF.

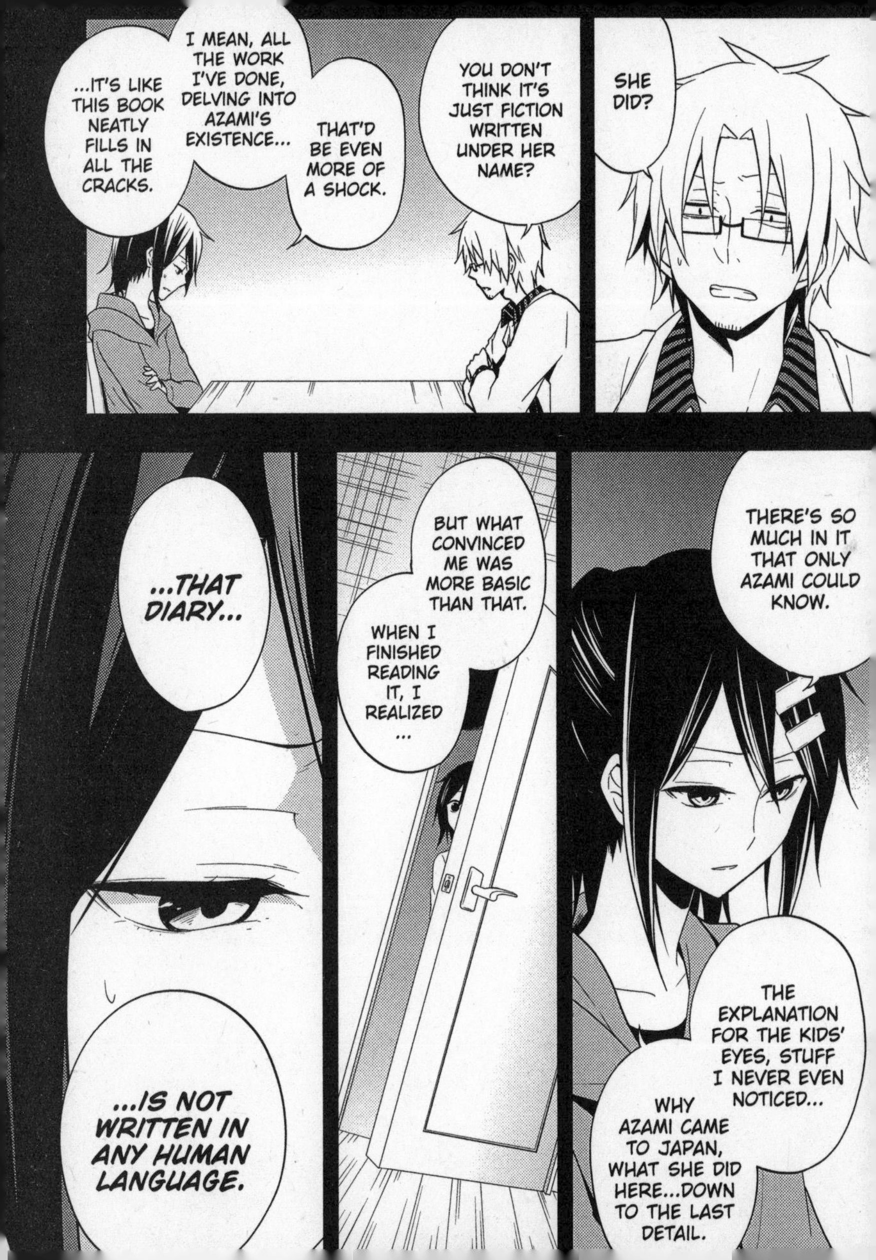
SHE DID?
YOU DON'T THINK IT'S JUST FICTION WRITTEN UNDER HER NAME?
THAT'D BE EVEN MORE OF A SHOCK.
I MEAN, ALL THE WORK I'VE DONE, DELVING INTO AZAMI'S EXISTENCE...
...IT'S LIKE THIS BOOK NEATLY FILLS IN ALL THE CRACKS.
THERE'S SO MUCH IN IT THAT ONLY AZAMI COULD KNOW.
THE EXPLANATION FOR THE KIDS' EYES, STUFF I NEVER EVEN NOTICED...
WHY AZAMI CAME TO JAPAN, WHAT SHE DID HERE...DOWN TO THE LAST DETAIL.
BUT WHAT CONVINCED ME WAS MORE BASIC THAN THAT.
WHEN I FINISHED READING IT, I REALIZED...
...THAT DIARY...
...IS NOT WRITTEN IN ANY HUMAN LANGUAGE.

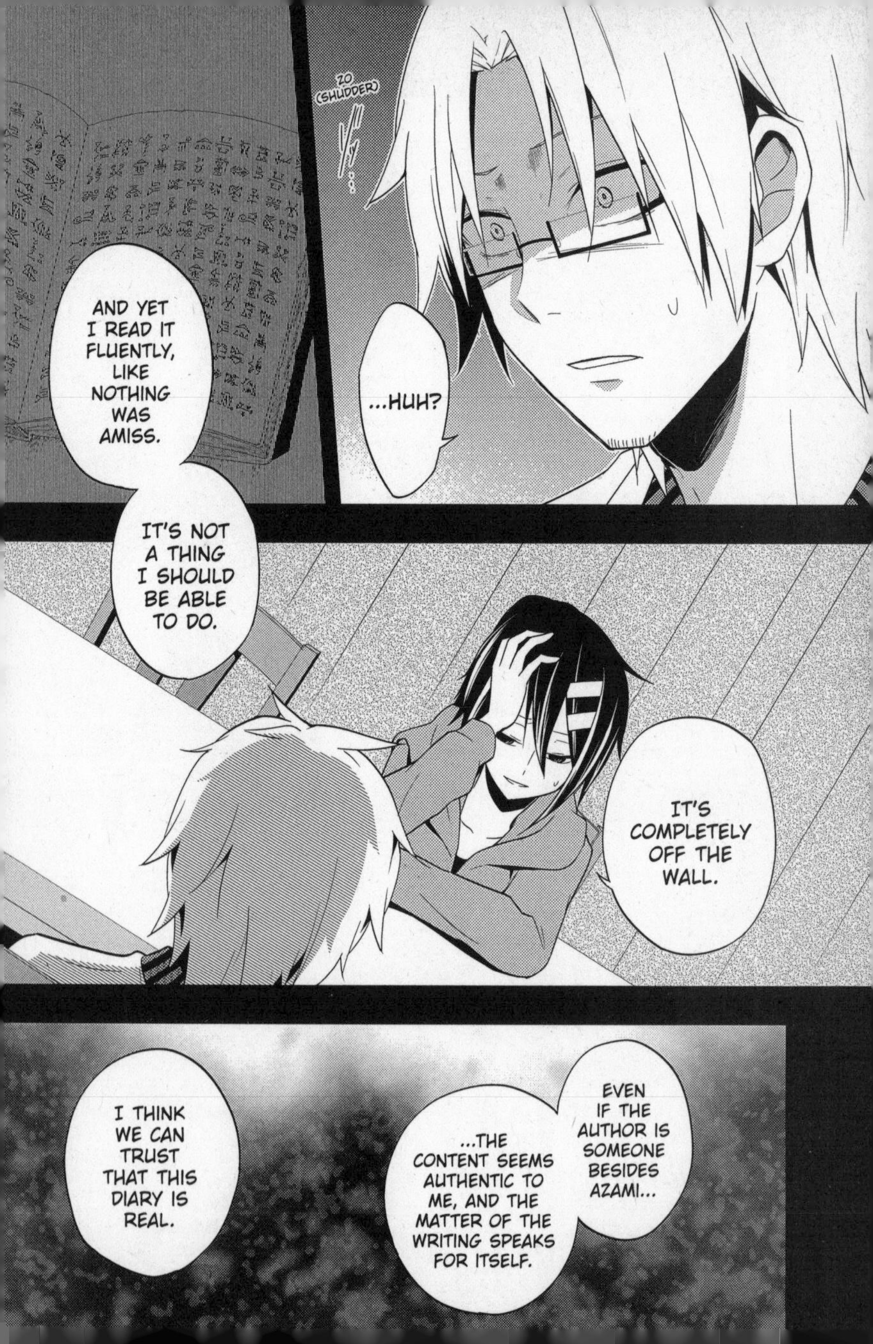
ZO (SHUDDER)
...HUH?
AND YET I READ IT FLUENTLY, LIKE NOTHING WAS AMISS.
IT'S NOT A THING I SHOULD BE ABLE TO DO.
IT'S COMPLETELY OFF THE WALL.
EVEN IF THE AUTHOR IS SOMEONE BESIDES AZAMI...
...THE CONTENT SEEMS AUTHENTIC TO ME, AND THE MATTER OF THE WRITING SPEAKS FOR ITSELF.
I THINK WE CAN TRUST THAT THIS DIARY IS REAL.

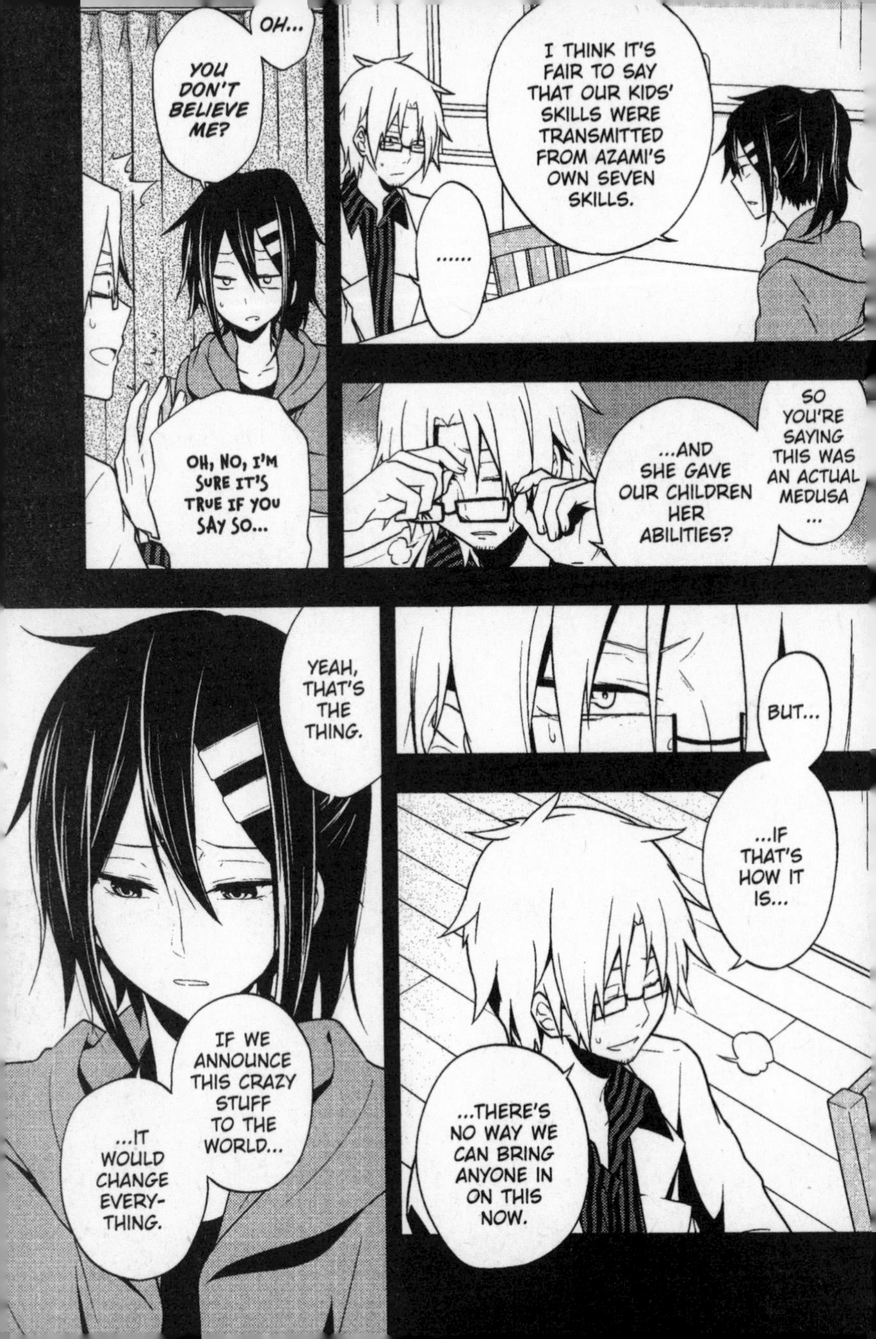
I THINK IT'S FAIR TO SAY THAT OUR KIDS' SKILLS WERE TRANSMITTED FROM AZAMI'S OWN SEVEN SKILLS.
......
SO YOU'RE SAYING THIS WAS AN ACTUAL MEDUSA...
...AND SHE GAVE OUR CHILDREN HER ABILITIES?
OH...
YOU DON'T BELIEVE ME?
OH, NO, I'M SURE IT'S TRUE IF YOU SAY SO...
BUT...
...IF THAT'S HOW IT IS...
...THERE'S NO WAY WE CAN BRING ANYONE IN ON THIS NOW.
YEAH, THAT'S THE THING.
IF WE ANNOUNCE THIS CRAZY STUFF TO THE WORLD...
...IT WOULD CHANGE EVERY-THING.

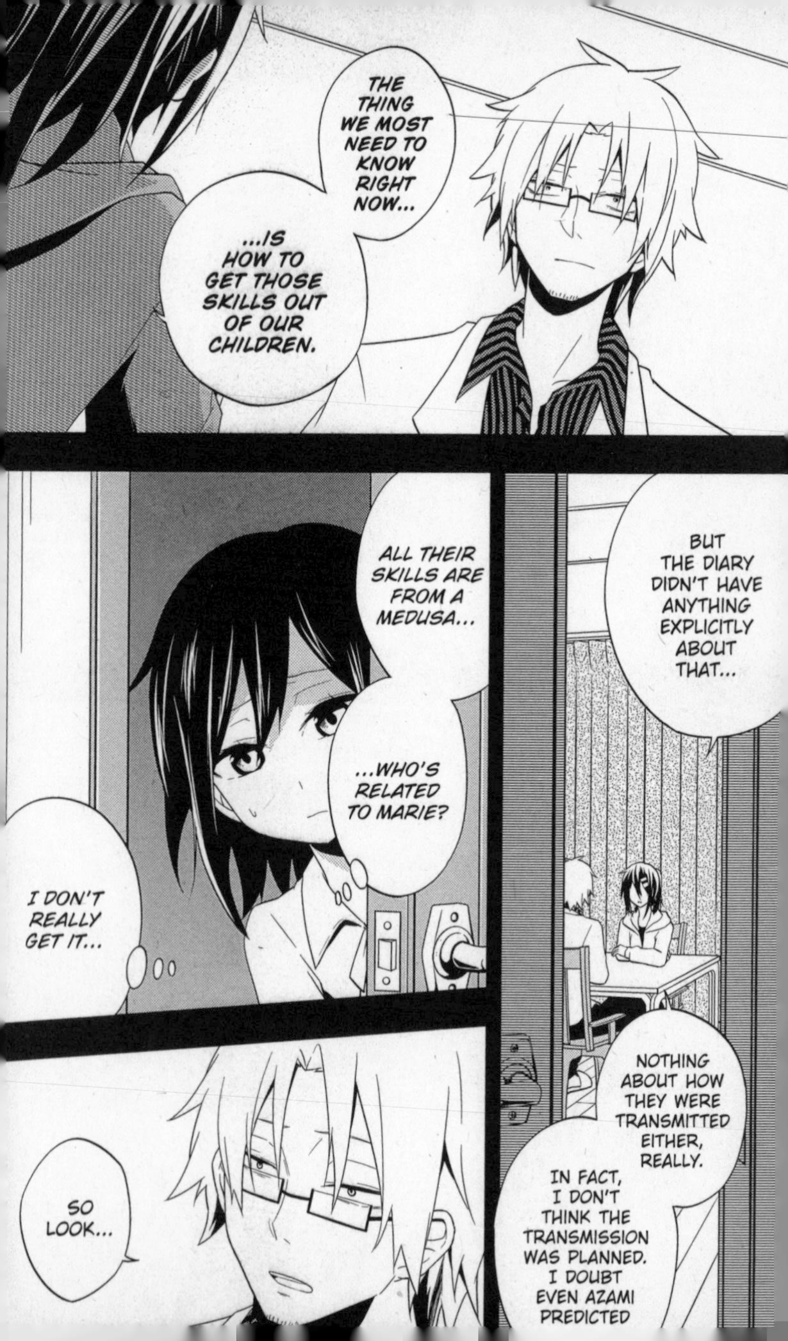
THE THING WE MOST NEED TO KNOW RIGHT NOW...
...IS HOW TO GET THOSE SKILLS OUT OF OUR CHILDREN.
BUT THE DIARY DIDN'T HAVE ANYTHING EXPLICITLY ABOUT THAT...
NOTHING ABOUT HOW THEY WERE TRANSMITTED EITHER, REALLY.
IN FACT, I DON'T THINK THE TRANSMISSION WAS PLANNED. I DOUBT EVEN AZAMI PREDICTED
ALL THEIR SKILLS ARE FROM A MEDUSA...
...WHO'S RELATED TO MARIE?
I DON'T REALLY GET IT...
SO LOOK...

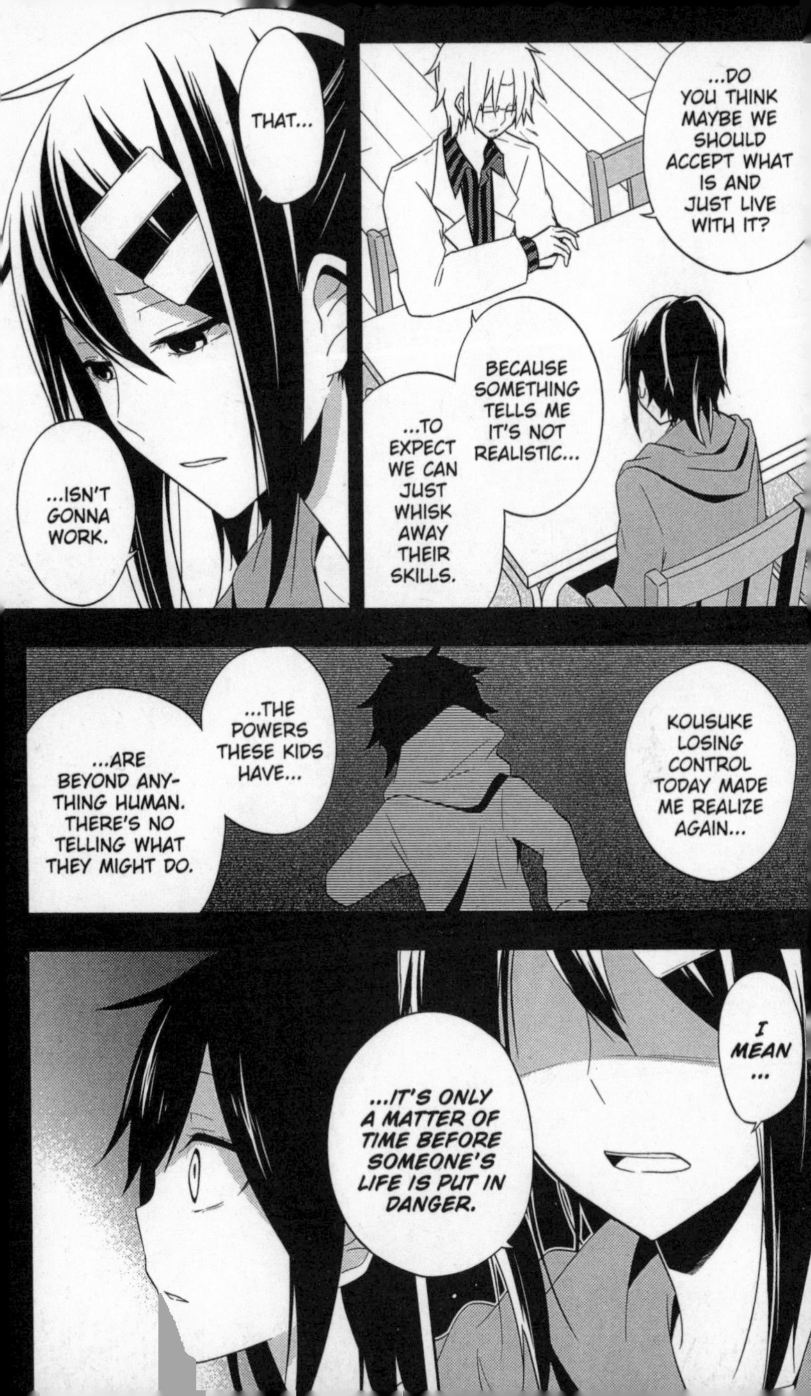
...DO YOU THINK MAYBE WE SHOULD ACCEPT WHAT IS AND JUST LIVE WITH IT?
BECAUSE SOMETHING TELLS ME IT'S NOT REALISTIC...
...TO EXPECT WE CAN JUST WHISK AWAY THEIR SKILLS.
THAT...
...ISN'T GONNA WORK.
KOUSUKE LOSING CONTROL TODAY MADE ME REALIZE AGAIN...
...THE POWERS THESE KIDS HAVE...
...ARE BEYOND ANY-THING HUMAN. THERE'S NO TELLING WHAT THEY MIGHT DO.
I MEAN...
...IT'S ONLY A MATTER OF TIME BEFORE SOMEONE'S LIFE IS PUT IN DANGER.

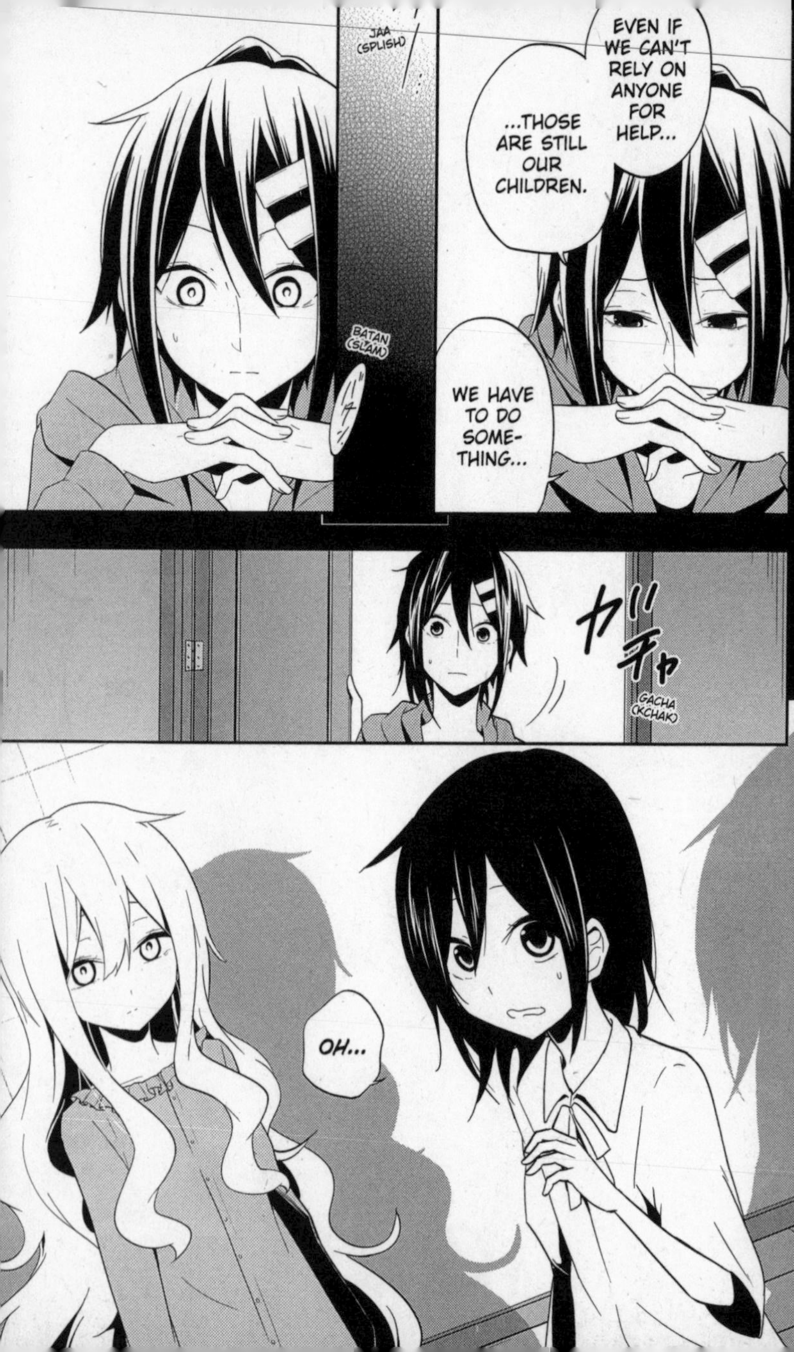
EVEN IF WE CAN'T RELY ON ANYONE FOR HELP...
...THOSE ARE STILL OUR CHILDREN.
WE HAVE TO DO SOMETHING...
JAA (SPLISH)
BATAN (SLAM)
ガチャ
GACHA (KCHAK)
OH...

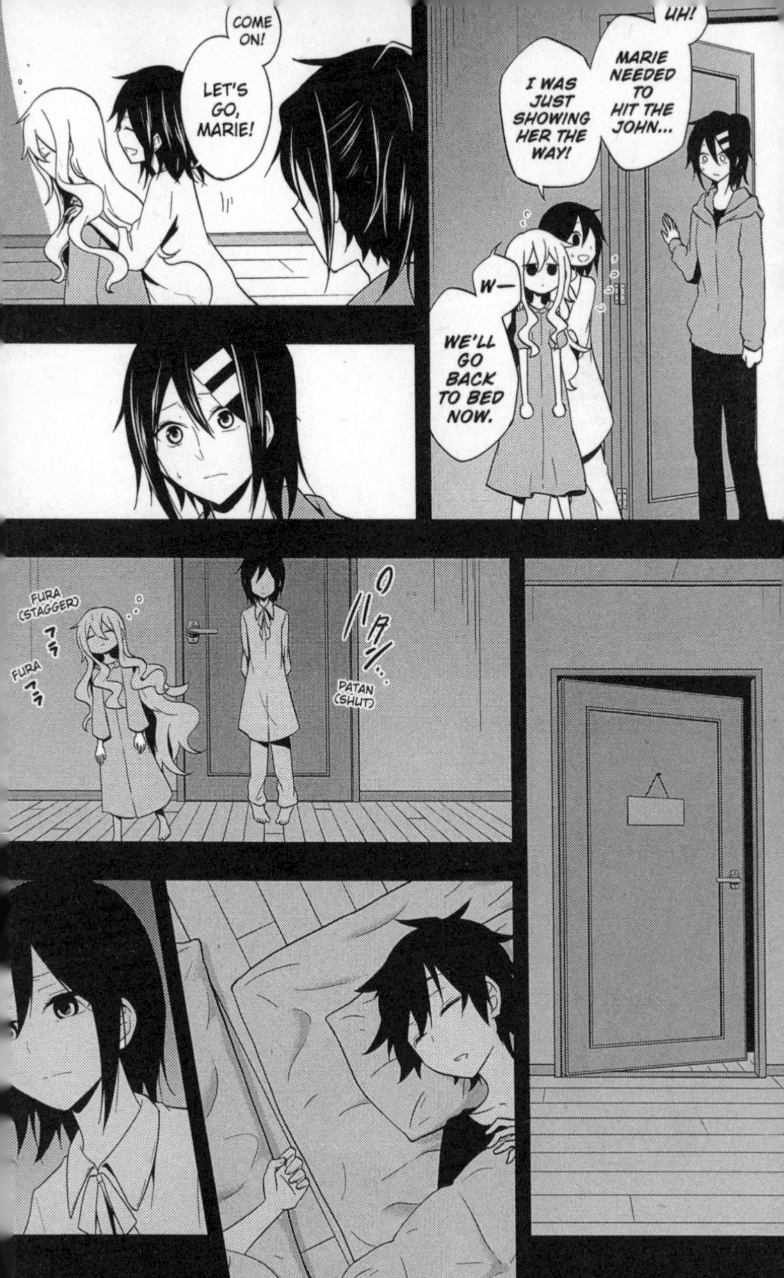
UH!
MARIE NEEDED TO HIT THE JOHN...
I WAS JUST SHOWING HER THE WAY!
W—
WE'LL GO BACK TO BED NOW.
COME ON!
LET'S GO, MARIE!
パタン…
PATAN (SHUT)
フラ
FURA (STAGGER)
フラ
FURA

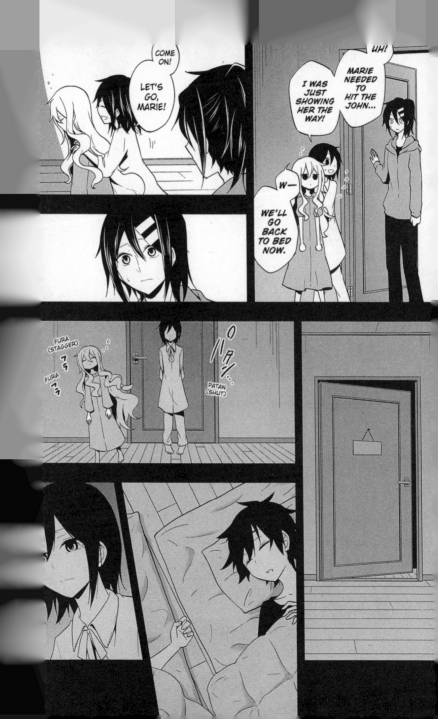

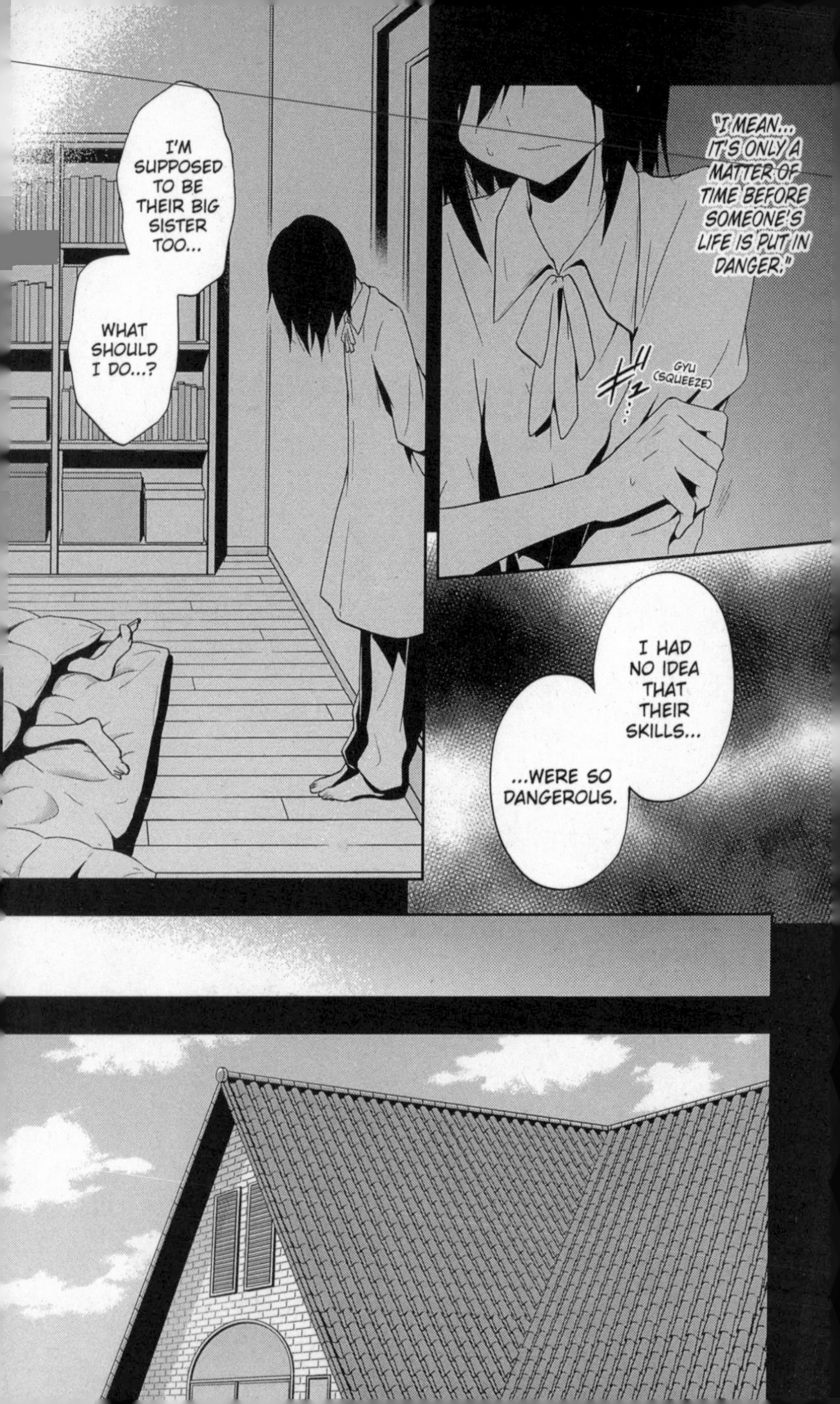
"I MEAN... IT'S ONLY A MATTER OF TIME BEFORE SOMEONE'S LIFE IS PUT IN DANGER."
GYU (SQUEEZE)
I HAD NO IDEA THAT THEIR SKILLS...
...WERE SO DANGEROUS.
I'M SUPPOSED TO BE THEIR BIG SISTER TOO...
WHAT SHOULD I DO...?

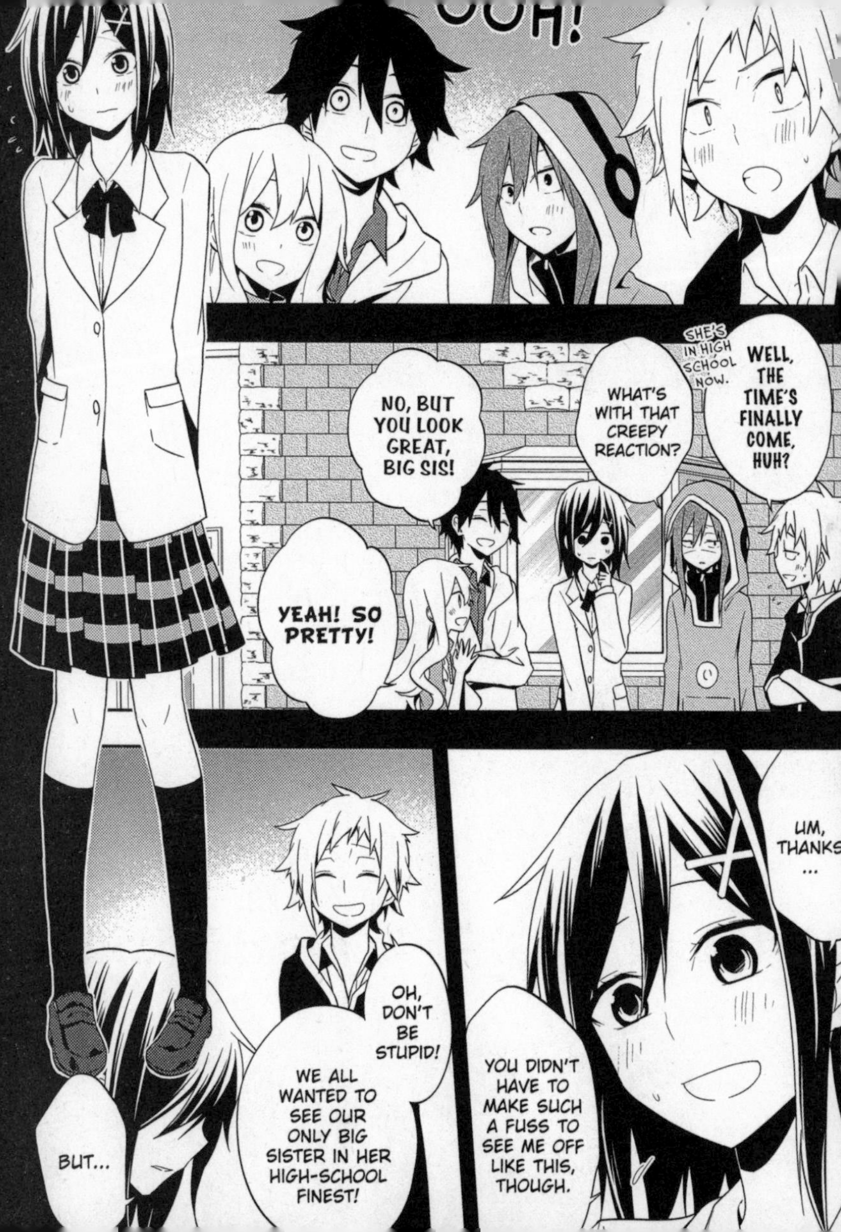

OOH!
WELL, THE TIME'S FINALLY COME, HUH?
SHE'S IN HIGH SCHOOL NOW.
WHAT'S WITH THAT CREEPY REACTION?
NO, BUT YOU LOOK GREAT, BIG SIS!
YEAH! SO PRETTY!
UM, THANKS...
YOU DIDN'T HAVE TO MAKE SUCH A FUSS TO SEE ME OFF LIKE THIS, THOUGH.
OH, DON'T BE STUPID!
WE ALL WANTED TO SEE OUR ONLY BIG SISTER IN HER HIGH-SCHOOL FINEST!
BUT...

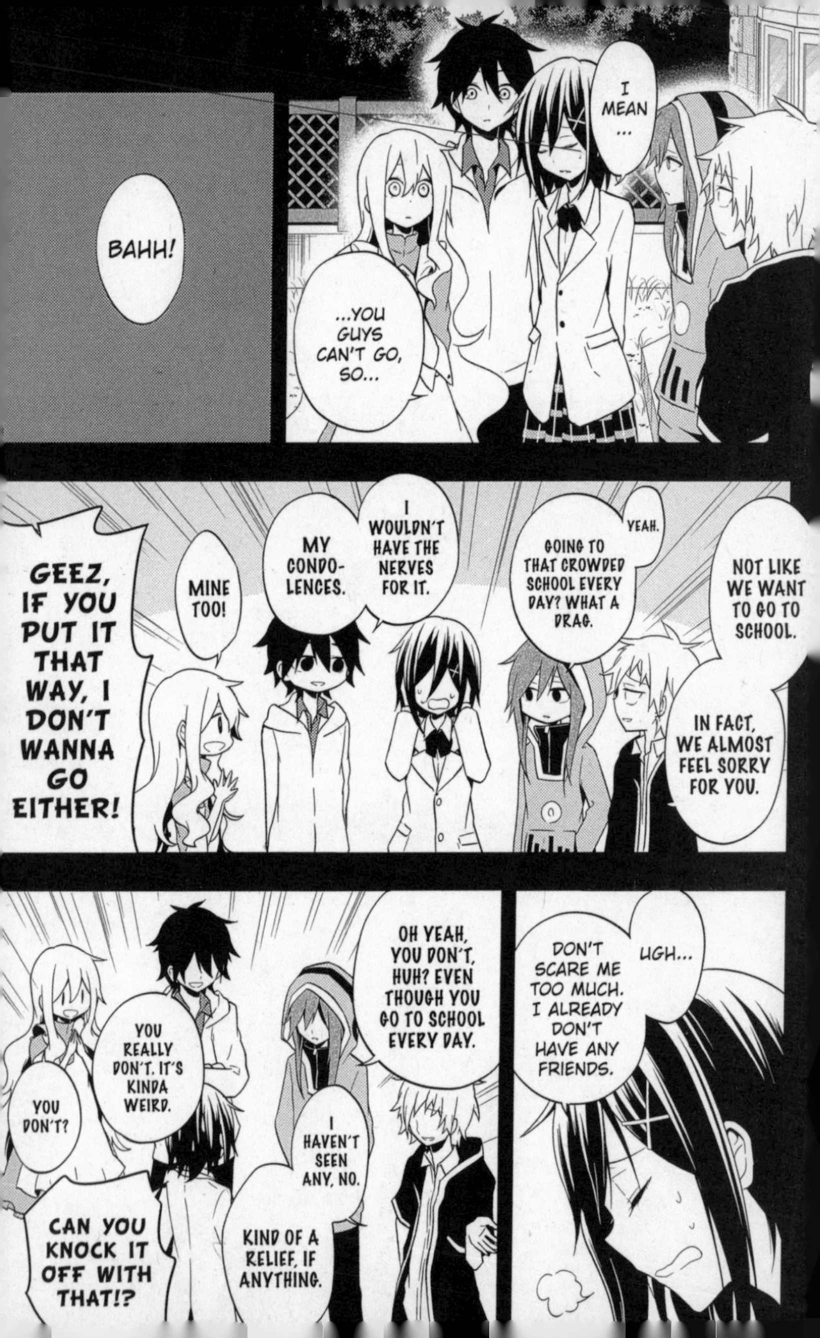
I MEAN ...
...YOU GUYS CAN'T GO, SO...
BAHH!
NOT LIKE WE WANT TO GO TO SCHOOL.
YEAH.
GOING TO THAT CROWDED SCHOOL EVERY DAY? WHAT A DRAG.
IN FACT, WE ALMOST FEEL SORRY FOR YOU.
I WOULDN'T HAVE THE NERVES FOR IT.
MY CONDOLENCES.
MINE TOO!
GEEZ, IF YOU PUT IT THAT WAY, I DON'T WANNA GO EITHER!
UGH...
DON'T SCARE ME TOO MUCH. I ALREADY DON'T HAVE ANY FRIENDS.
OH YEAH, YOU DON'T, HUH? EVEN THOUGH YOU GO TO SCHOOL EVERY DAY.
YOU REALLY DON'T. IT'S KINDA WEIRD.
YOU DON'T?
I HAVEN'T SEEN ANY, NO.
KIND OF A RELIEF, IF ANYTHING.
CAN YOU KNOCK IT OFF WITH THAT!?

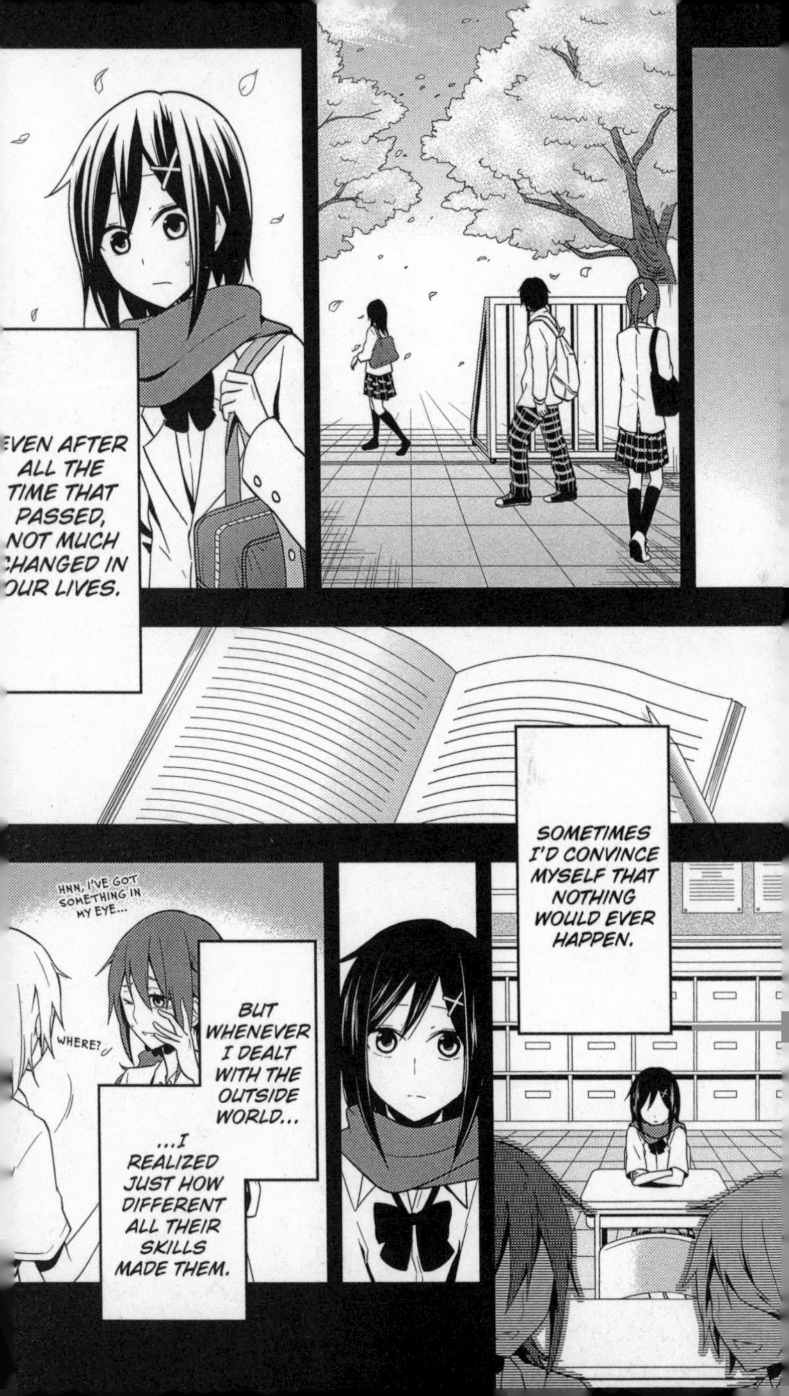
EVEN AFTER ALL THE TIME THAT PASSED, NOT MUCH CHANGED IN OUR LIVES.
SOMETIMES I'D CONVINCE MYSELF THAT NOTHING WOULD EVER HAPPEN.
HNN, I'VE GOT SOMETHING IN MY EYE...
WHERE?
BUT WHENEVER I DEALT WITH THE OUTSIDE WORLD...
...I REALIZED JUST HOW DIFFERENT ALL THEIR SKILLS MADE THEM.

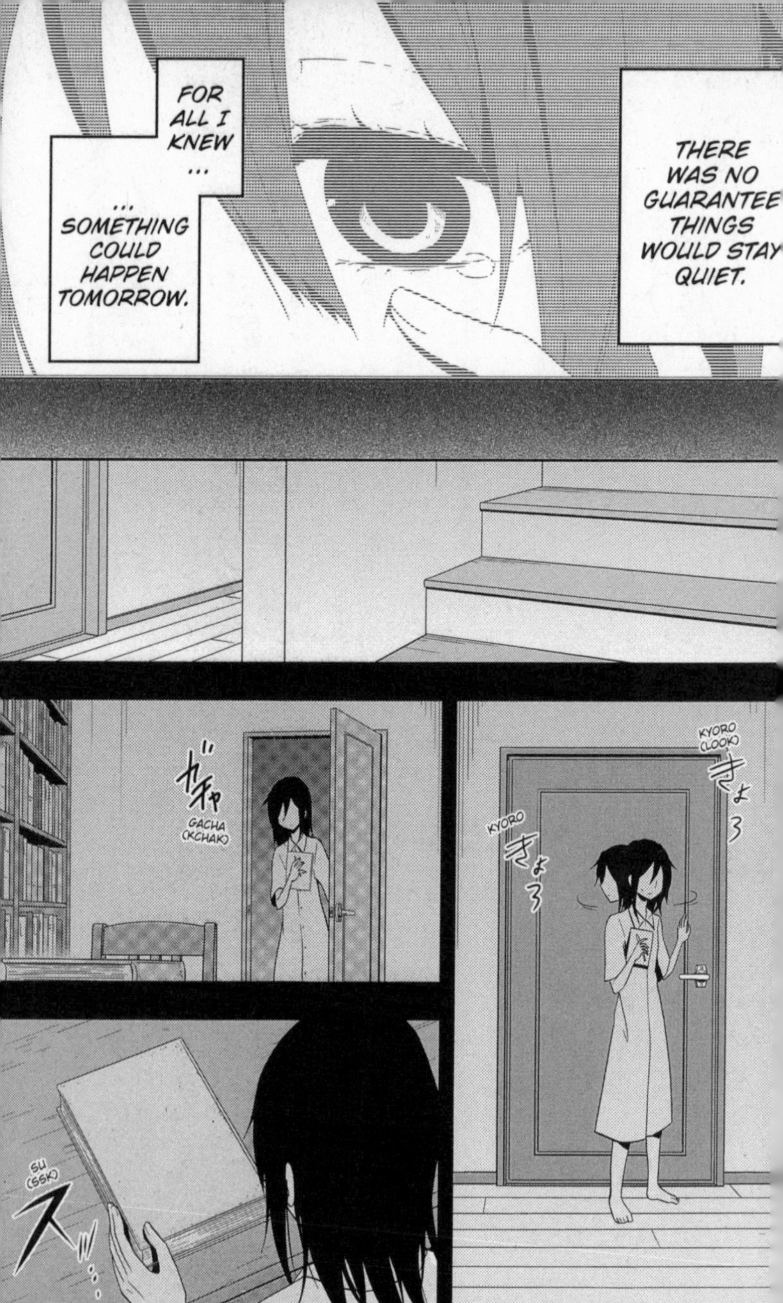
THERE WAS NO GUARANTEE THINGS WOULD STAY QUIET.
FOR ALL I KNEW ...
... SOMETHING COULD HAPPEN TOMORROW.
きょろ
KYORO (LOOK)
きょろ
KYORO
ガチャ
GACHA (KCHAK)
スッ…
SU (SSK)

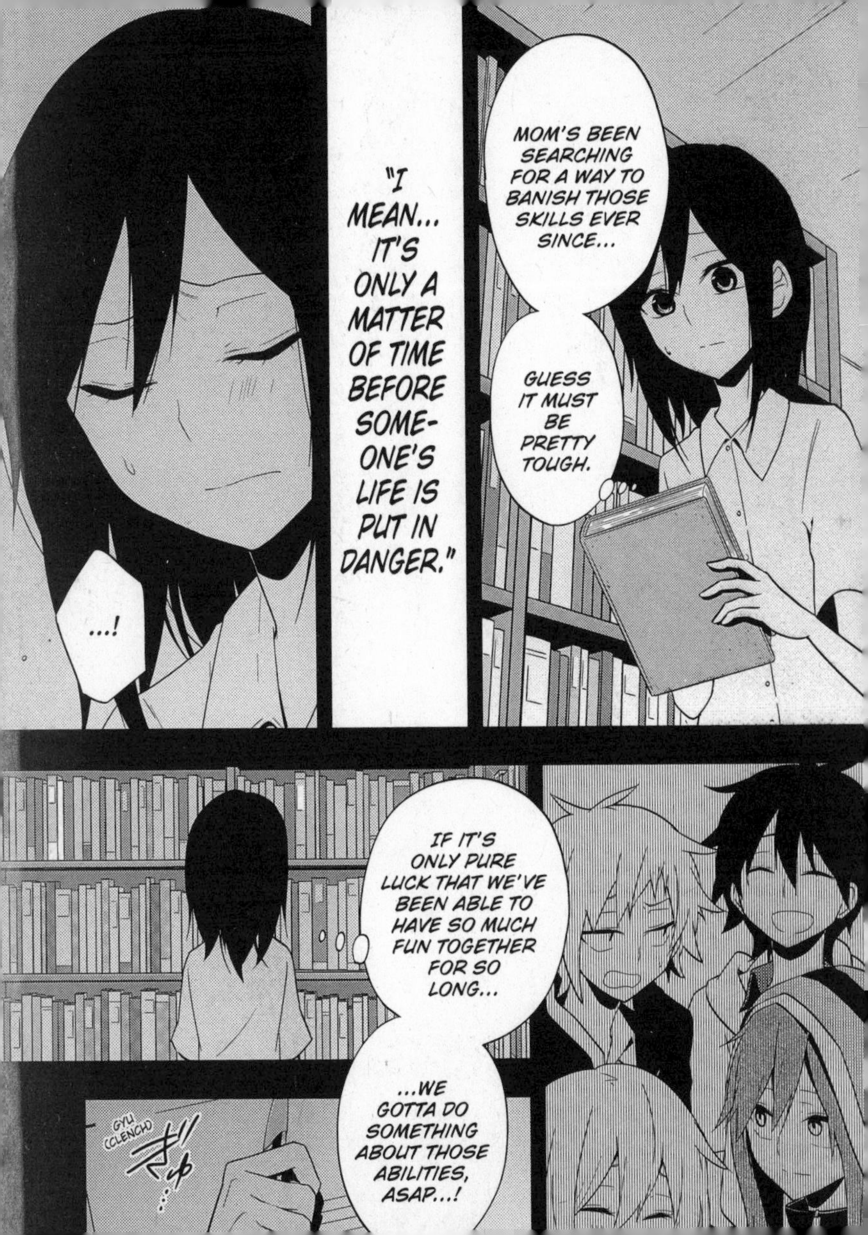
MOM'S BEEN SEARCHING FOR A WAY TO BANISH THOSE SKILLS EVER SINCE...
GUESS IT MUST BE PRETTY TOUGH.
"I MEAN... IT'S ONLY A MATTER OF TIME BEFORE SOME-ONE'S LIFE IS PUT IN DANGER."
...!
IF IT'S ONLY PURE LUCK THAT WE'VE BEEN ABLE TO HAVE SO MUCH FUN TOGETHER FOR SO LONG...
...WE GOTTA DO SOMETHING ABOUT THOSE ABILITIES, ASAP...!
GYU (CLENCH)

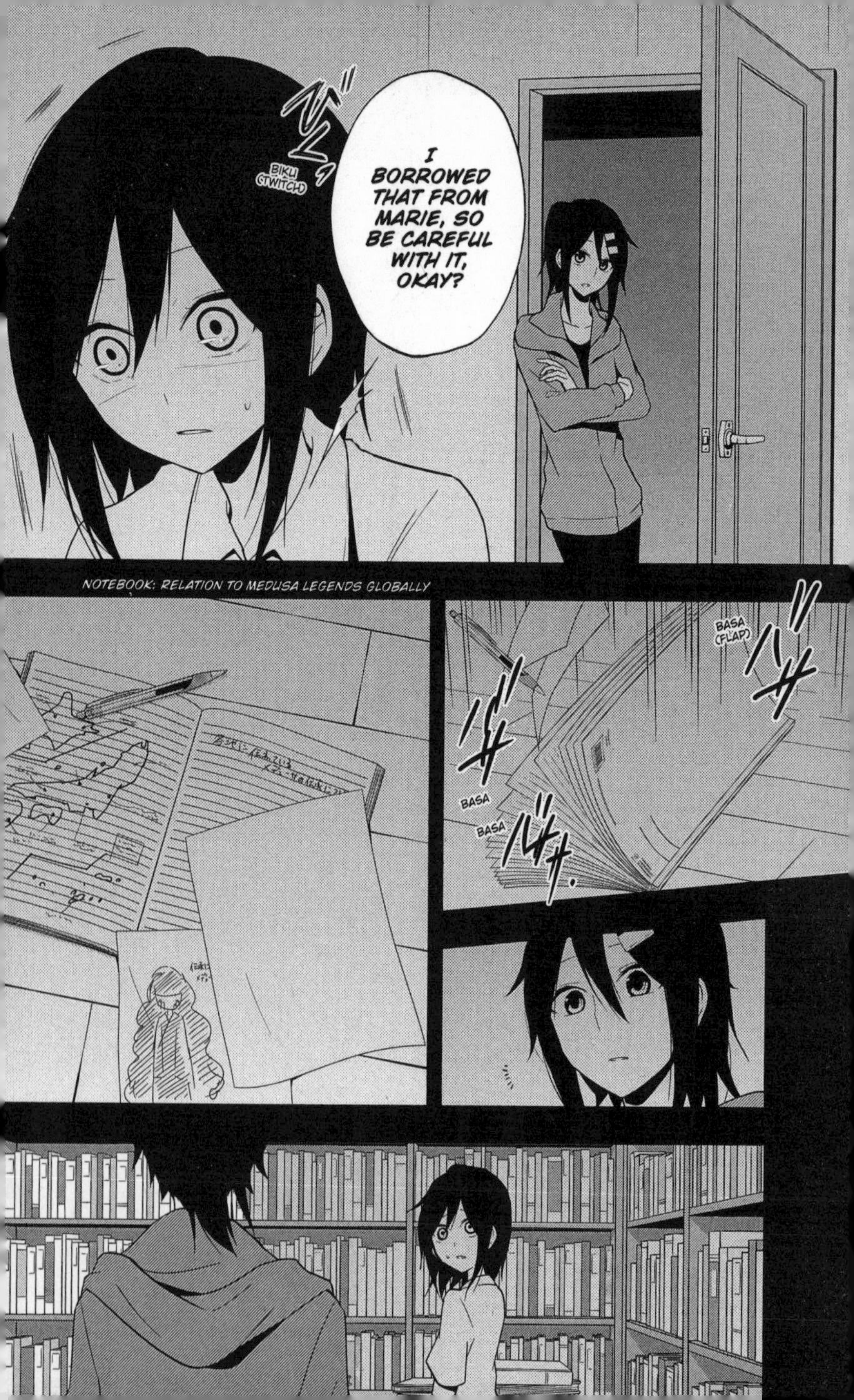
BIKU (TWITCH)
I BORROWED THAT FROM MARIE, SO BE CAREFUL WITH IT, OKAY?
BASA (FLAP)
BASA
BASA
NOTEBOOK: RELATION TO MEDUSA LEGENDS GLOBALLY

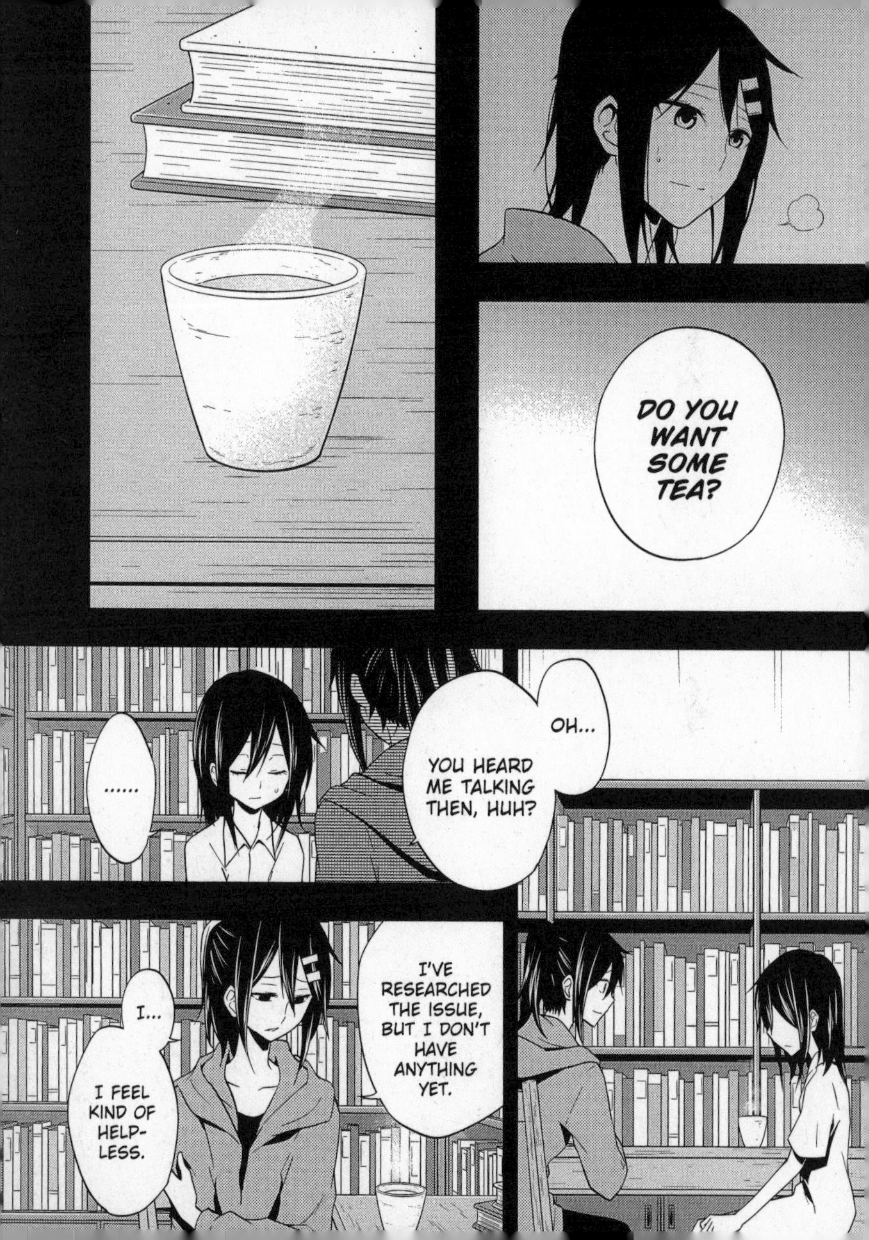
DO YOU WANT SOME TEA?
OH... YOU HEARD ME TALKING THEN, HUH?
......
I'VE RESEARCHED THE ISSUE, BUT I DON'T HAVE ANYTHING YET.
I... I FEEL KIND OF HELP-LESS.

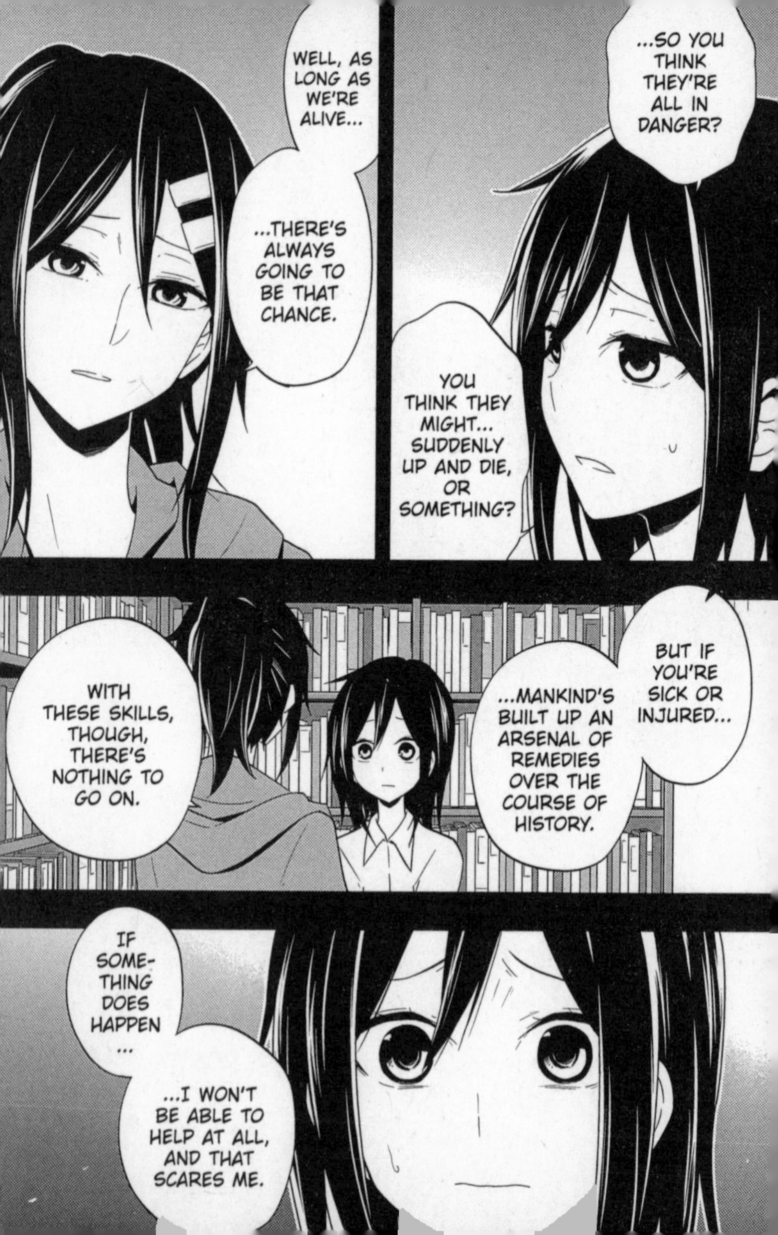
...SO YOU THINK THEY'RE ALL IN DANGER?
YOU THINK THEY MIGHT... SUDDENLY UP AND DIE, OR SOMETHING?
WELL, AS LONG AS WE'RE ALIVE...
...THERE'S ALWAYS GOING TO BE THAT CHANCE.
BUT IF YOU'RE SICK OR INJURED...
...MANKIND'S BUILT UP AN ARSENAL OF REMEDIES OVER THE COURSE OF HISTORY.
WITH THESE SKILLS, THOUGH, THERE'S NOTHING TO GO ON.
IF SOME-THING DOES HAPPEN...
...I WON'T BE ABLE TO HELP AT ALL, AND THAT SCARES ME.

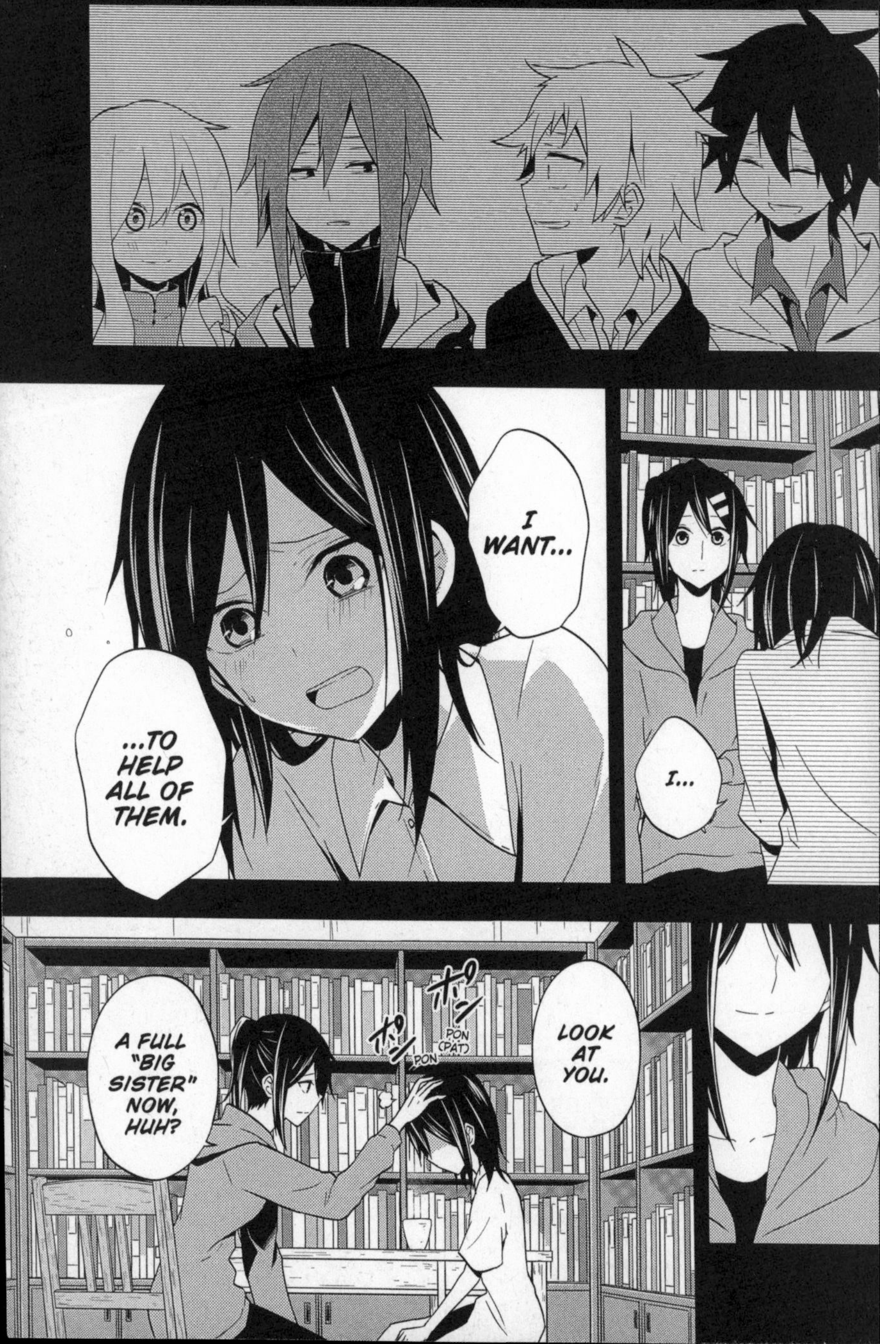
I...
I WANT...
...TO HELP ALL OF THEM.
LOOK AT YOU.
PON (PAT)
PON
A FULL "BIG SISTER" NOW, HUH?

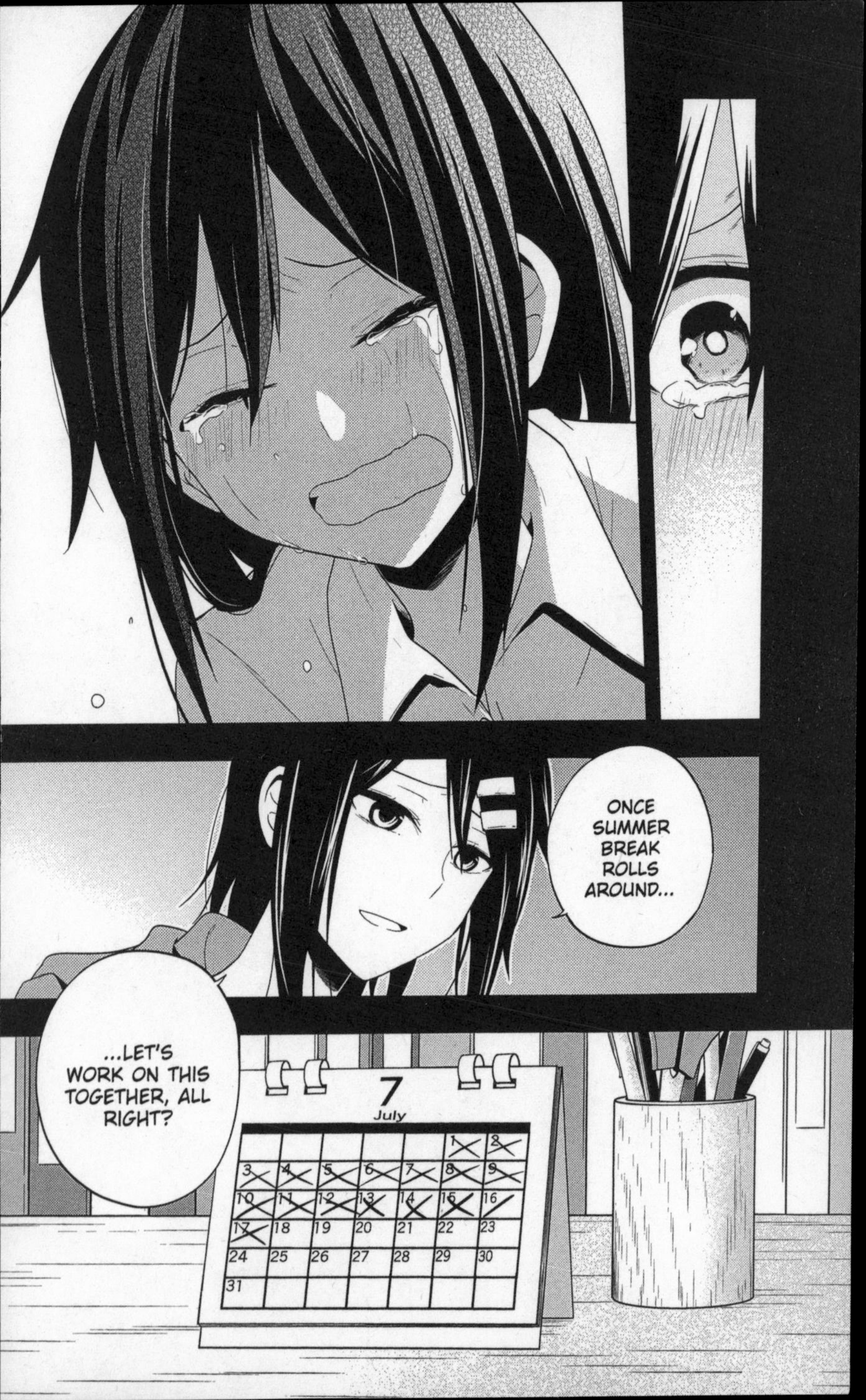
ONCE SUMMER BREAK ROLLS AROUND...
...LET'S WORK ON THIS TOGETHER, ALL RIGHT?
7
July

KAGEROU DAZE

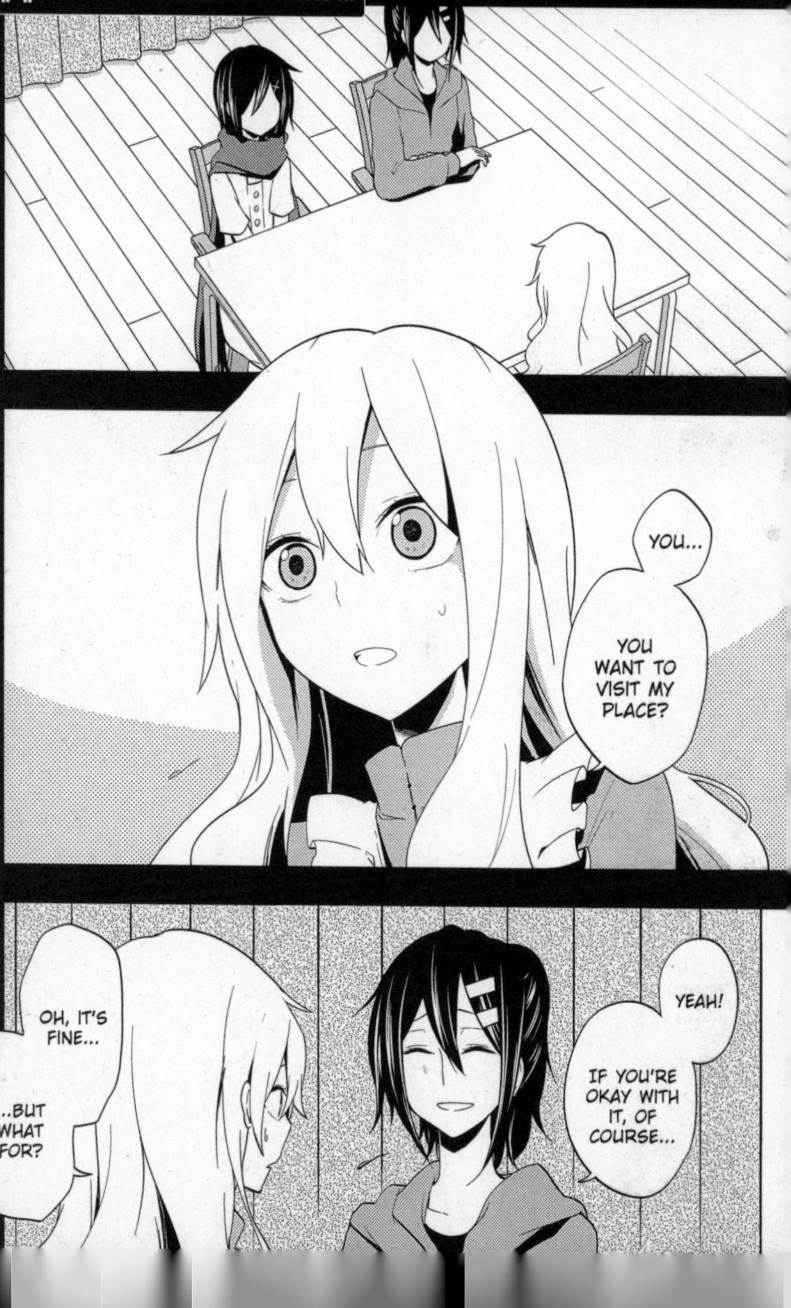
YOU...
YOU WANT TO VISIT MY PLACE?
YEAH!
IF YOU'RE OKAY WITH IT, OF COURSE...
OH, IT'S FINE...
...BUT WHAT FOR?

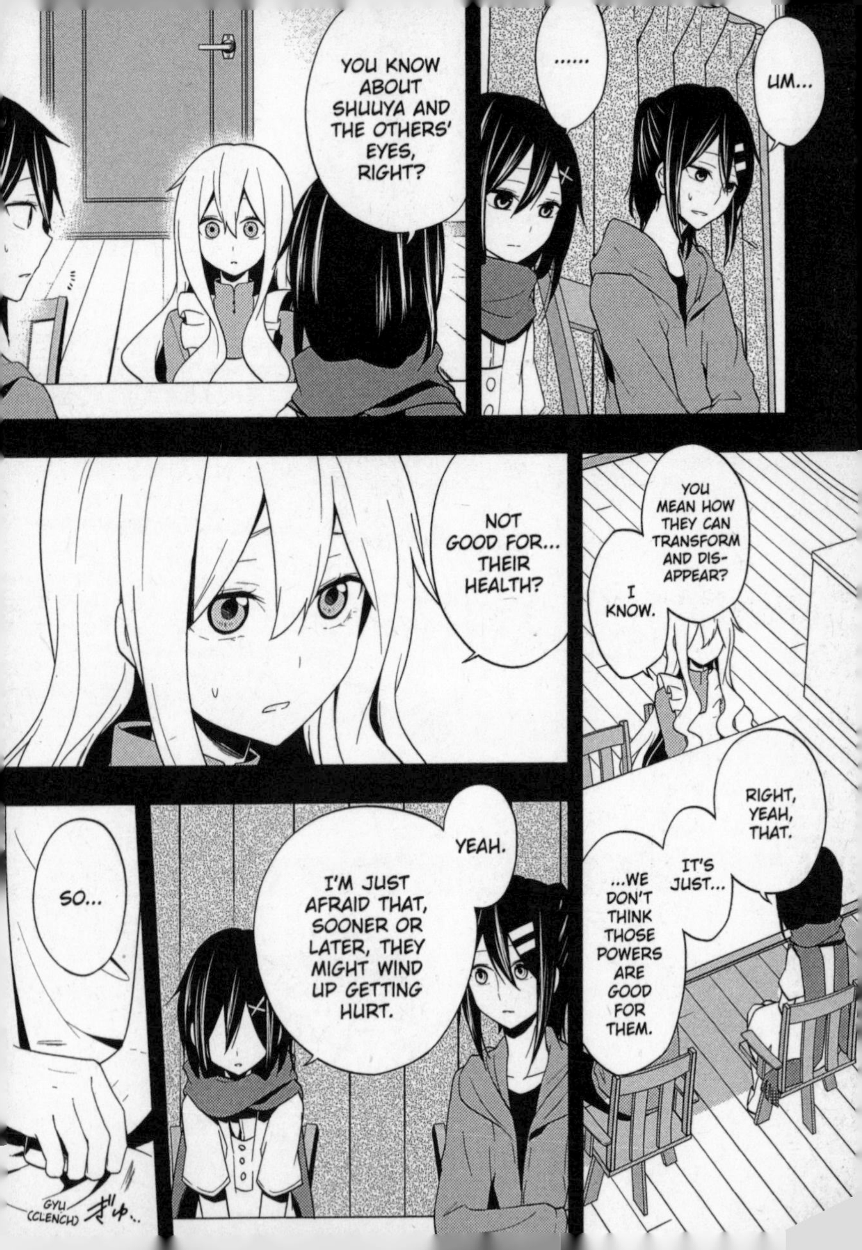
UM...
......
YOU KNOW ABOUT SHUUYA AND THE OTHERS' EYES, RIGHT?
YOU MEAN HOW THEY CAN TRANSFORM AND DIS-APPEAR?
I KNOW.
RIGHT, YEAH, THAT.
IT'S JUST...
...WE DON'T THINK THOSE POWERS ARE GOOD FOR THEM.
NOT GOOD FOR... THEIR HEALTH?
YEAH.
I'M JUST AFRAID THAT, SOONER OR LATER, THEY MIGHT WIND UP GETTING HURT.
SO...
GYU (CLENCH)
ぎゅ..

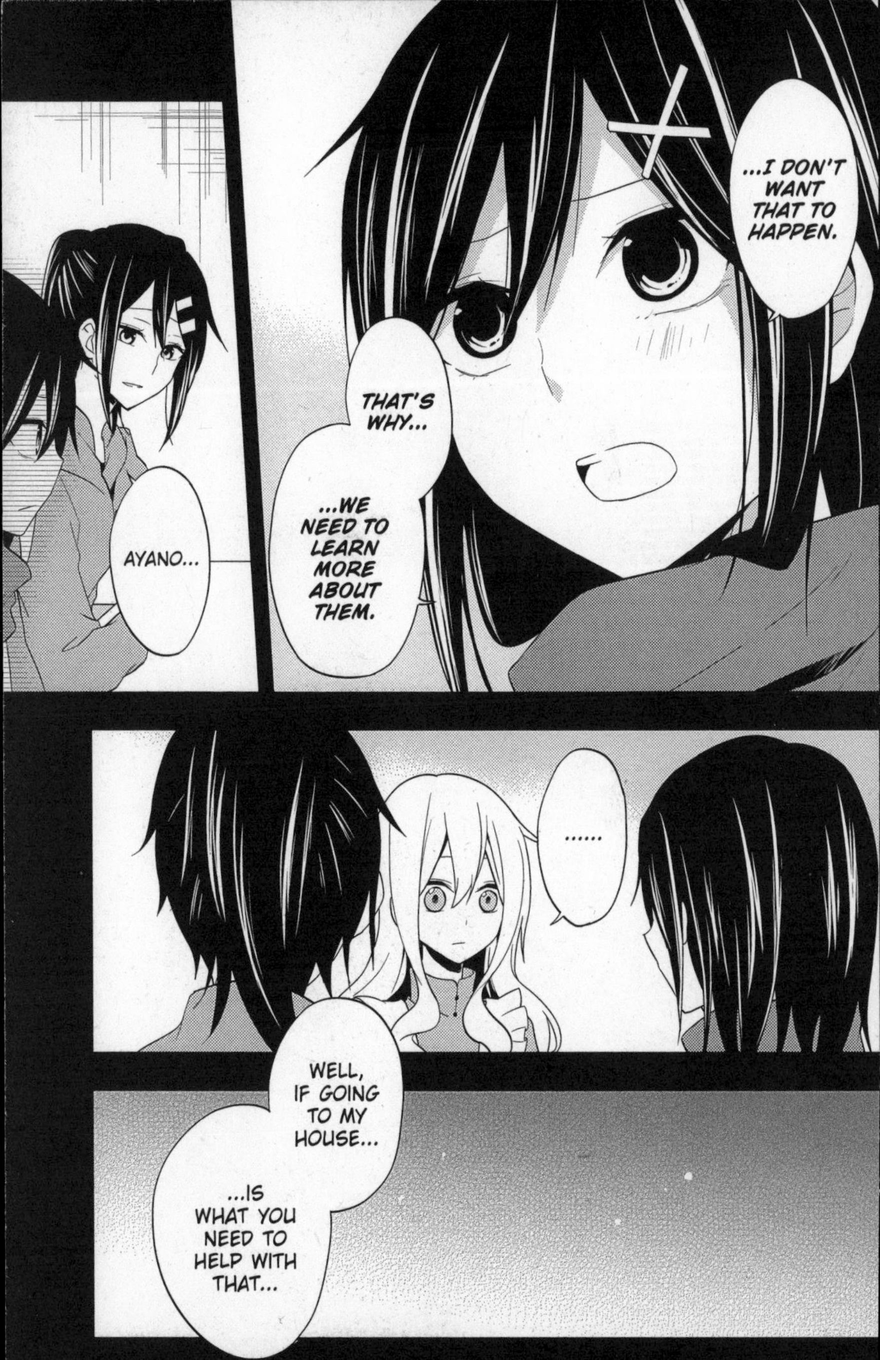
...I DON'T WANT THAT TO HAPPEN.
THAT'S WHY...
...WE NEED TO LEARN MORE ABOUT THEM.
AYANO...
......
WELL, IF GOING TO MY HOUSE...
...IS WHAT YOU NEED TO HELP WITH THAT...

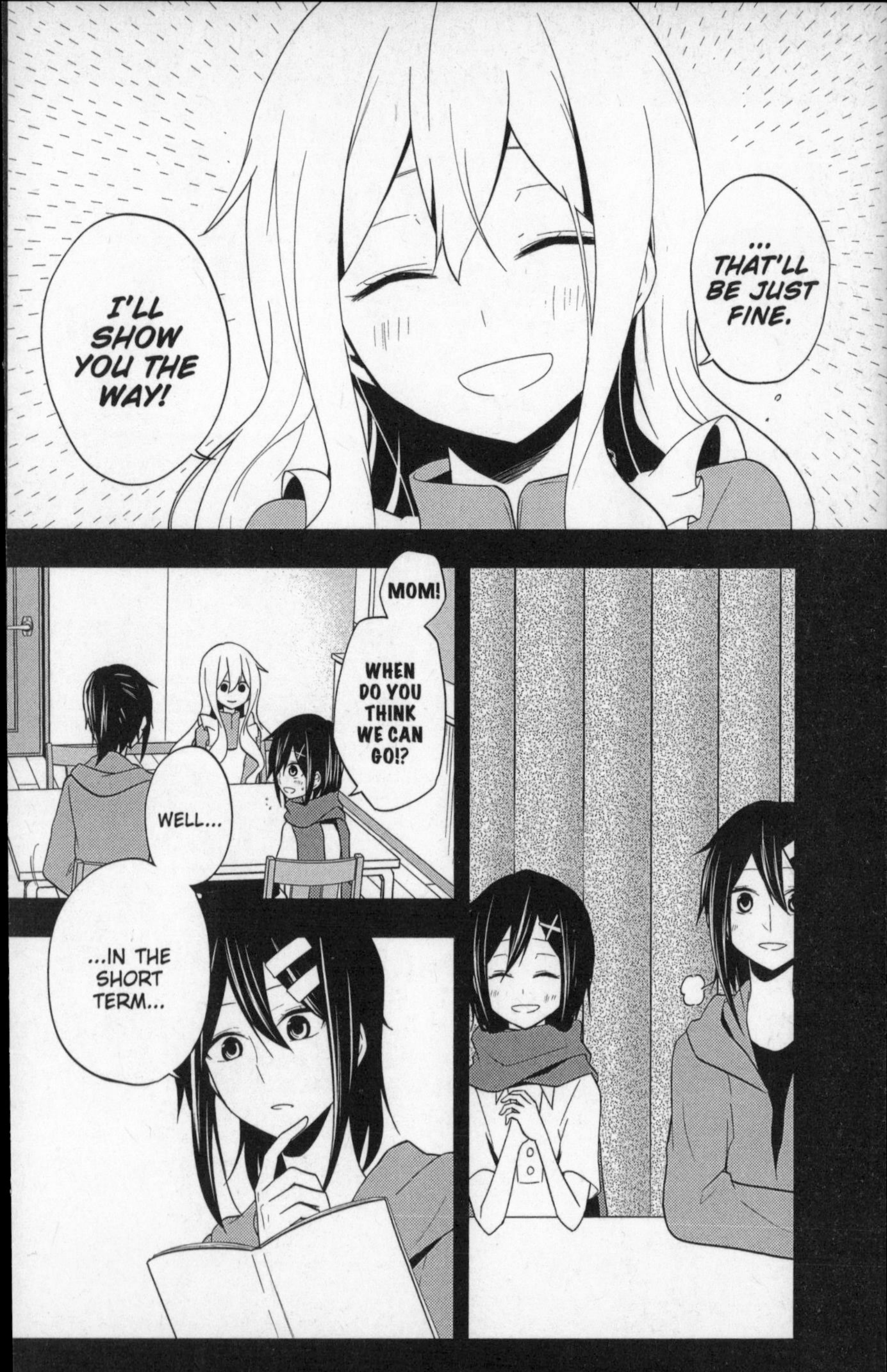
...THAT'LL BE JUST FINE.
I'LL SHOW YOU THE WAY!
MOM!
WHEN DO YOU THINK WE CAN GO!?
WELL...
...IN THE SHORT TERM...

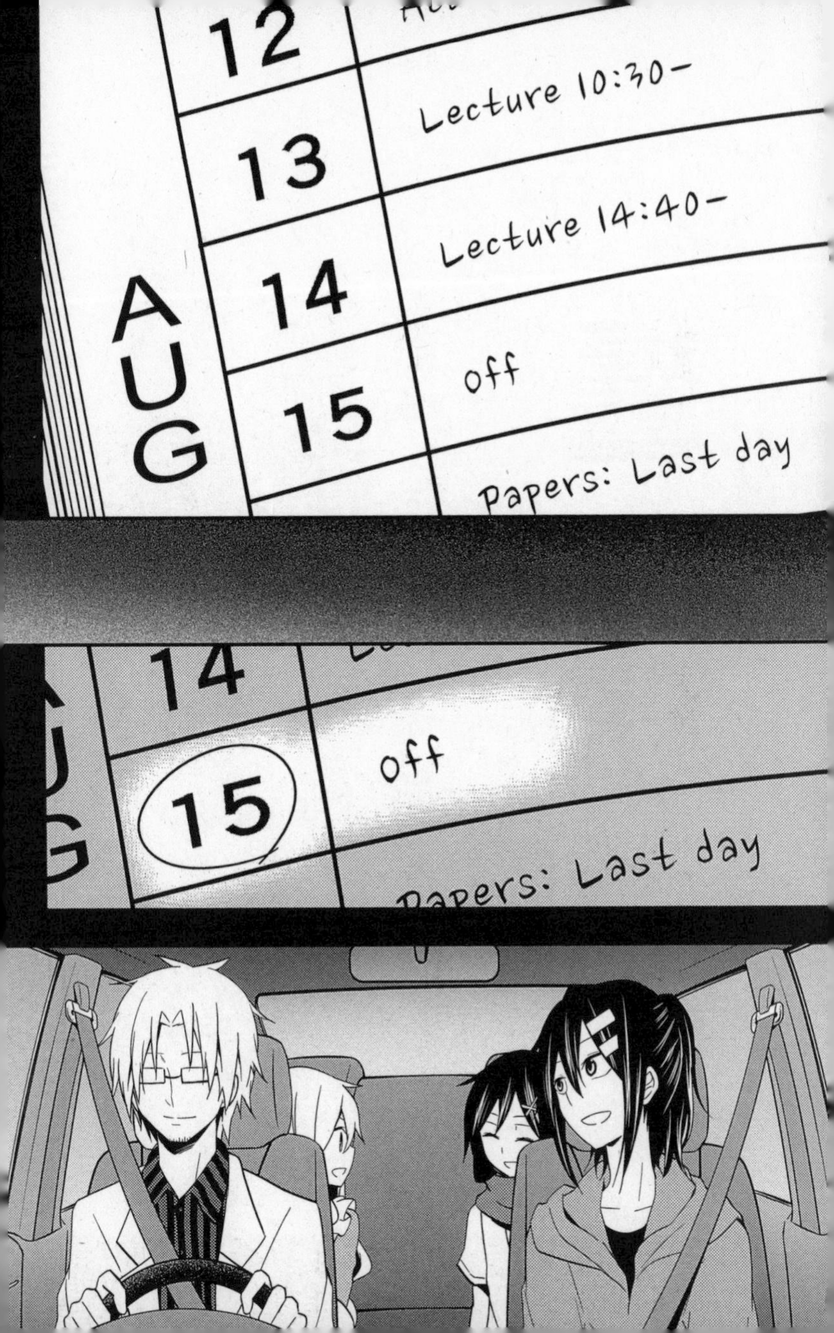

AUG
12
13
Lecture 10:30-
14
Lecture 14:40-
15
off
Papers: Last day
14
15
off
Last day

BACK THEN...

...I REMEMBER THAT ME AND MY MOM...

...THOUGHT ALL THEIR SKILLS HAD COME TO THEM BY CHANCE.

THAT WAS OUR THEORY.

WE THOUGHT SOMETHING IN MARIE'S HOME COULD HELP US RESCUE THEM.

THAT IF WE FOUND THAT MISSING PIECE, WE COULD HELP THE OTHERS.

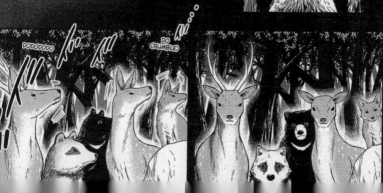

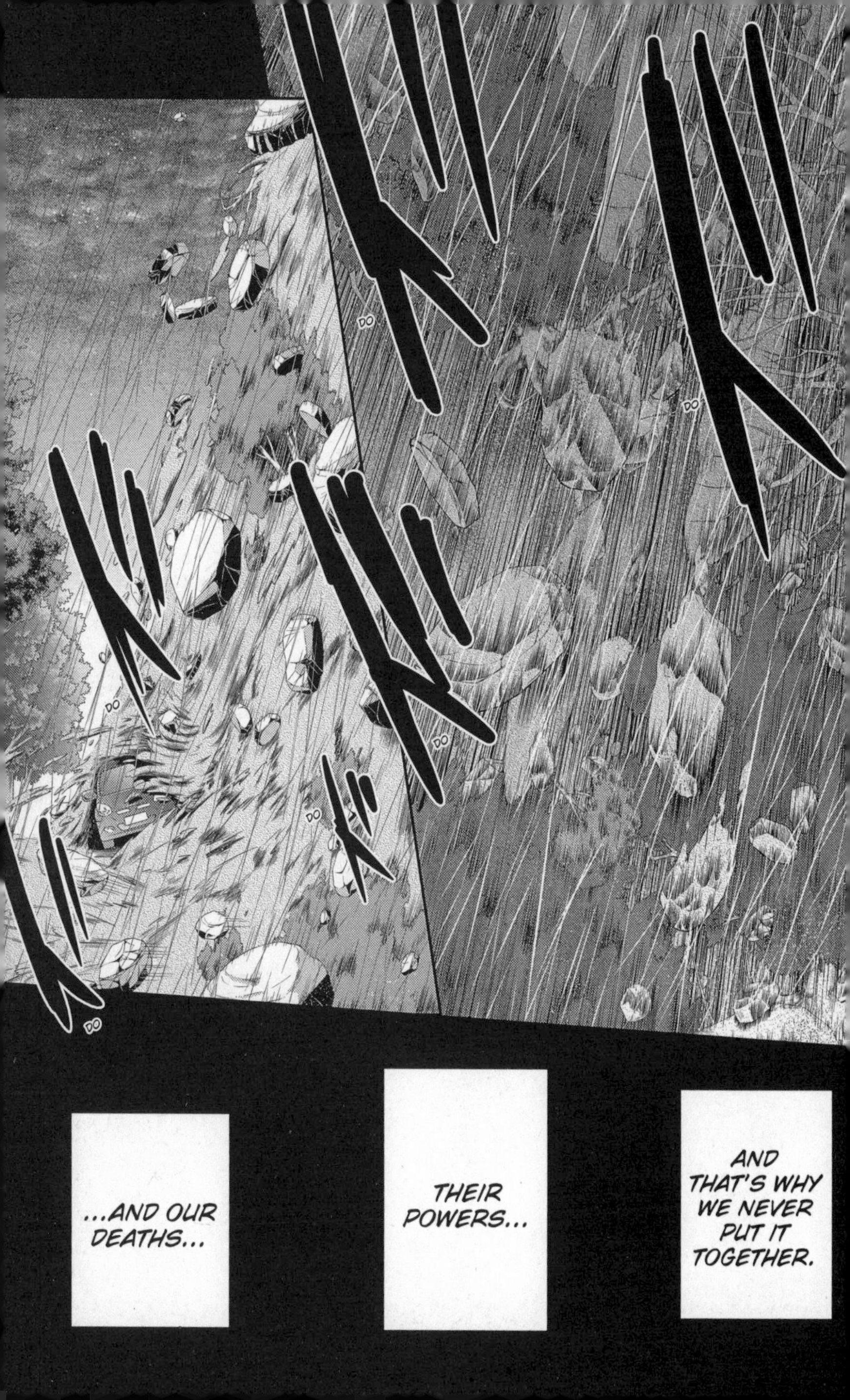
DO
DO
DO
DO
DO
DO
AND THAT'S WHY WE NEVER PUT IT TOGETHER.
THEIR POWERS...
...AND OUR DEATHS...

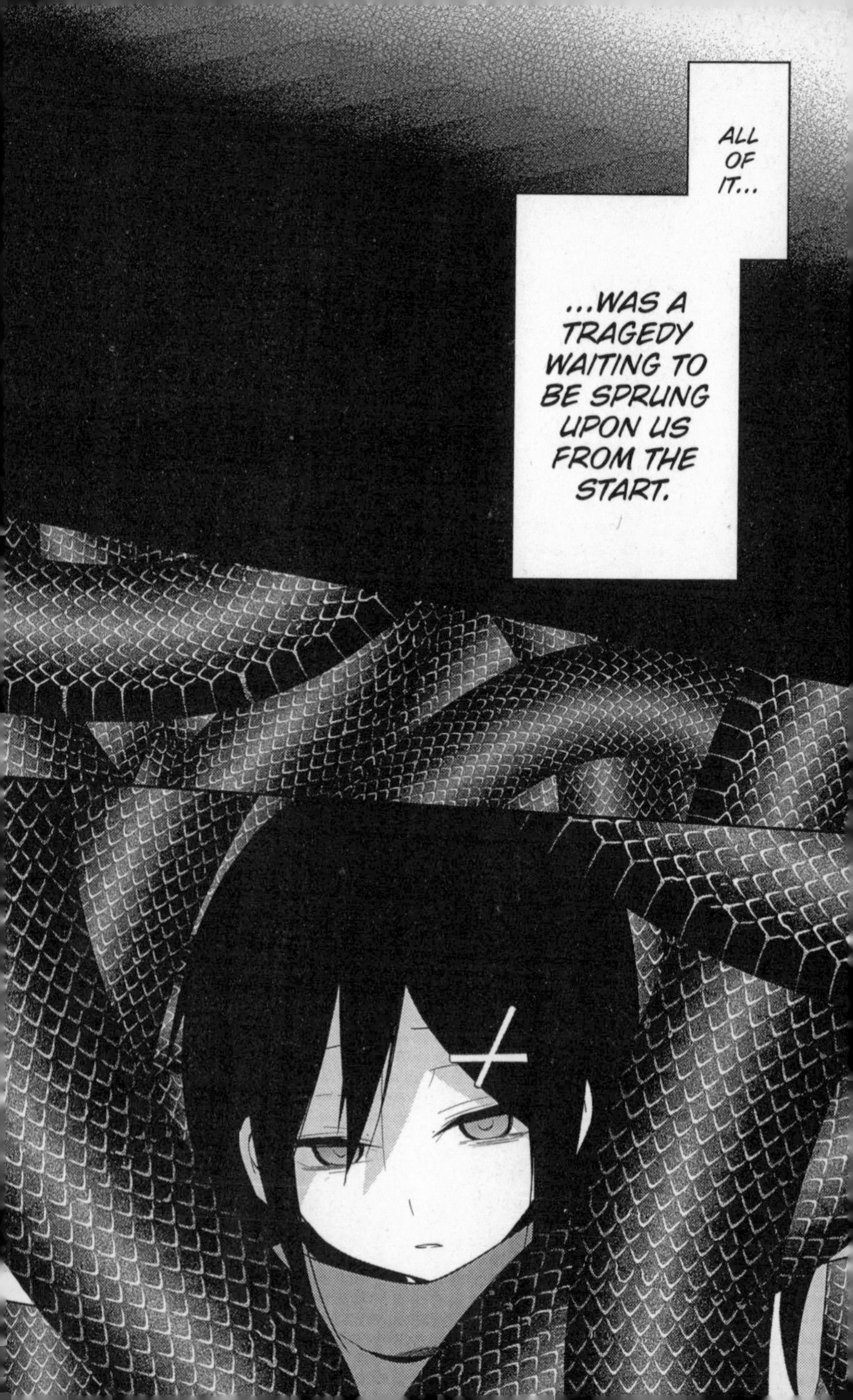
ALL OF IT...
...WAS A TRAGEDY WAITING TO BE SPRUNG UPON US FROM THE START.

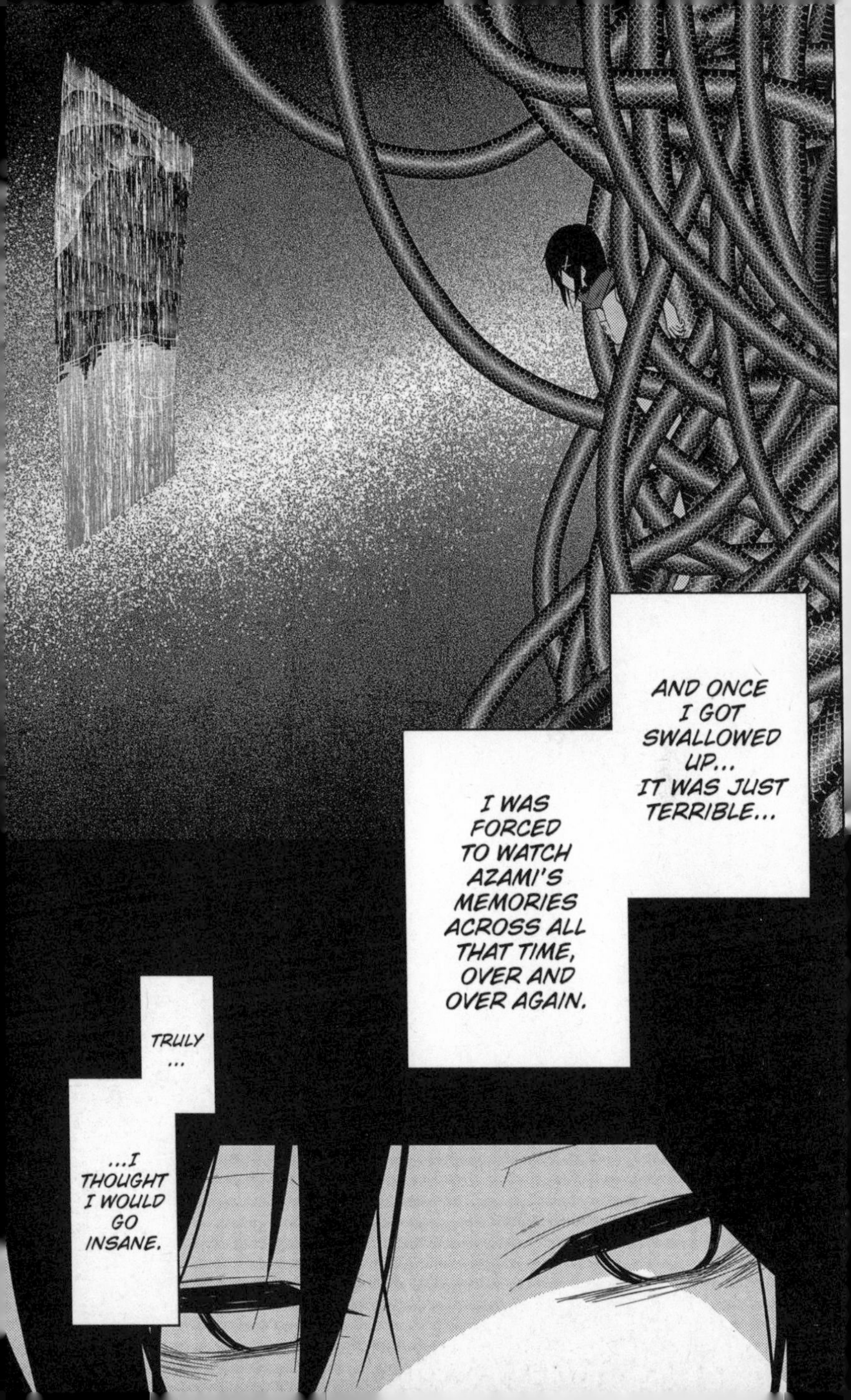
AND ONCE I GOT SWALLOWED UP... IT WAS JUST TERRIBLE...
I WAS FORCED TO WATCH AZAMI'S MEMORIES ACROSS ALL THAT TIME, OVER AND OVER AGAIN.
TRULY ...
...I THOUGHT I WOULD GO INSANE.

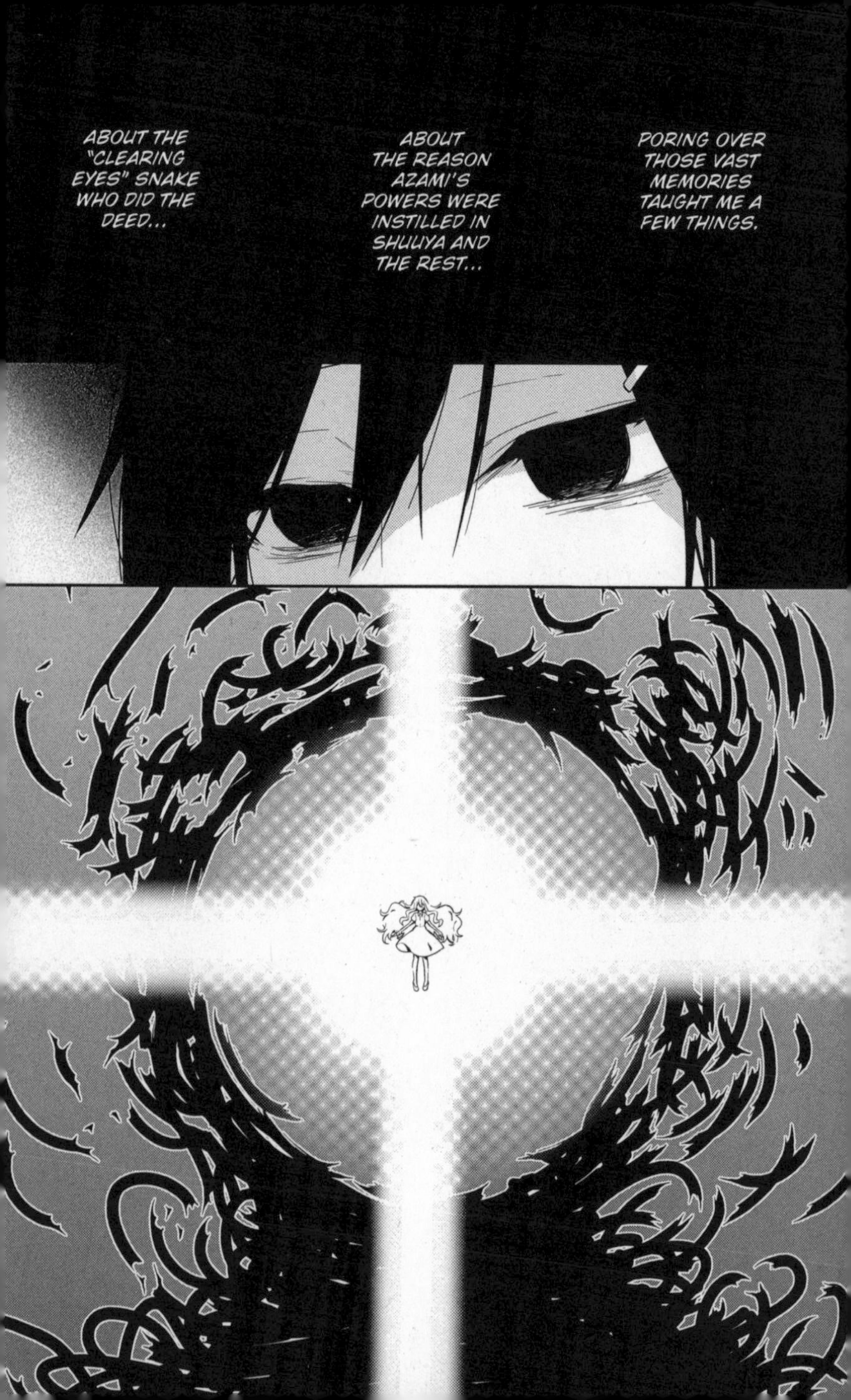
PORING OVER THOSE VAST MEMORIES TAUGHT ME A FEW THINGS.
ABOUT THE REASON AZAMI'S POWERS WERE INSTILLED IN SHUUYA AND THE REST...
ABOUT THE "CLEARING EYES" SNAKE WHO DID THE DEED...

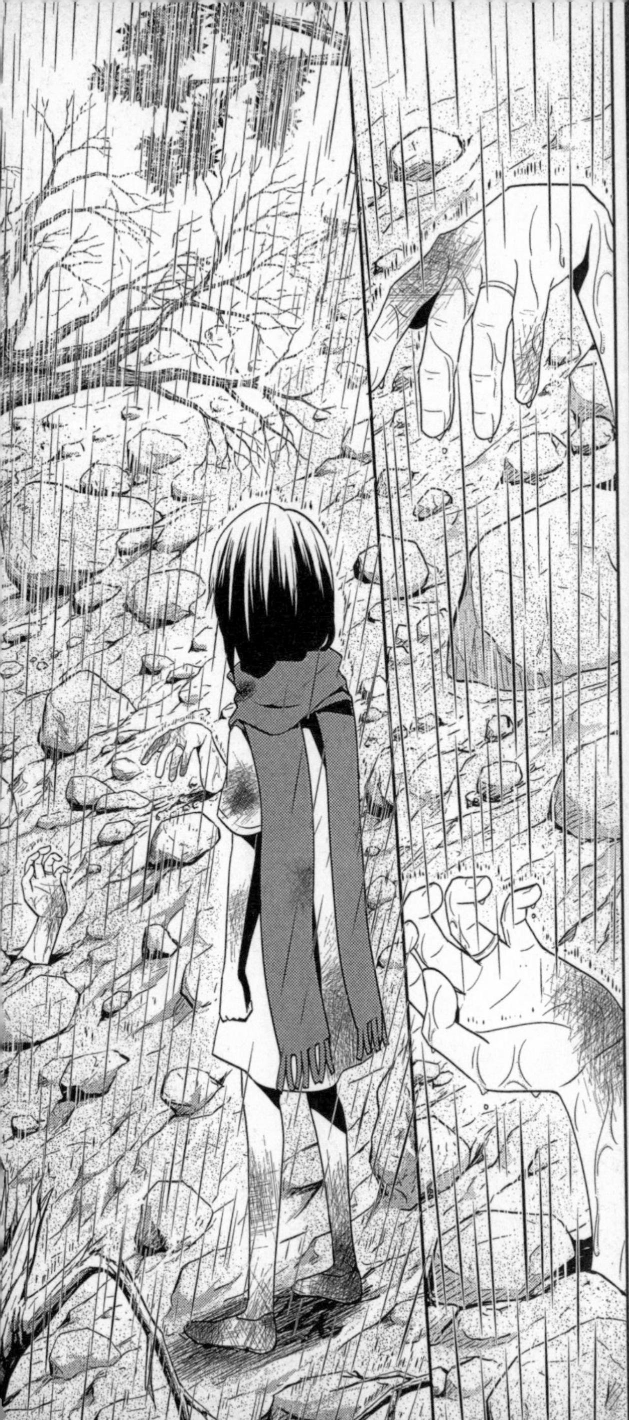

ABOUT WHAT WE CAN DO TO END THIS TRAGEDY FOR GOOD...

...AND WHAT IT WILL TAKE TO PULL THAT OFF.

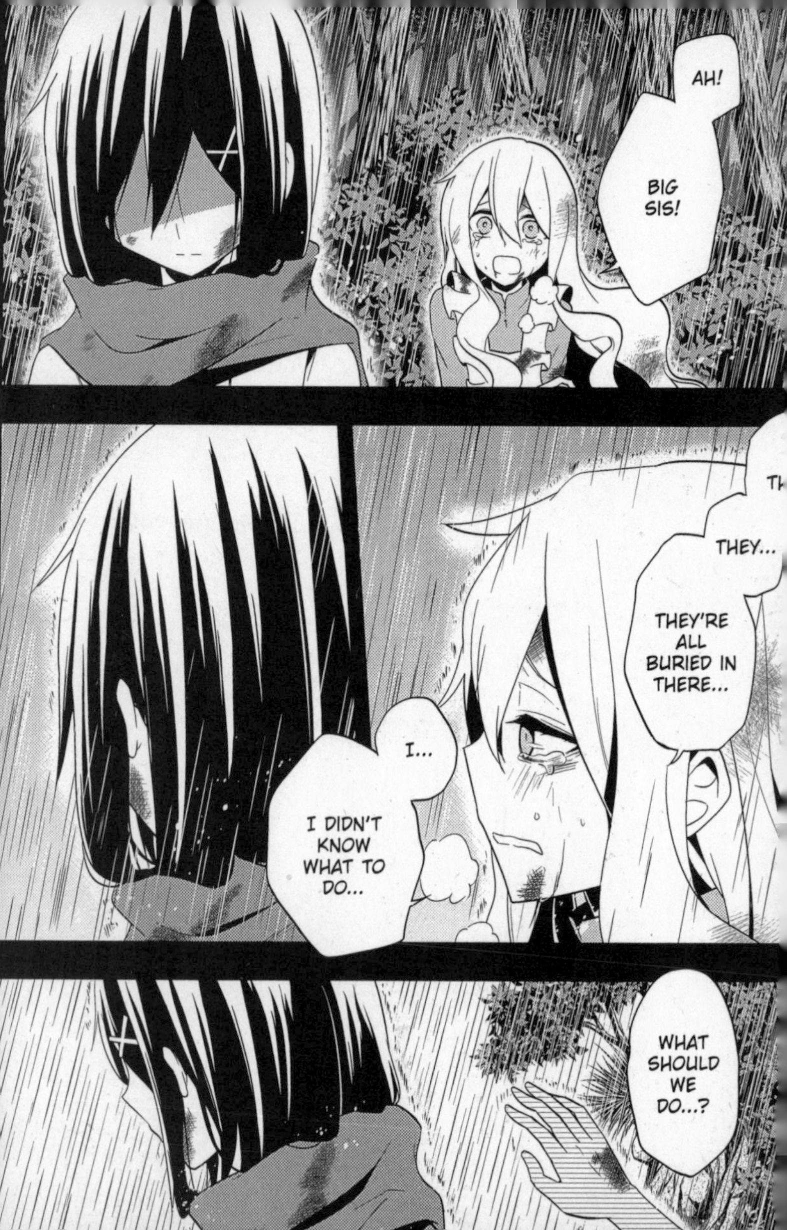
AH!
BIG SIS!
THEY...
THEY'RE ALL BURIED IN THERE...
I...
I DIDN'T KNOW WHAT TO DO...
WHAT SHOULD WE DO...?

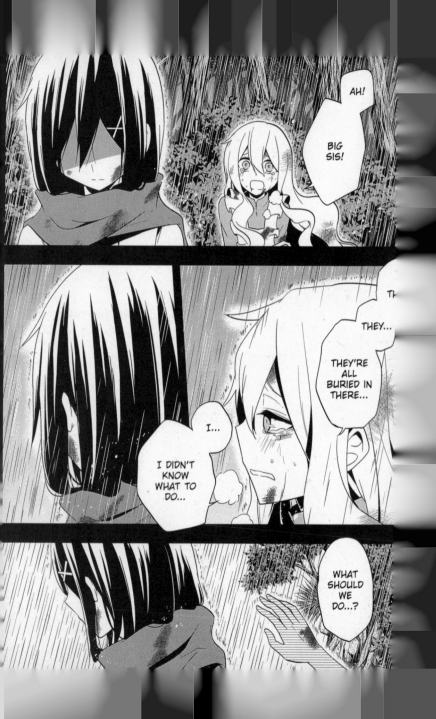

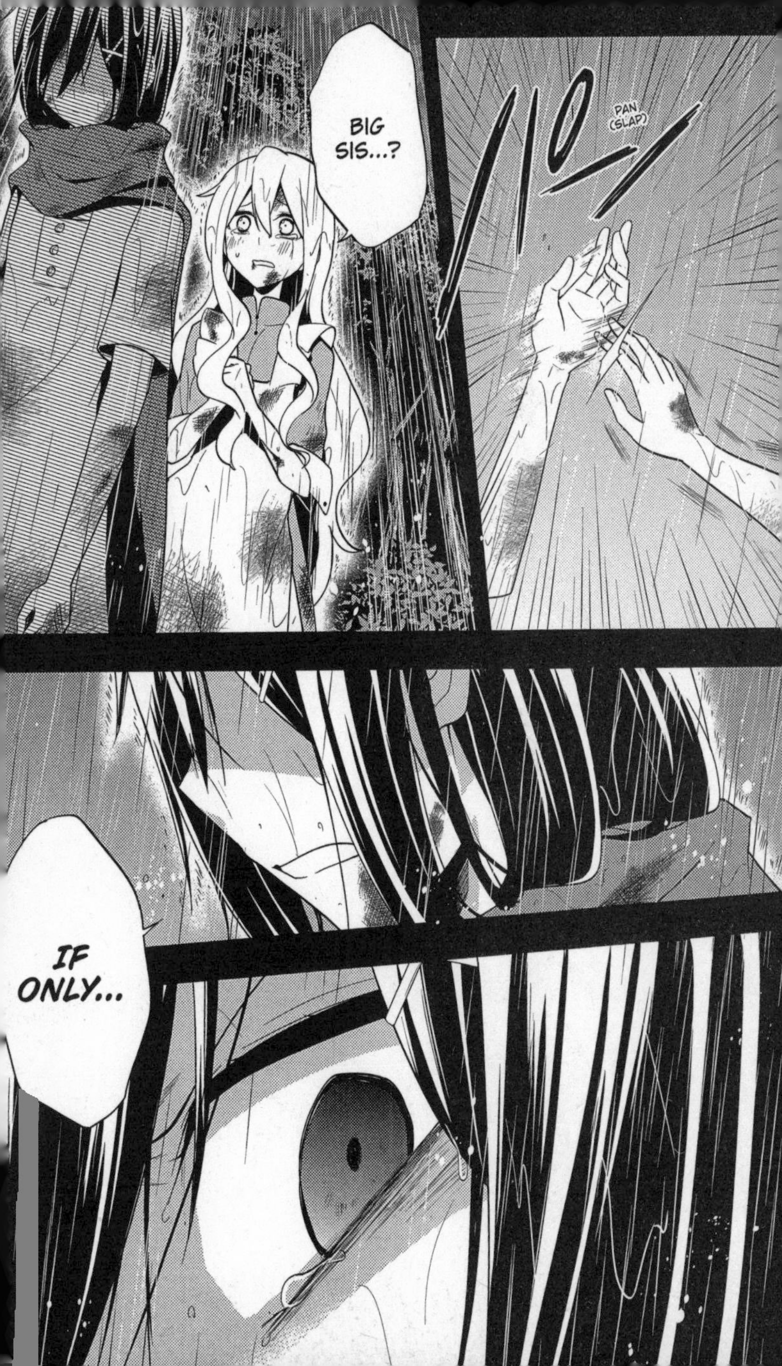
PAN (SLAP)
BIG SIS...?
IF ONLY...

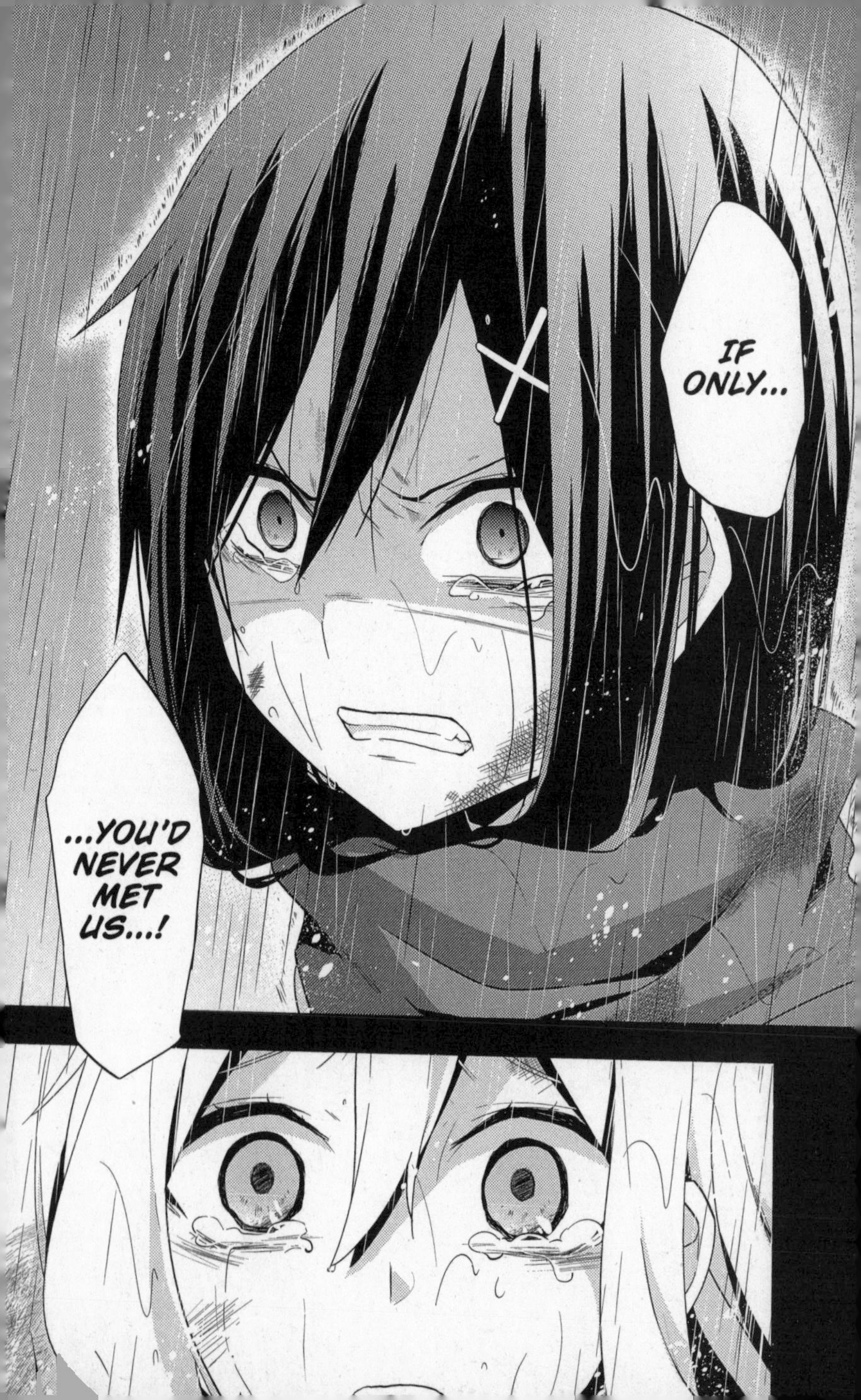
IF ONLY...
...YOU'D NEVER MET US...!

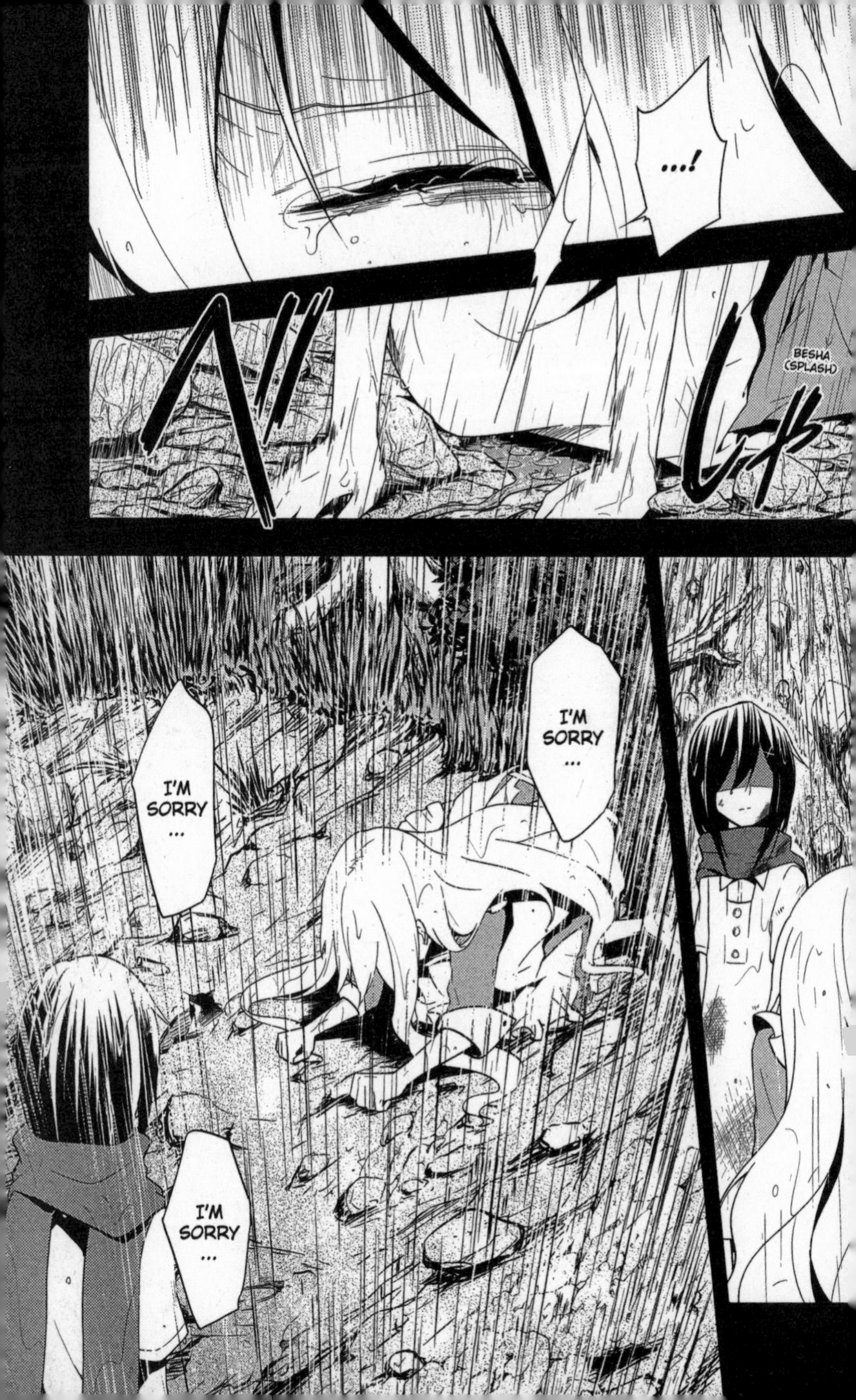
...!
BESHA (SPLASH)
I'M SORRY ...
I'M SORRY ...
I'M SORRY ...

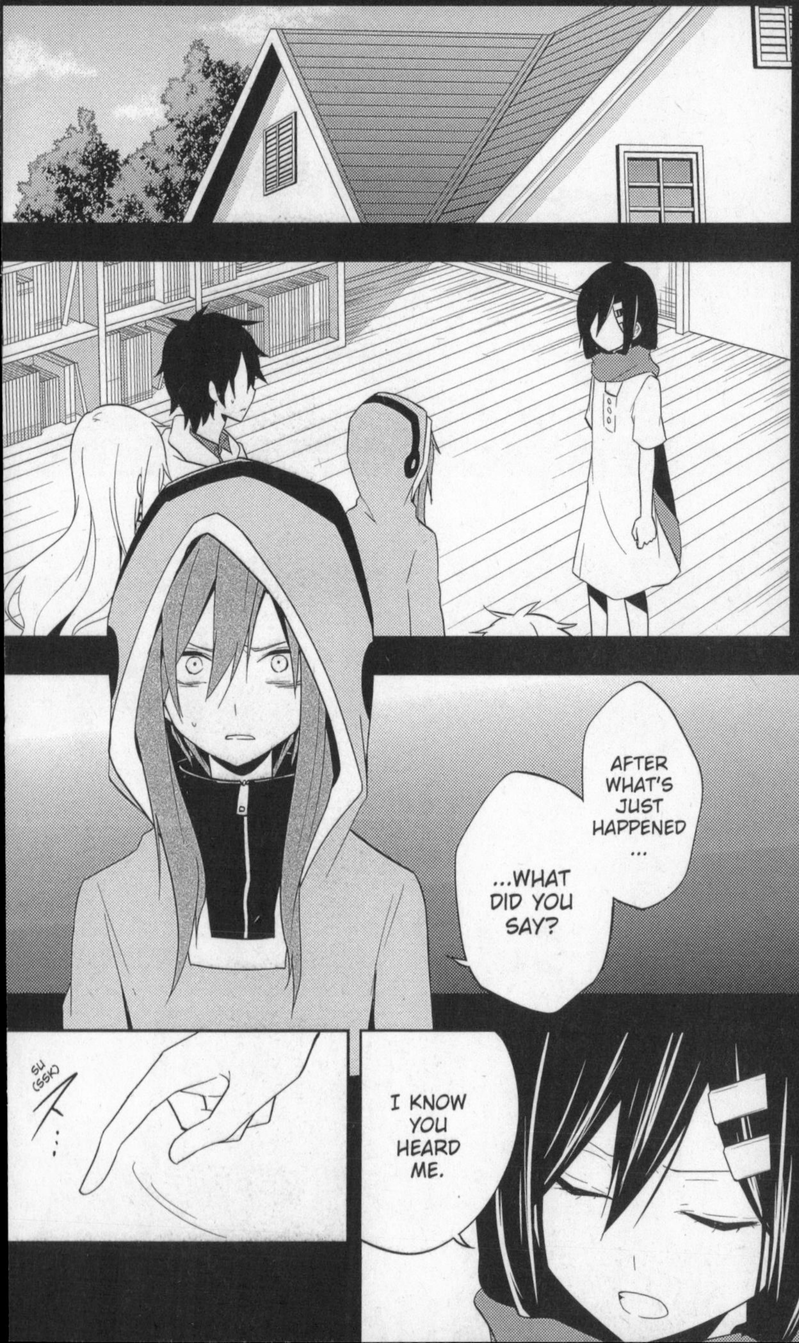
AFTER WHAT'S JUST HAPPENED ...
...WHAT DID YOU SAY?
I KNOW YOU HEARD ME.
SU (SSK)
ス…

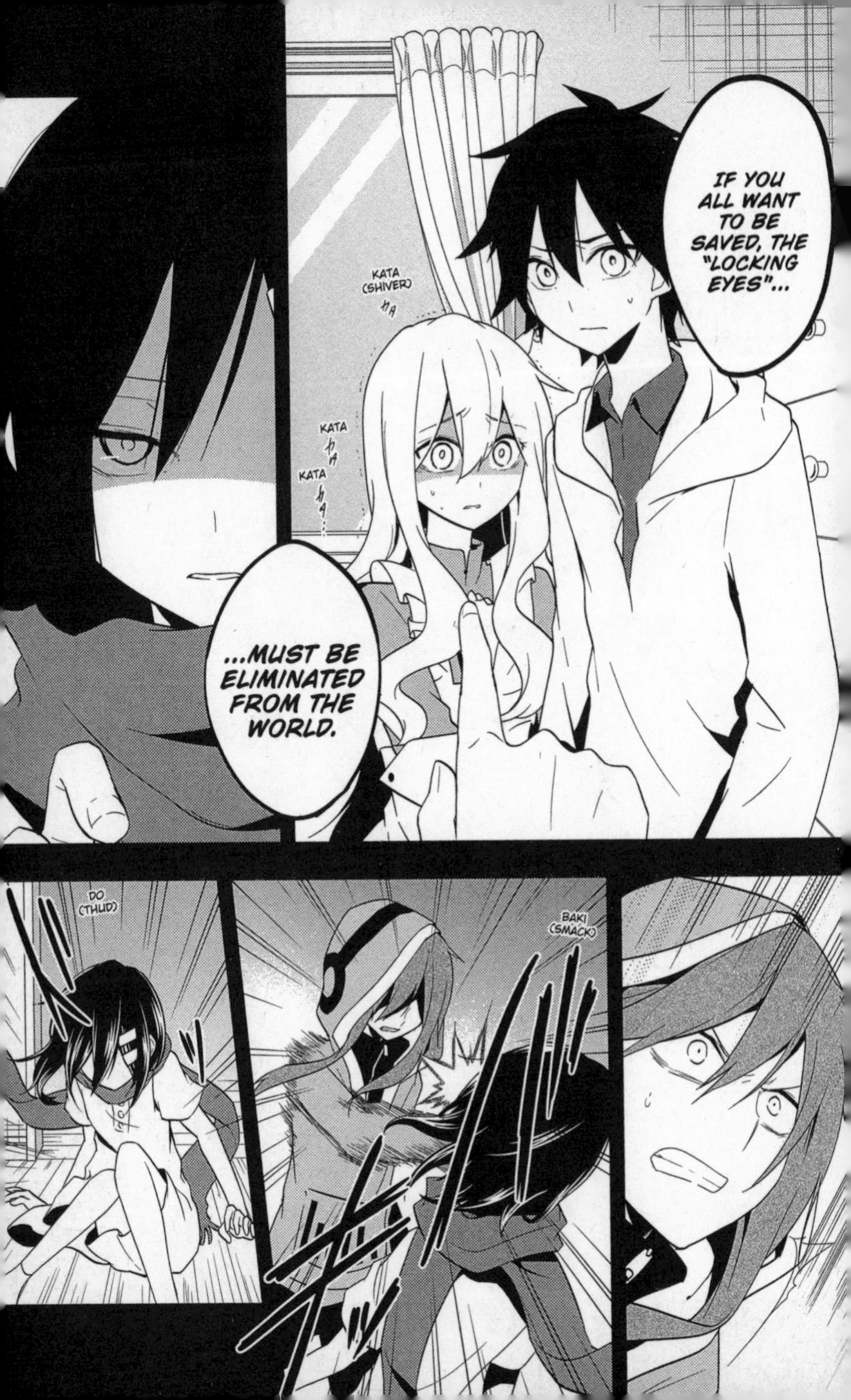
IF YOU ALL WANT TO BE SAVED, THE "LOCKING EYES"...
KATA (SHIVER)
KATA
KATA
...MUST BE ELIMINATED FROM THE WORLD.
BAKI (SMACK)
DO (THUD)

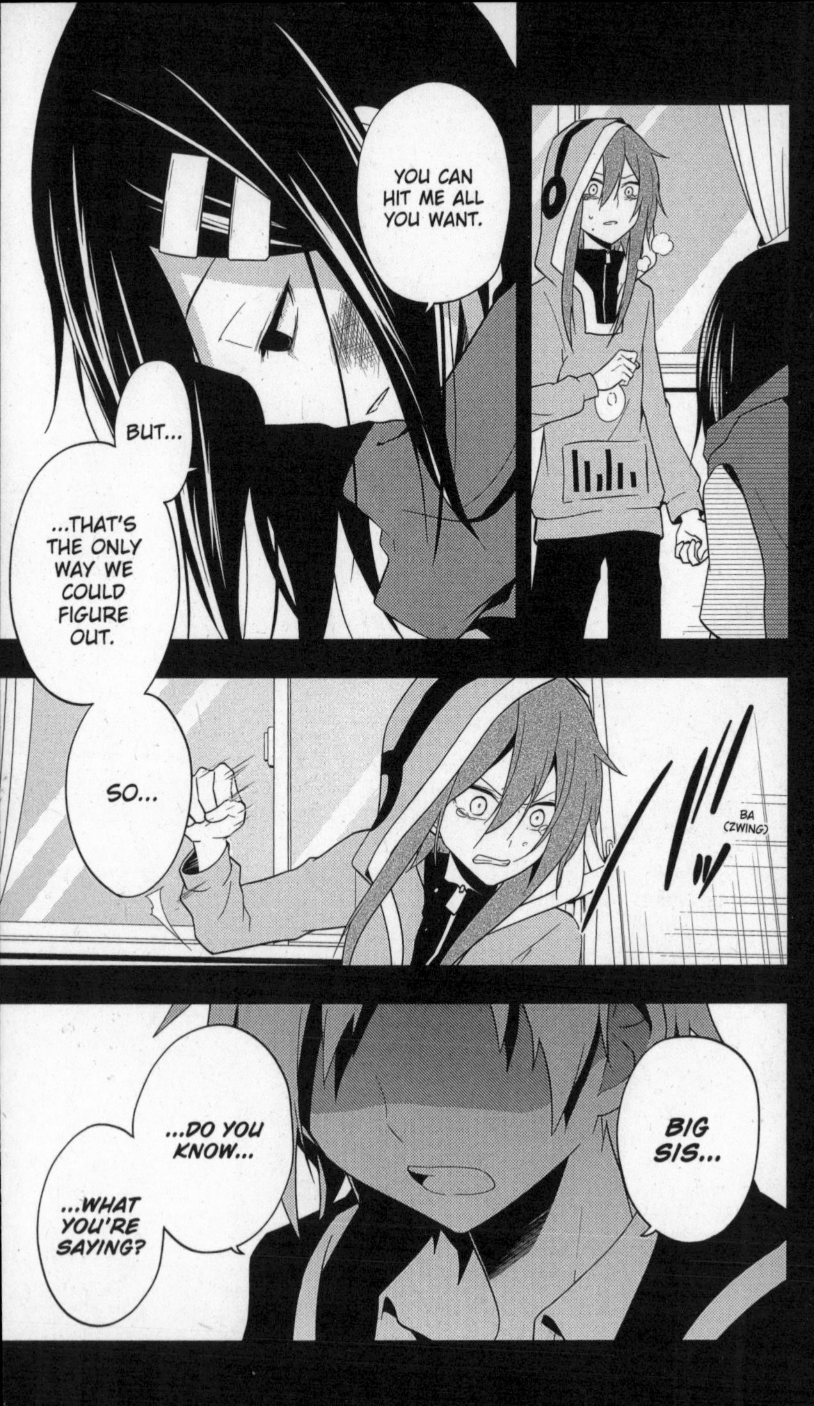
YOU CAN HIT ME ALL YOU WANT.
BUT...
...THAT'S THE ONLY WAY WE COULD FIGURE OUT.
SO...
BA (ZWING)
BIG SIS...
...DO YOU KNOW...
...WHAT YOU'RE SAYING?

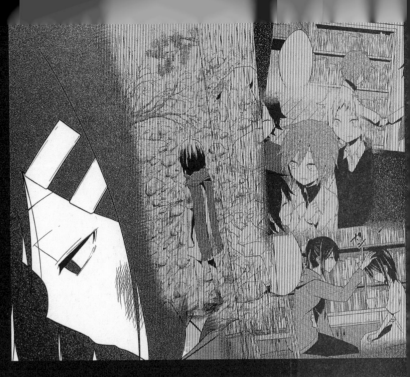

SHUUYA...

...YOUR BIG SIS WILL ALWAYS BE WITH YOU...

I DO...

I TOLD YOU...

...DIDN'T I...?

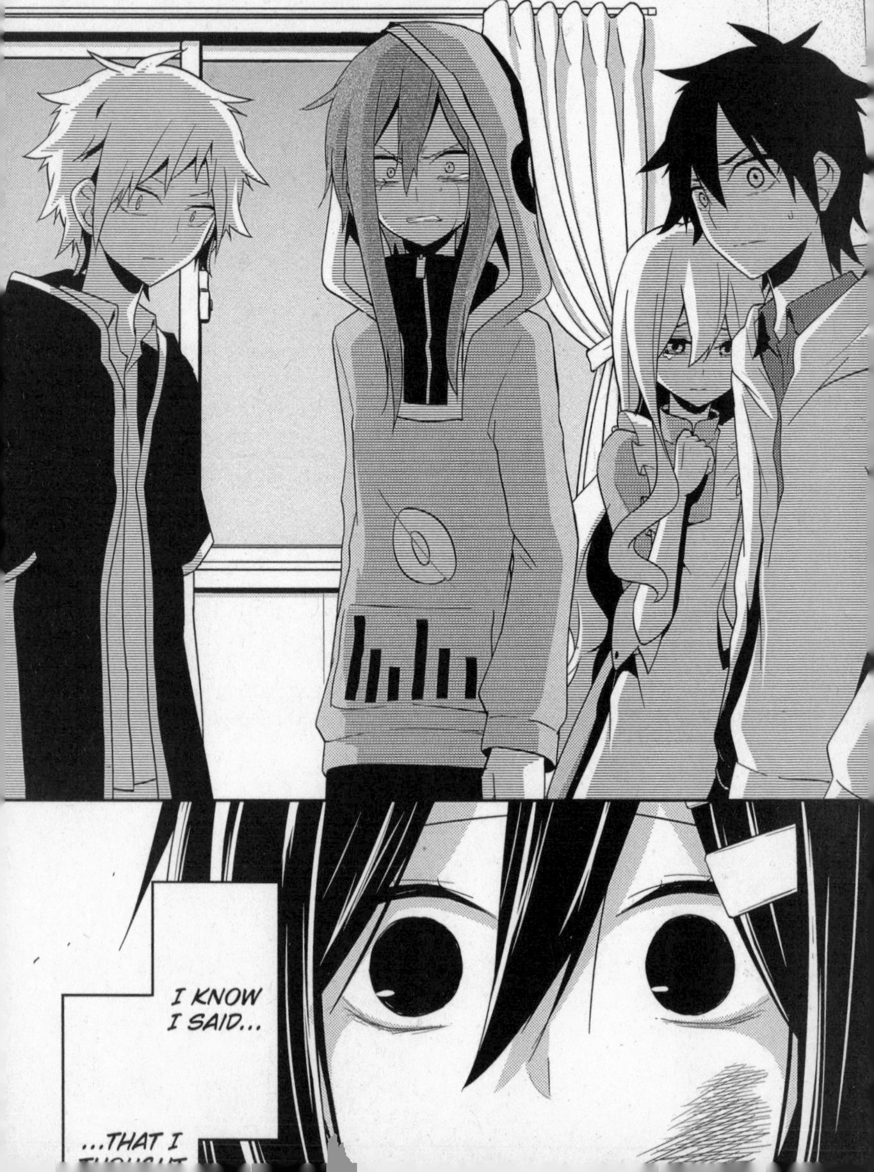
I KNOW I SAID...
...THAT I

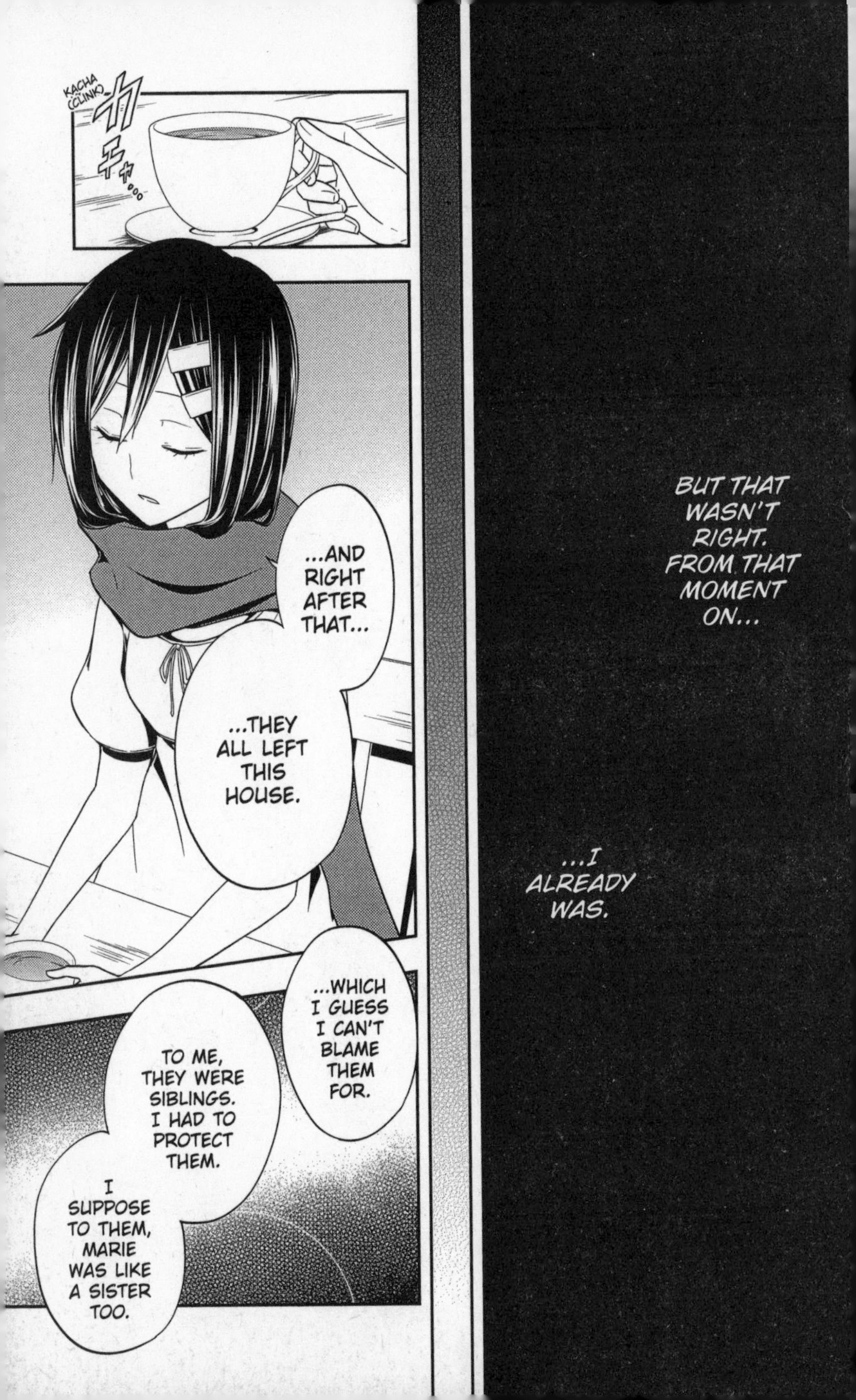
KACHA (CLINK)
...AND RIGHT AFTER THAT...
...THEY ALL LEFT THIS HOUSE.
...WHICH I GUESS I CAN'T BLAME THEM FOR.
TO ME, THEY WERE SIBLINGS. I HAD TO PROTECT THEM.
I SUPPOSE TO THEM, MARIE WAS LIKE A SISTER TOO.
BUT THAT WASN'T RIGHT. FROM THAT MOMENT ON...
...I ALREADY WAS.

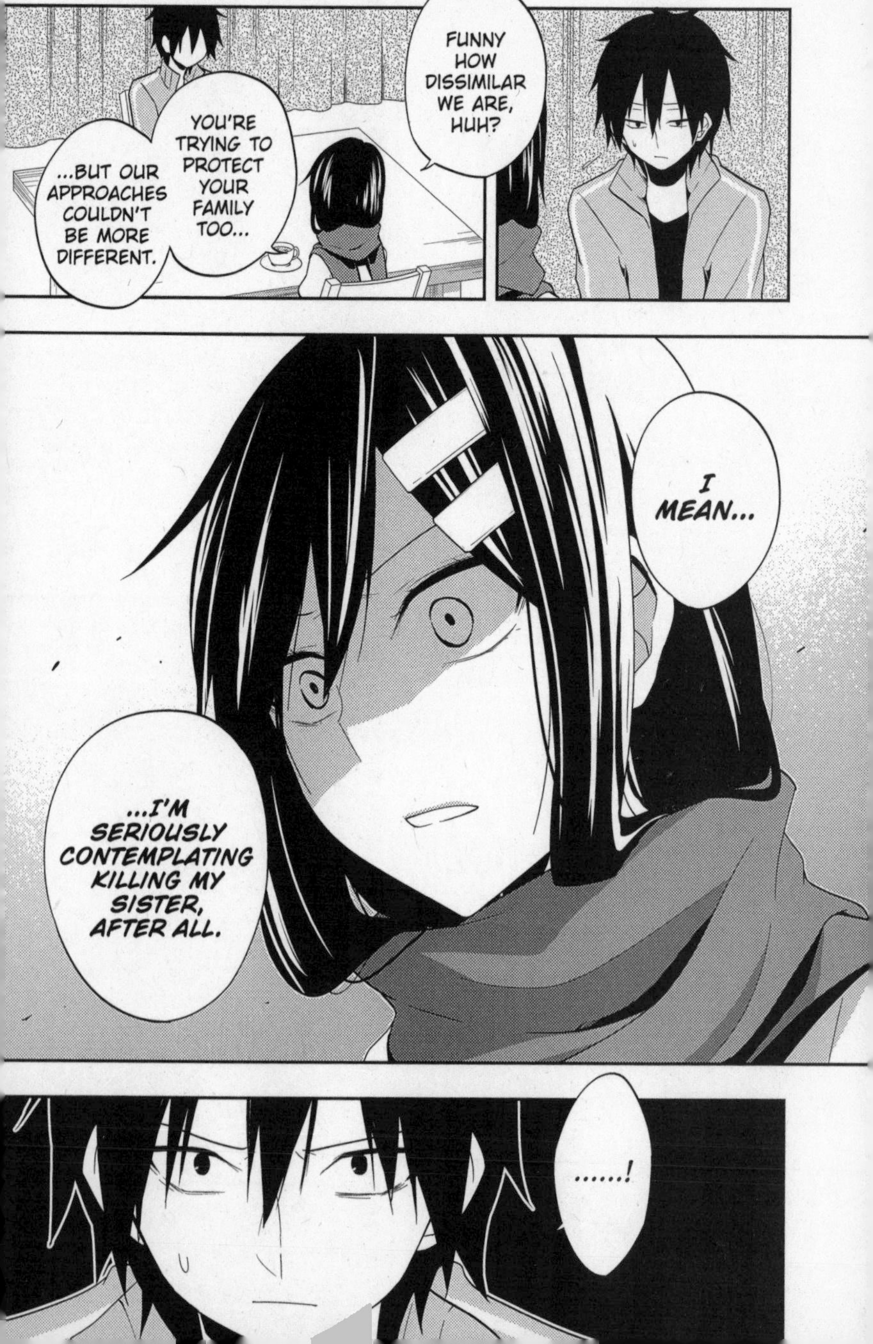
FUNNY HOW DISSIMILAR WE ARE, HUH?
YOU'RE TRYING TO PROTECT YOUR FAMILY TOO...
...BUT OUR APPROACHES COULDN'T BE MORE DIFFERENT.
I MEAN...
...I'M SERIOUSLY CONTEMPLATING KILLING MY SISTER, AFTER ALL.
......!

KAGEROU DAZE

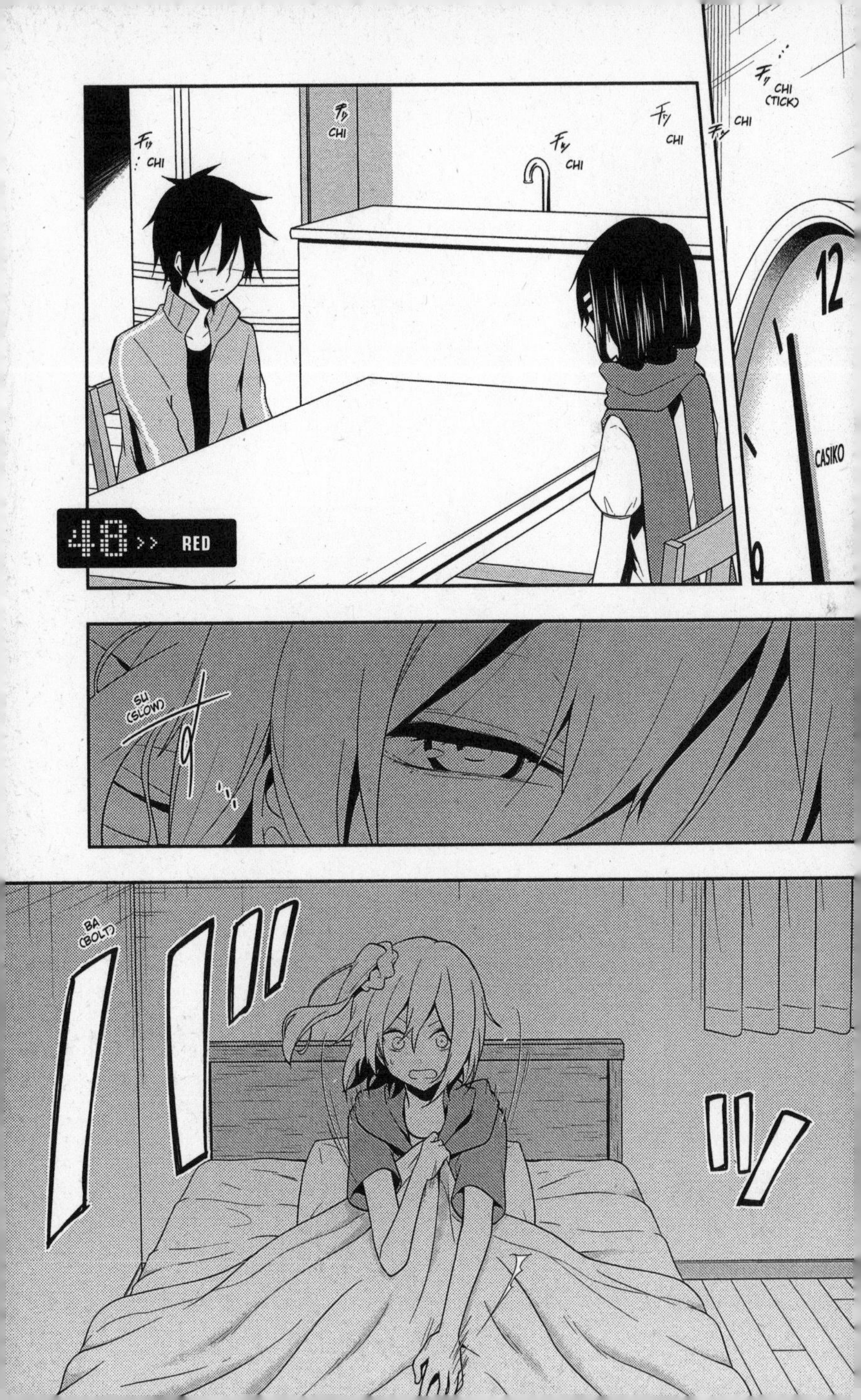

...
CHI (TICK)
CHI
CHI
CHI
CHI
CHI
12
CASIKO
48 >> RED
SU (SLOW)
...
BA (BOLT)

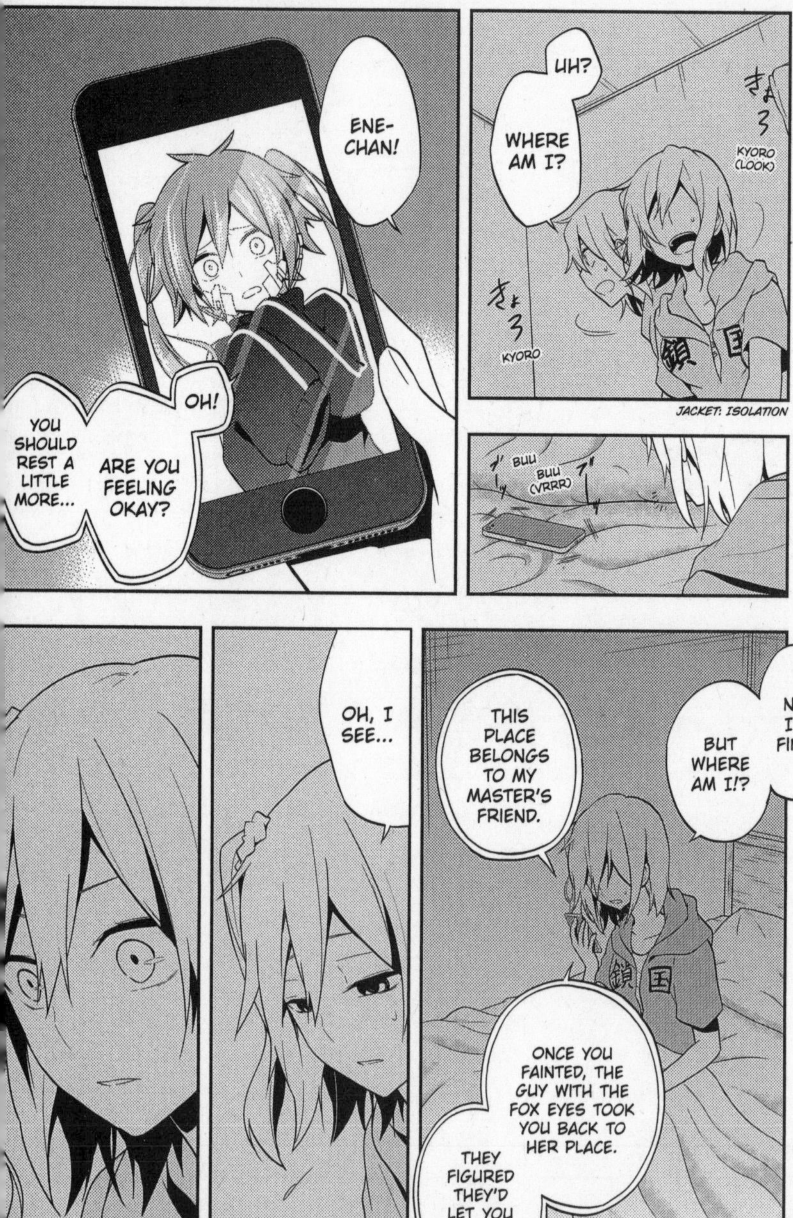

UH?
WHERE AM I?
きょろ
KYORO (LOOK)
きょろ
KYORO
JACKET: ISOLATION
BUU BUU (VRRR)
ENE-CHAN!
OH!
ARE YOU FEELING OKAY?
YOU SHOULD REST A LITTLE MORE...
NO, I'M FINE.
BUT WHERE AM I!?
THIS PLACE BELONGS TO MY MASTER'S FRIEND.
ONCE YOU FAINTED, THE GUY WITH THE FOX EYES TOOK YOU BACK TO HER PLACE.
THEY FIGURED THEY'D LET YOU REST A LITTLE.
OH, I SEE...

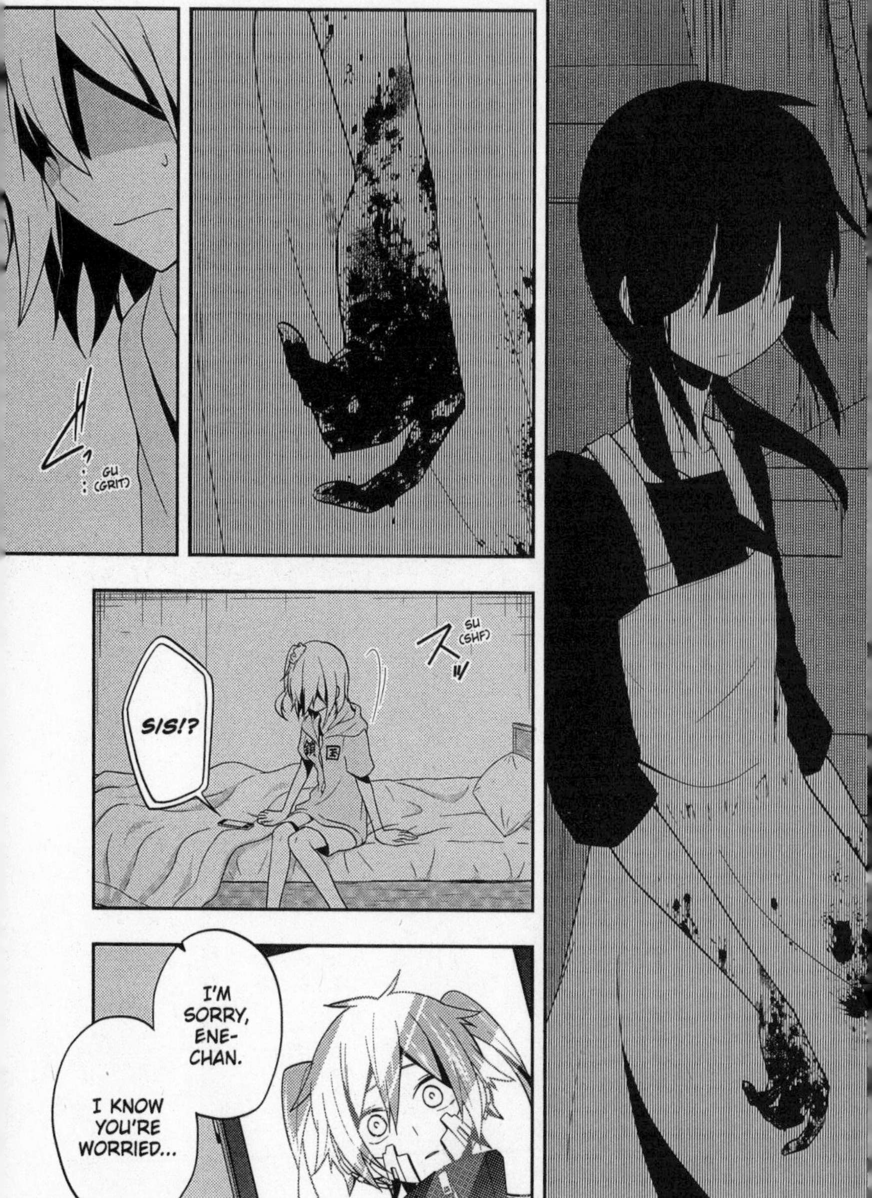
GU (GRIT)
SU (SHF)
SIS!?
I'M SORRY, ENE-CHAN.
I KNOW YOU'RE WORRIED...

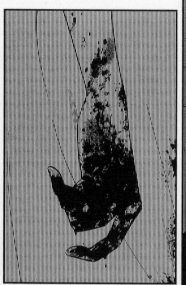

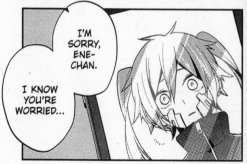

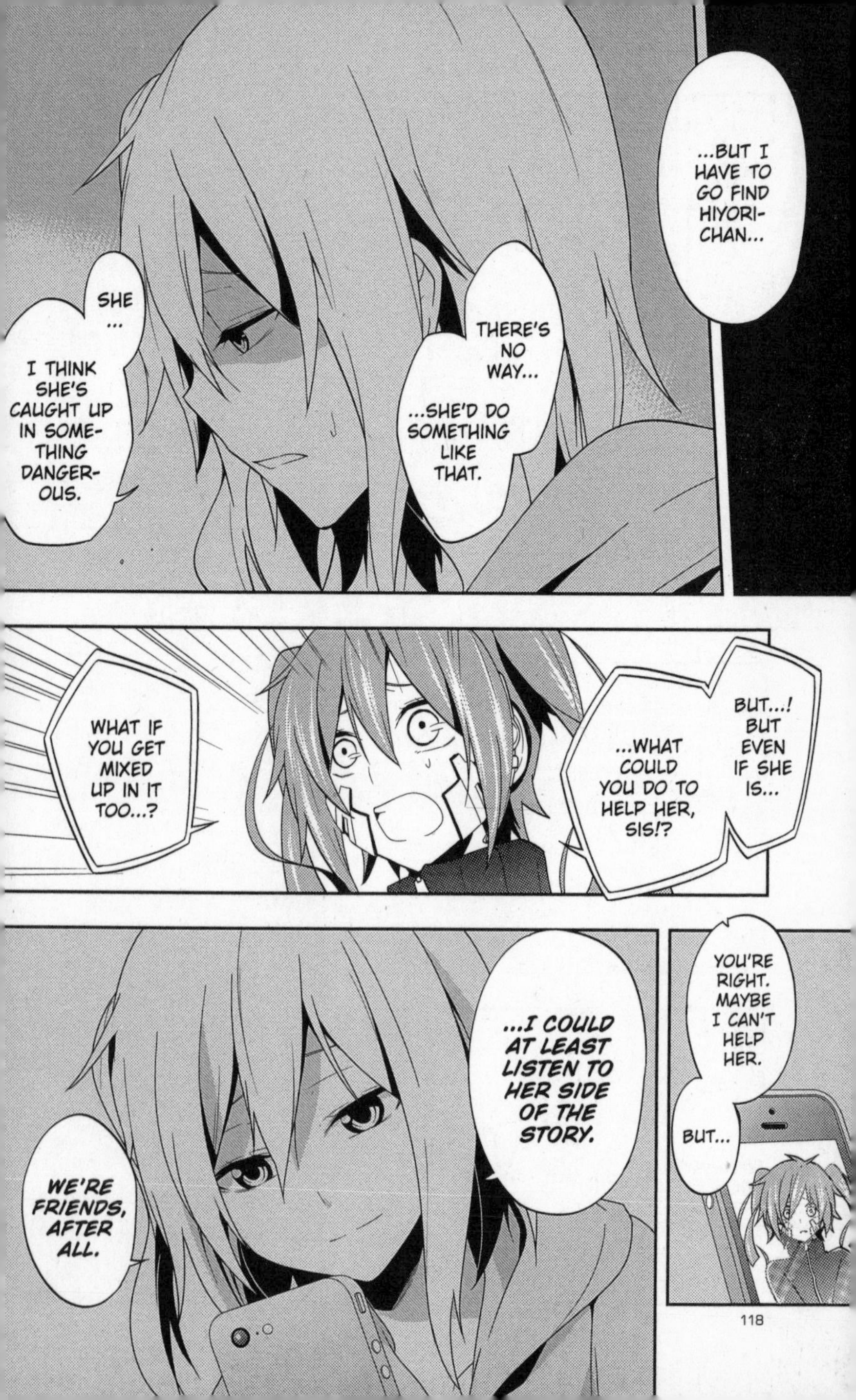
...BUT I HAVE TO GO FIND HIYORI-CHAN...
THERE'S NO WAY...
...SHE'D DO SOMETHING LIKE THAT.
SHE ...
I THINK SHE'S CAUGHT UP IN SOMETHING DANGEROUS.
BUT...! BUT EVEN IF SHE IS...
...WHAT COULD YOU DO TO HELP HER, SIS!?
WHAT IF YOU GET MIXED UP IN IT TOO...?
YOU'RE RIGHT. MAYBE I CAN'T HELP HER.
BUT...
...I COULD AT LEAST LISTEN TO HER SIDE OF THE STORY.
WE'RE FRIENDS, AFTER ALL.

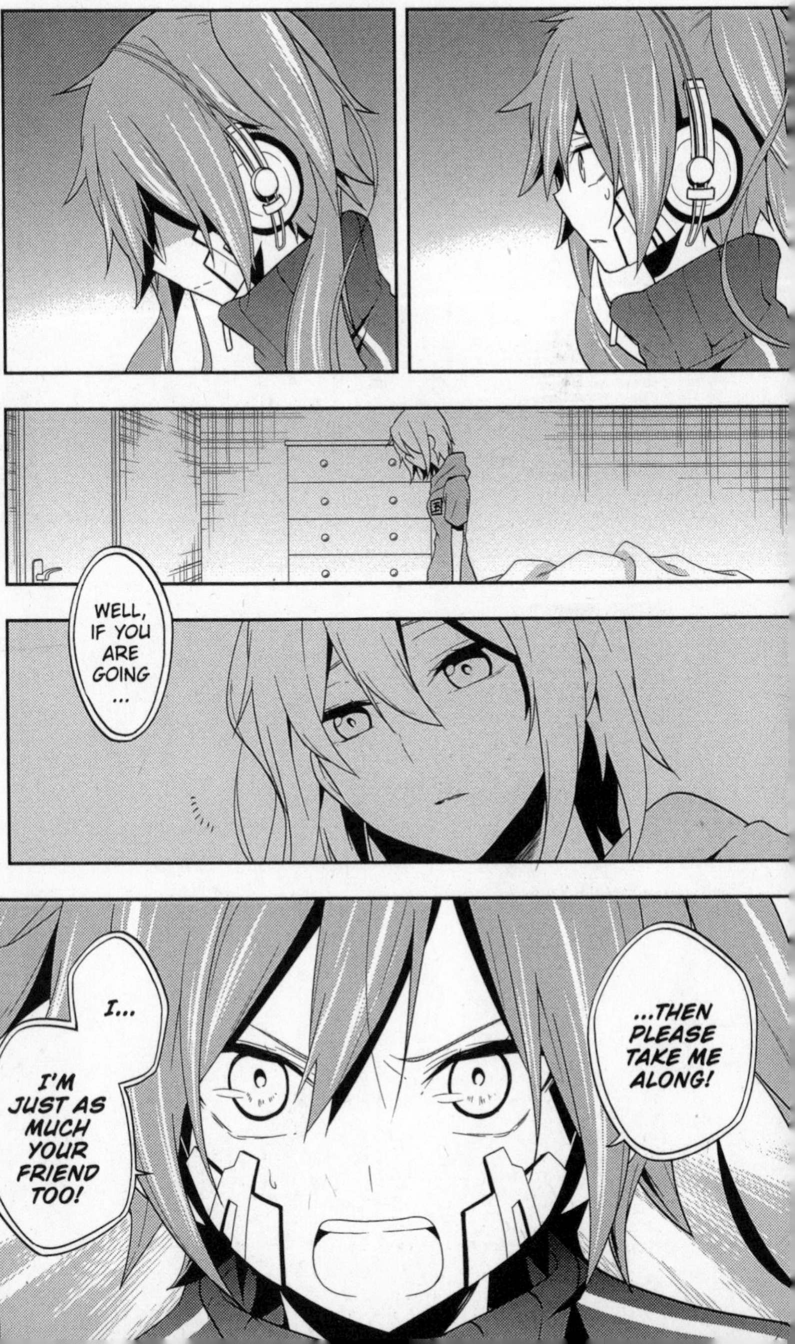
WELL, IF YOU ARE GOING ...
...THEN PLEASE TAKE ME ALONG!
I...
I'M JUST AS MUCH YOUR FRIEND TOO!

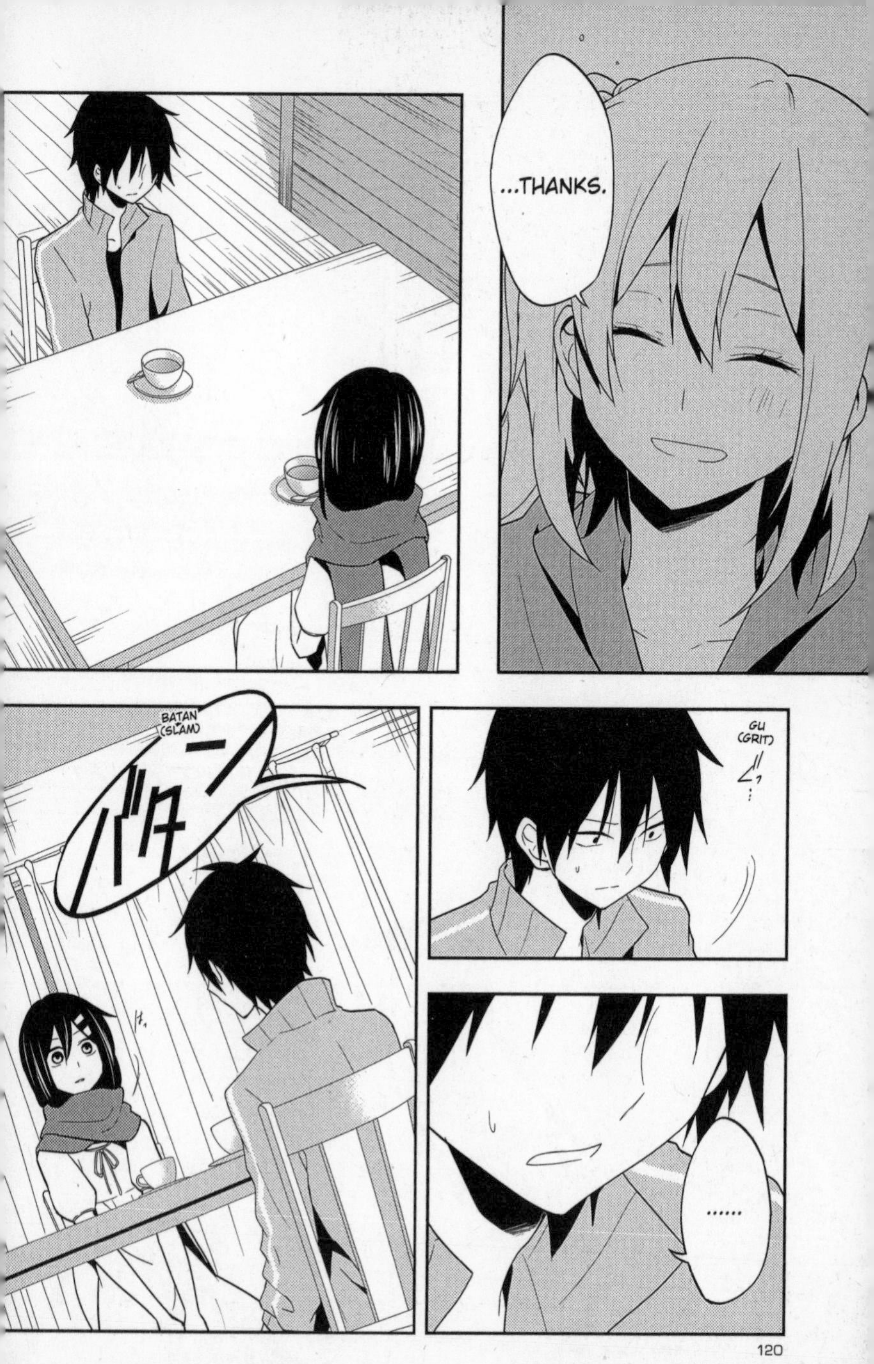
...THANKS.
GU (GRIT)
......
BATAN (SLAM)

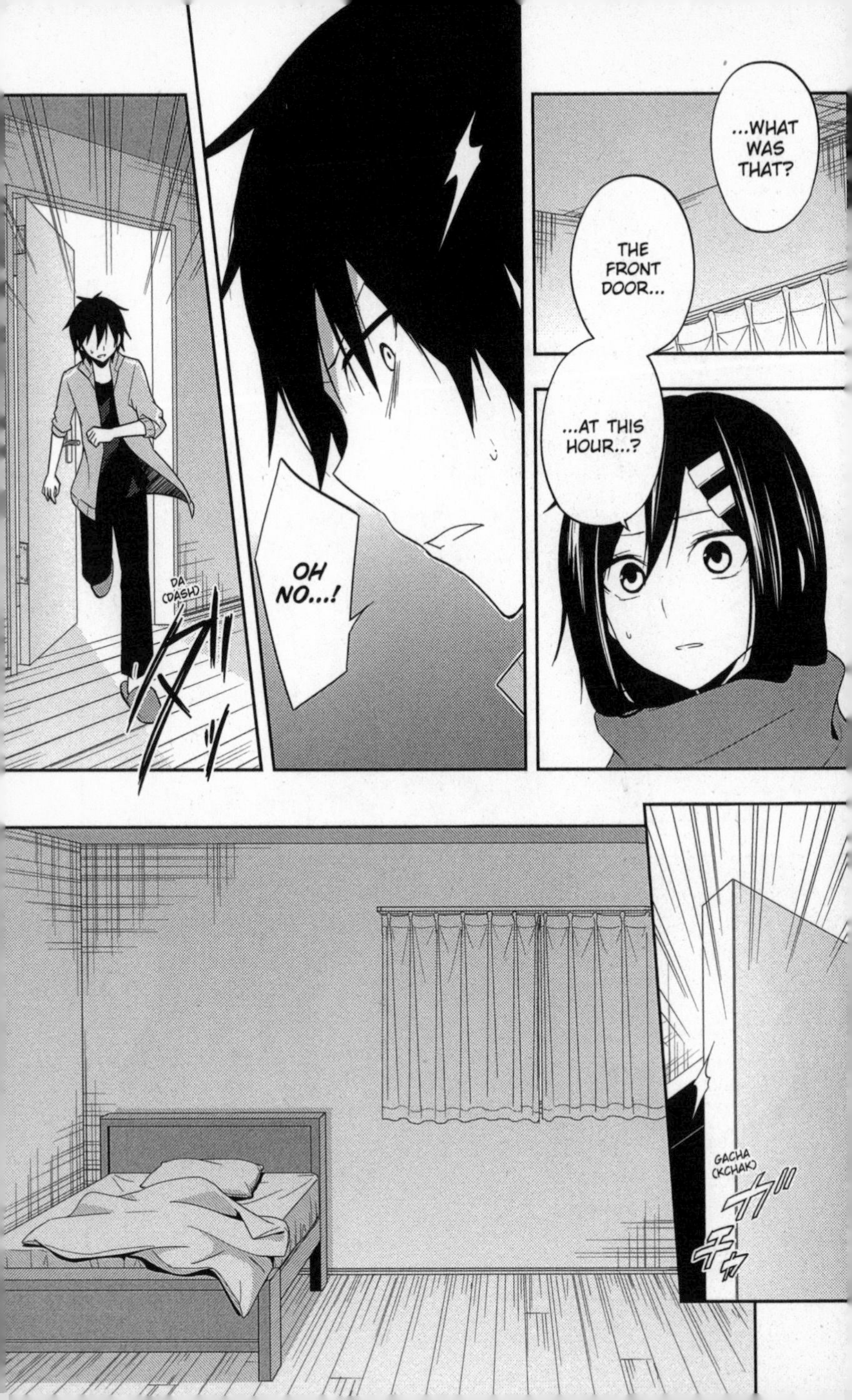
...WHAT WAS THAT?
THE FRONT DOOR...
...AT THIS HOUR...?
OH NO...!
DA (DASH)
GACHA (KCHAK)

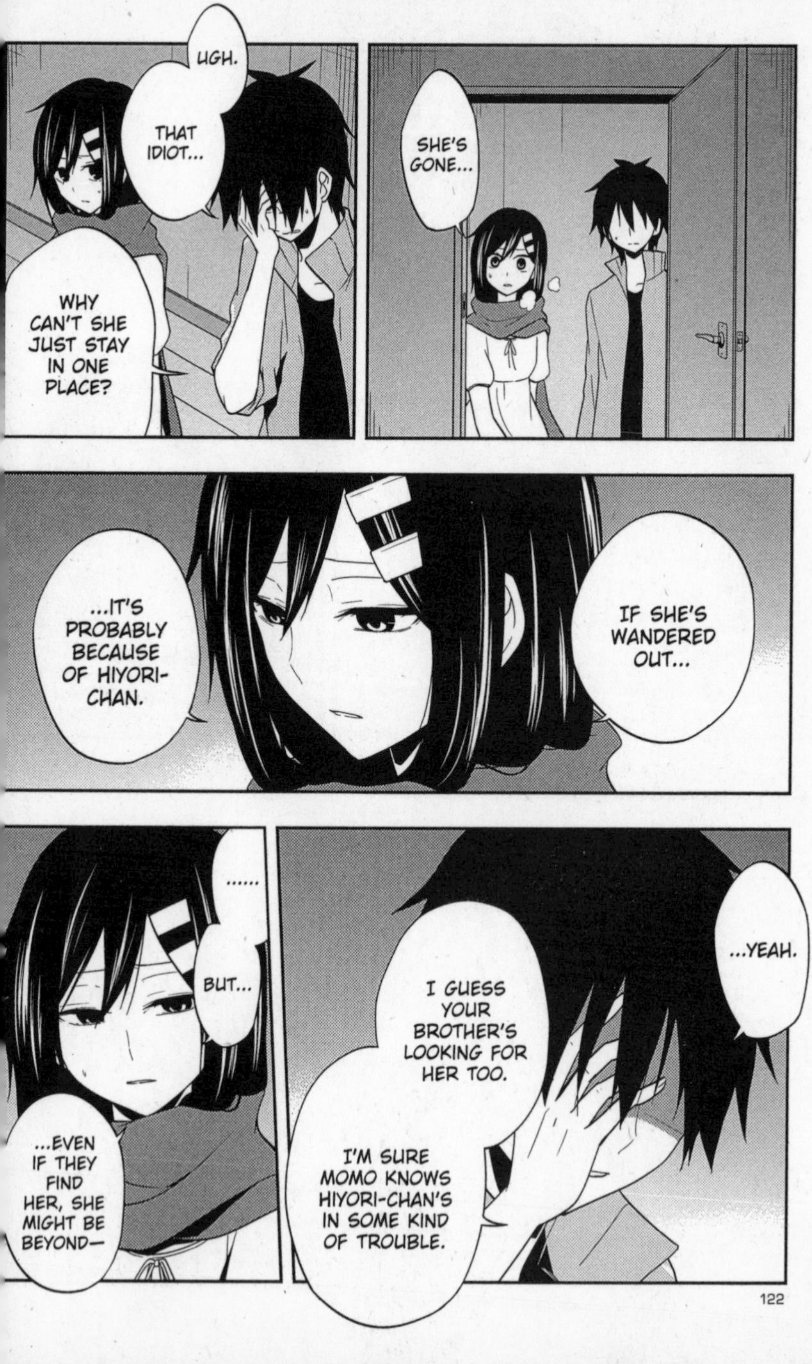
SHE'S GONE...
UGH.
THAT IDIOT...
WHY CAN'T SHE JUST STAY IN ONE PLACE?
IF SHE'S WANDERED OUT...
...IT'S PROBABLY BECAUSE OF HIYORI-CHAN.
...YEAH.
I GUESS YOUR BROTHER'S LOOKING FOR HER TOO.
I'M SURE MOMO KNOWS HIYORI-CHAN'S IN SOME KIND OF TROUBLE.
......
BUT...
...EVEN IF THEY FIND HER, SHE MIGHT BE BEYOND—

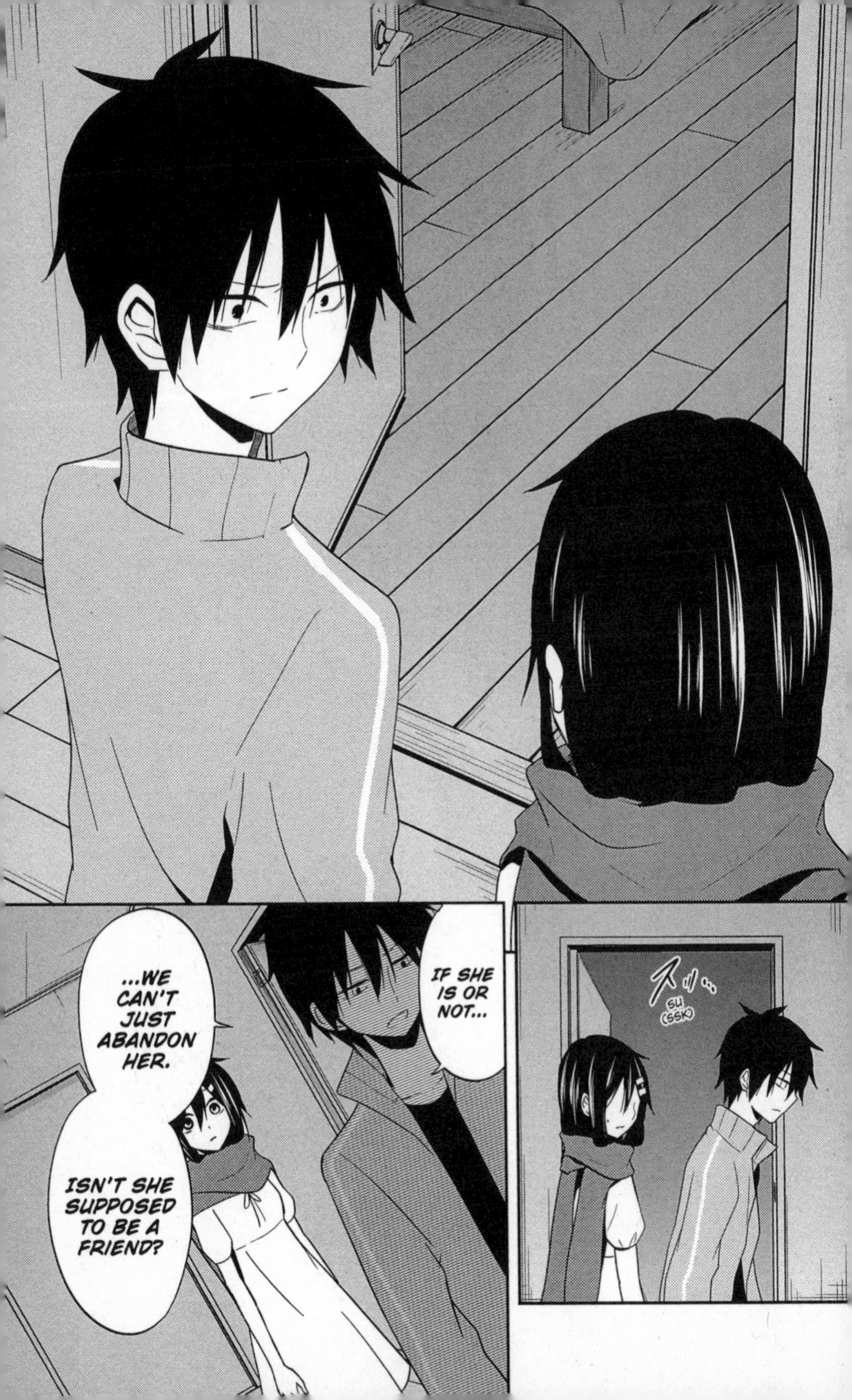
スッ…
SU (SSK)
IF SHE IS OR NOT...
...WE CAN'T JUST ABANDON HER.
ISN'T SHE SUPPOSED TO BE A FRIEND?

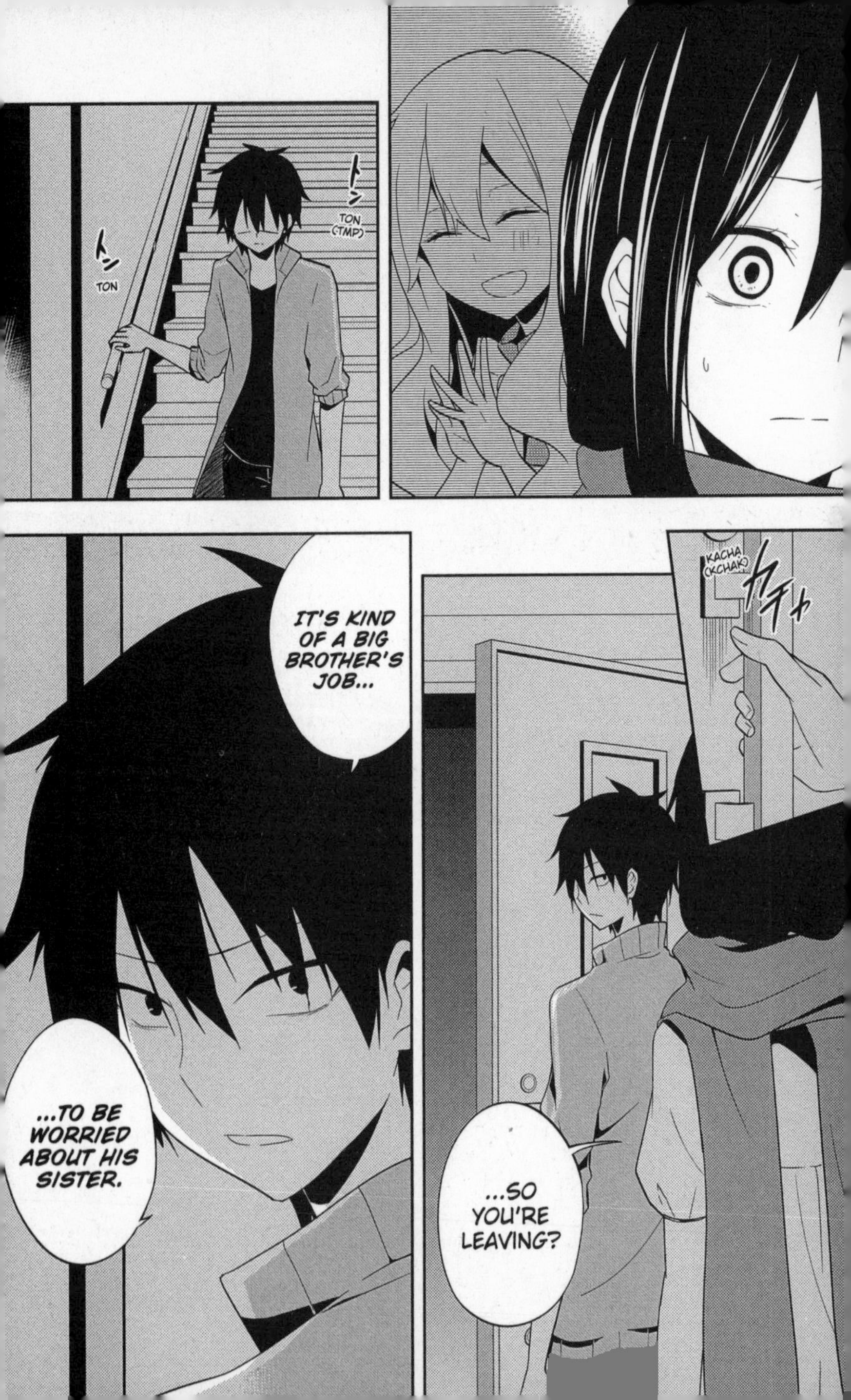
トン
TON (TMP)
トン
TON
KACHA (KCHAK)
カチャ
...SO YOU'RE LEAVING?
IT'S KIND OF A BIG BROTHER'S JOB...
...TO BE WORRIED ABOUT HIS SISTER.

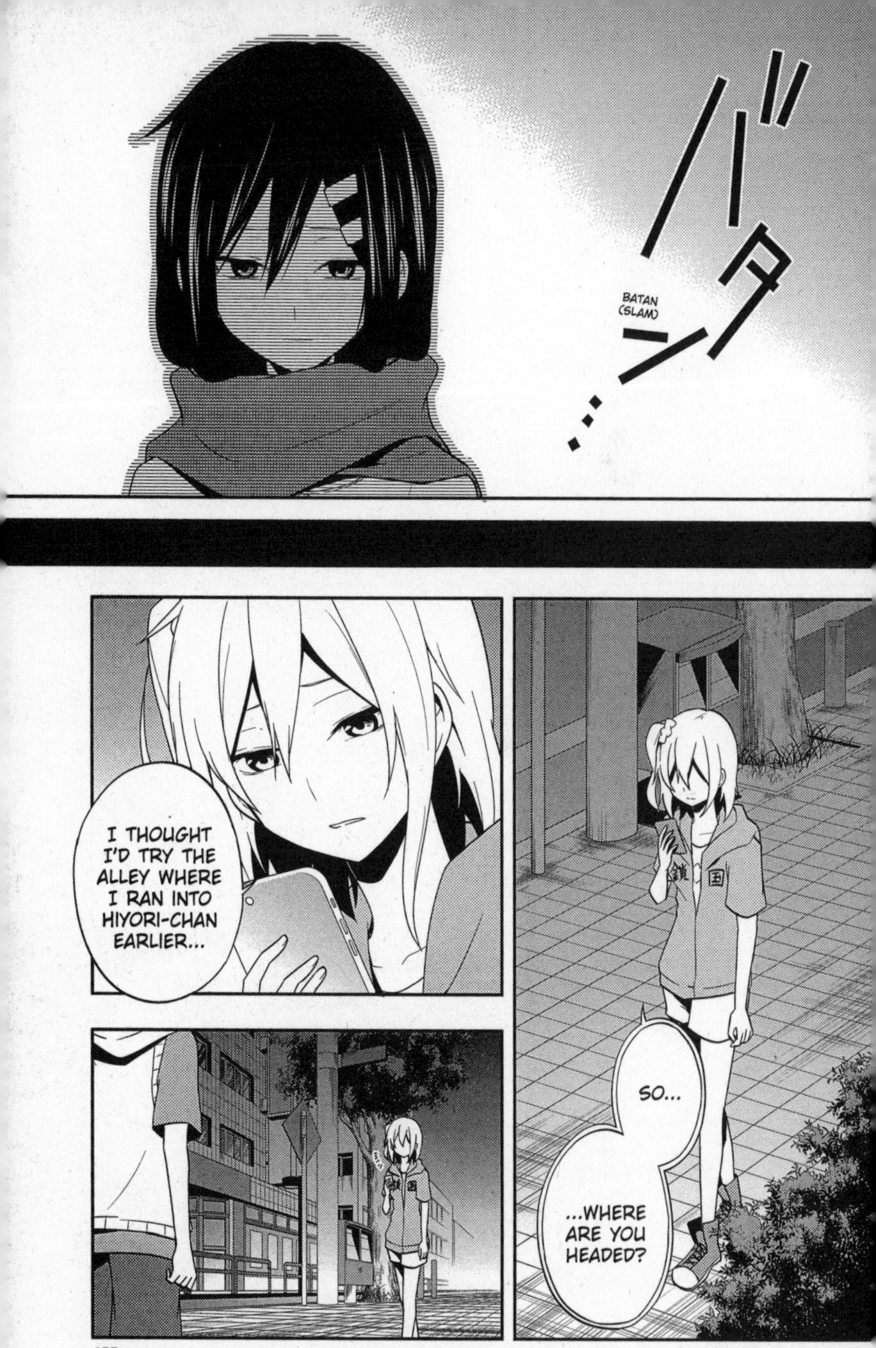
BATAN (SLAM)
SO...
...WHERE ARE YOU HEADED?
I THOUGHT I'D TRY THE ALLEY WHERE I RAN INTO HIYORI-CHAN EARLIER...

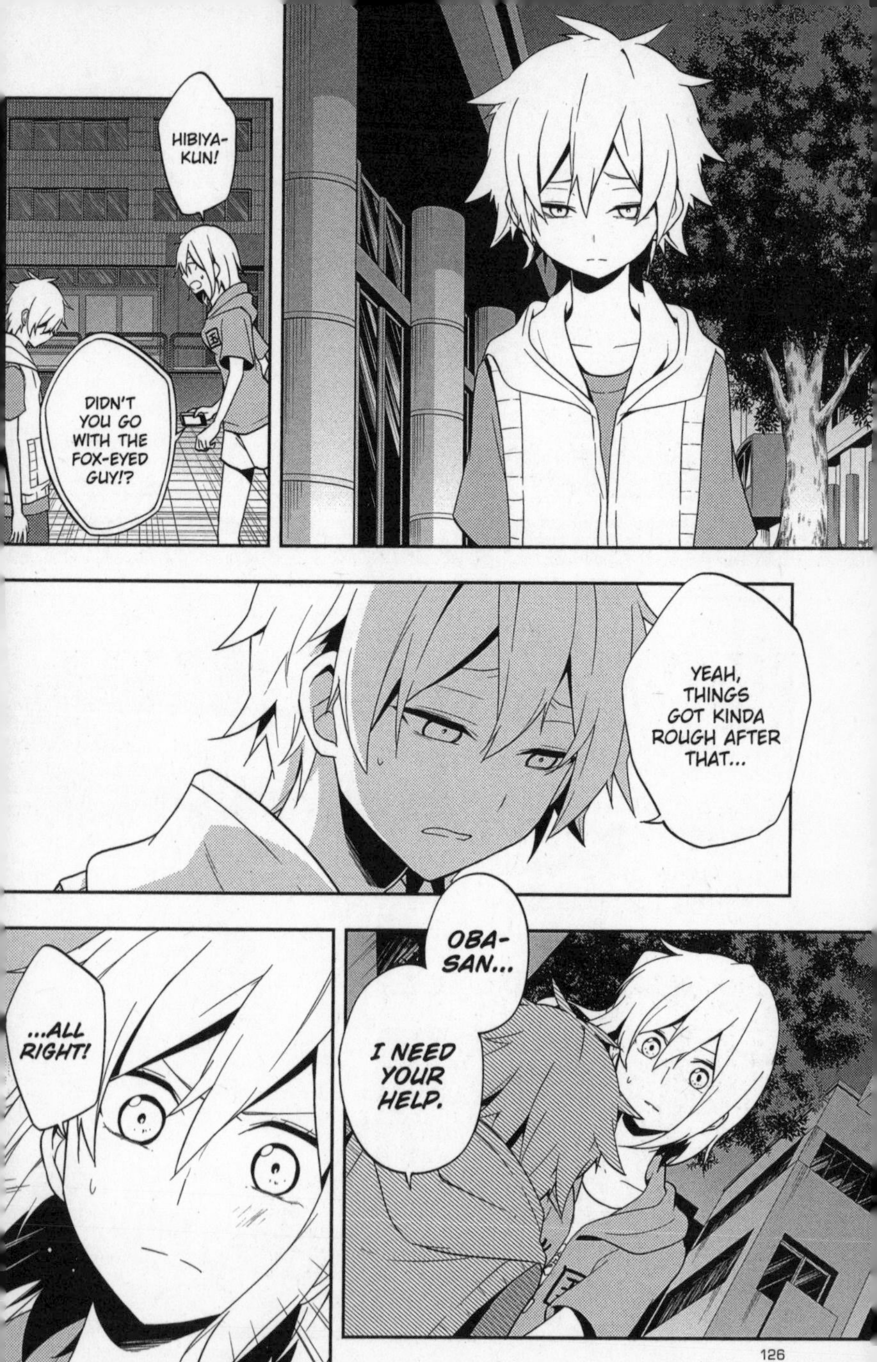
HIBIYA-KUN!
DIDN'T YOU GO WITH THE FOX-EYED GUY!?
YEAH, THINGS GOT KINDA ROUGH AFTER THAT...
OBA-SAN...
I NEED YOUR HELP.
...ALL RIGHT!

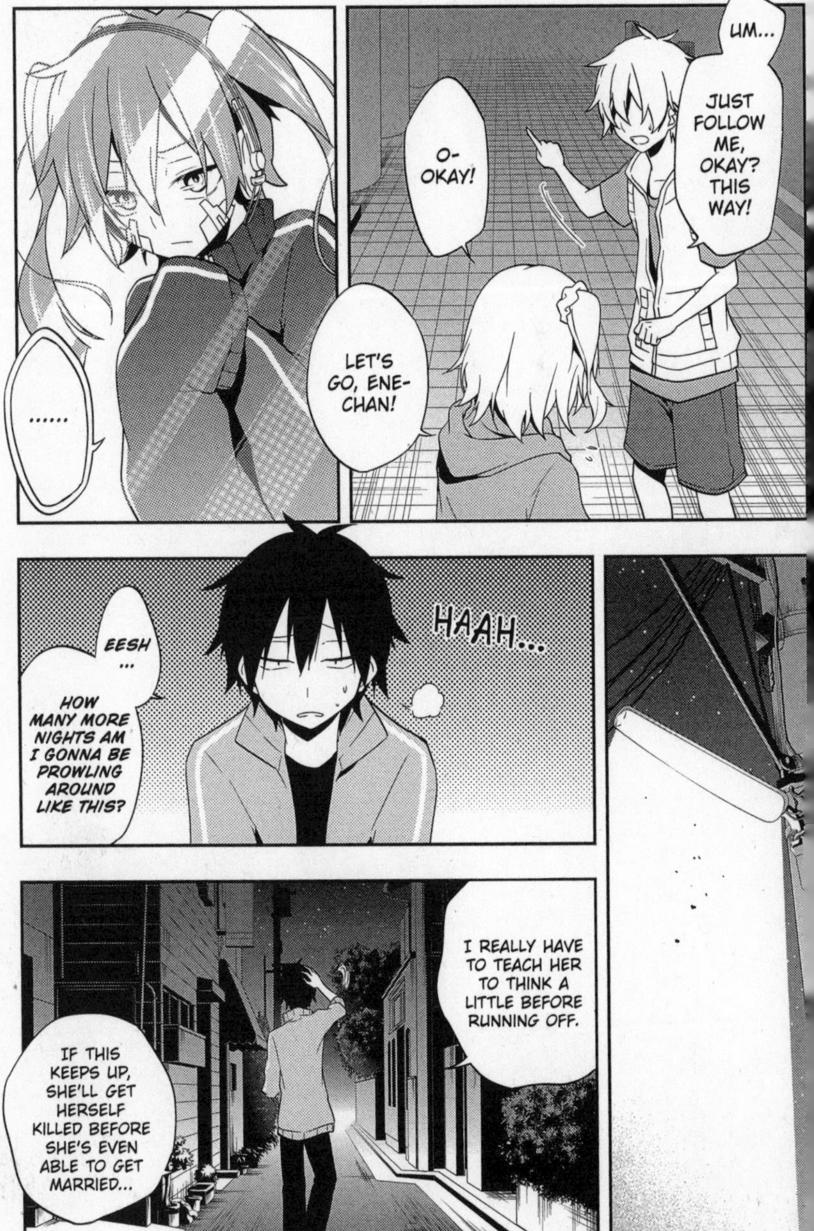
UM...
JUST FOLLOW ME, OKAY? THIS WAY!
O-OKAY!
LET'S GO, ENE-CHAN!
......
HAAH...
EESH... HOW MANY MORE NIGHTS AM I GONNA BE PROWLING AROUND LIKE THIS?
I REALLY HAVE TO TEACH HER TO THINK A LITTLE BEFORE RUNNING OFF.
IF THIS KEEPS UP, SHE'LL GET HERSELF KILLED BEFORE SHE'S EVEN ABLE TO GET MARRIED...

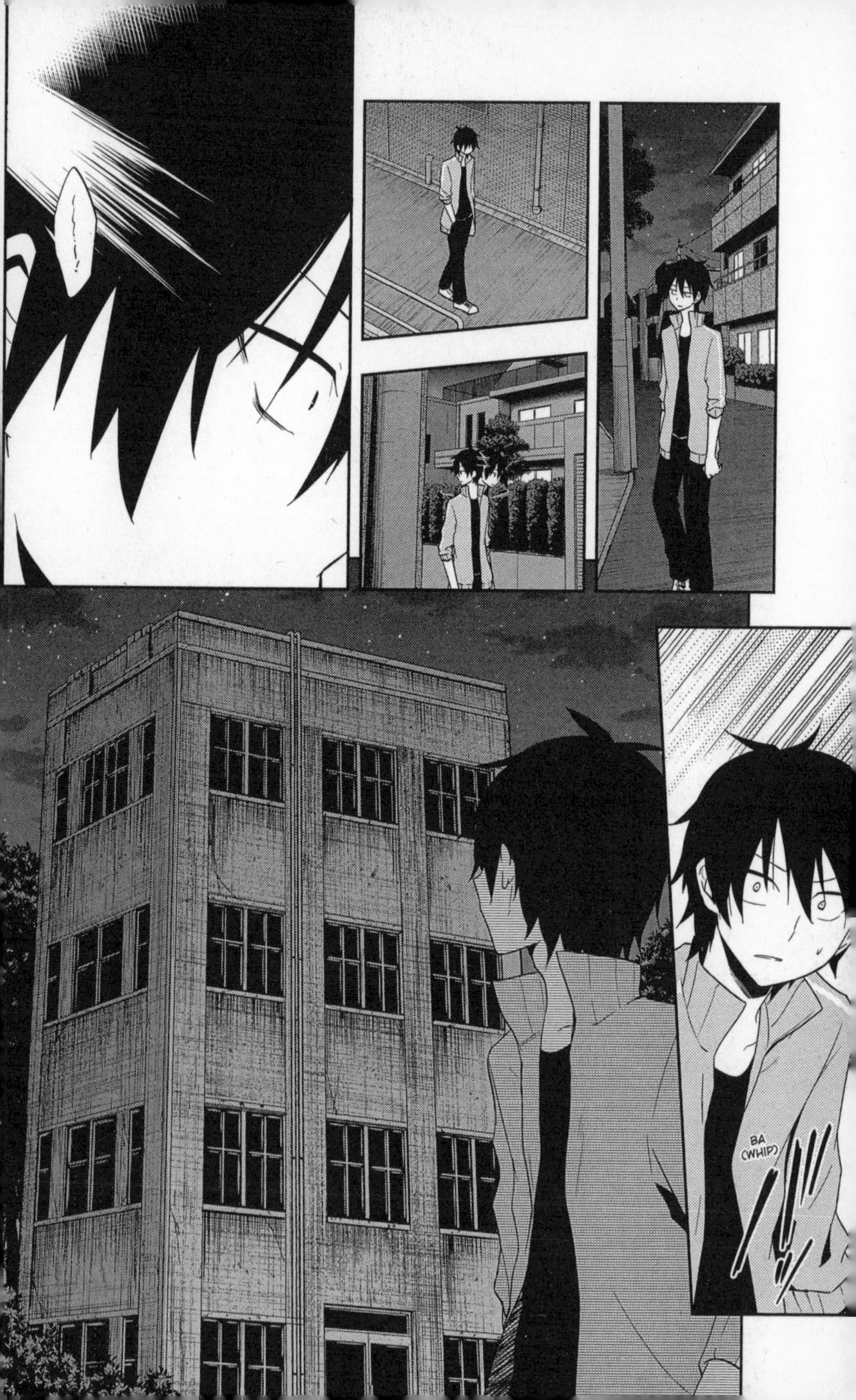
BA
(WHIP)

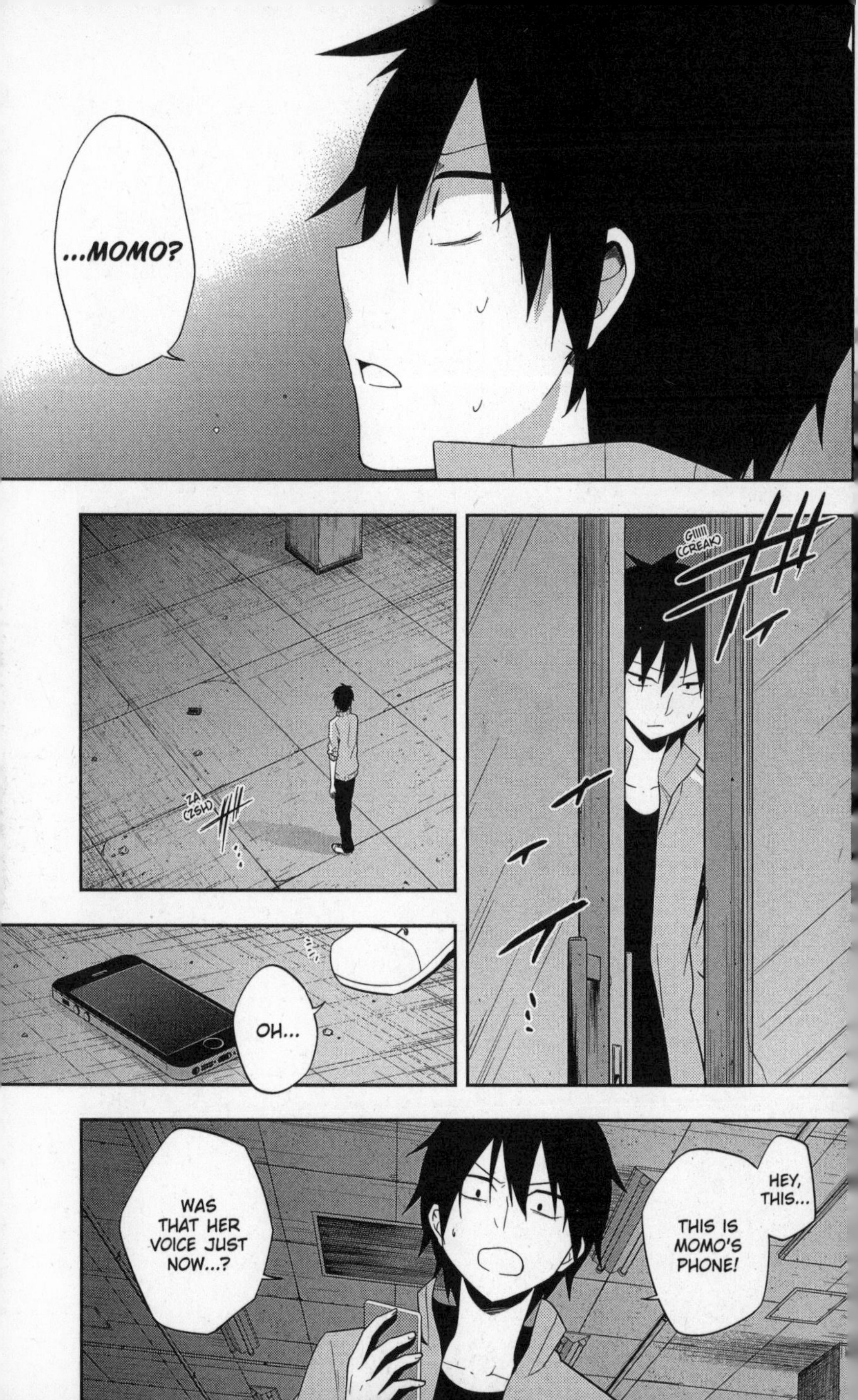
...MOMO?
GIIII (CREAK)
ZA (ZSH)
OH...
HEY, THIS...
THIS IS MOMO'S PHONE!
WAS THAT HER VOICE JUST NOW...?

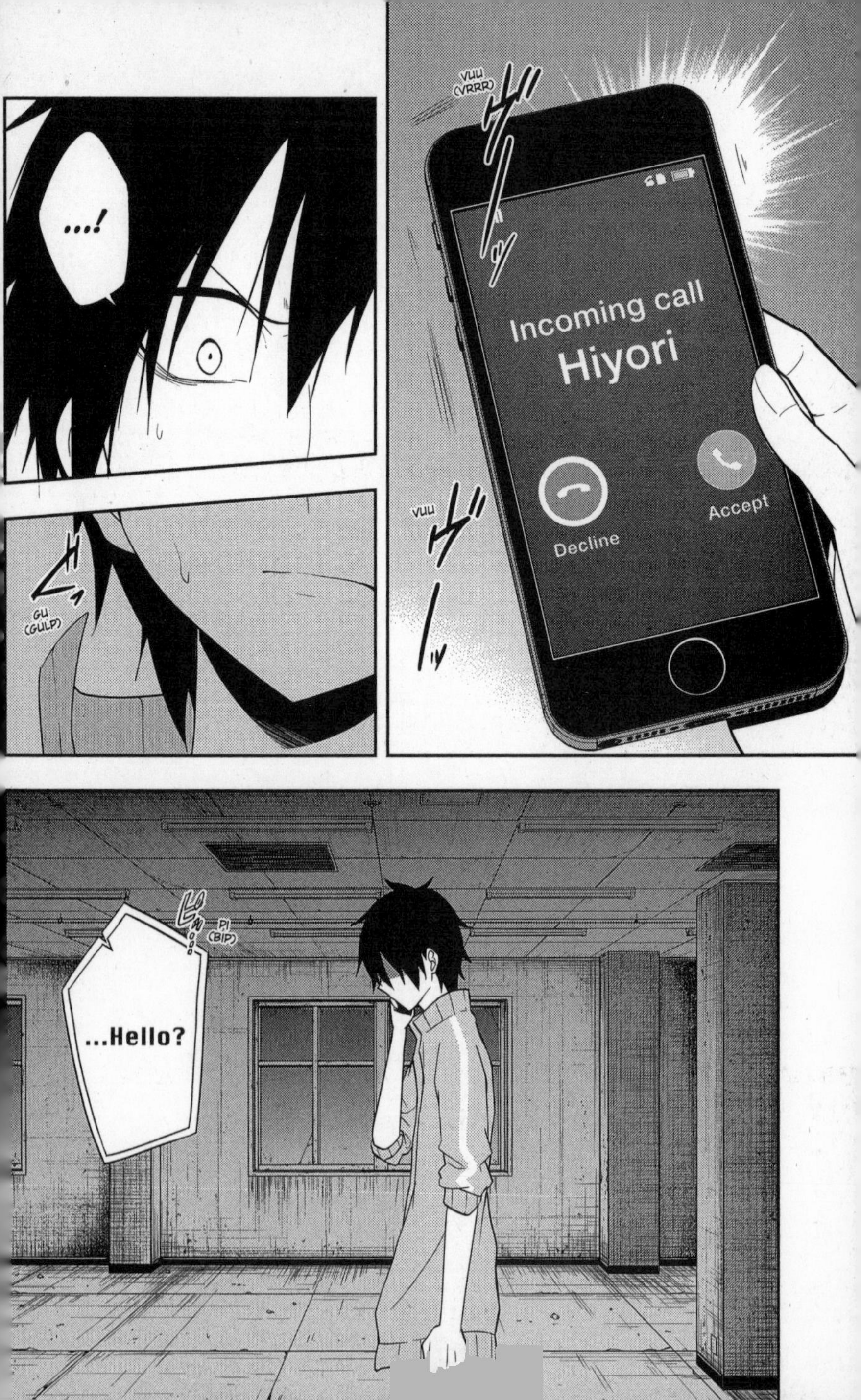
VUU (VRRR)
Incoming call
Hiyori
Decline
Accept
VUU
...!
GU (GULP)
PI (BIP)
...Hello?

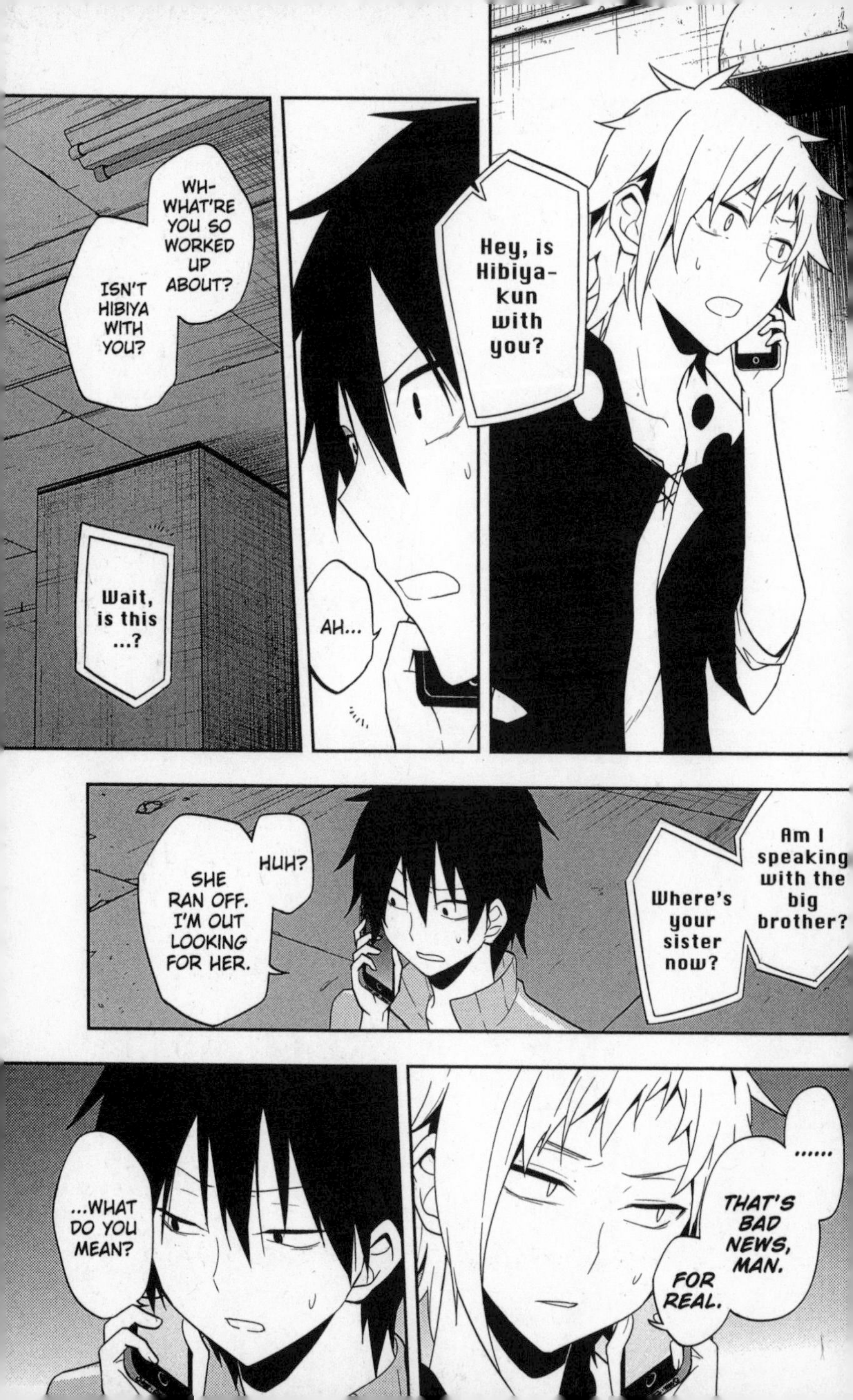
Hey, is Hibiya-kun with you?
AH...
WH-WHAT'RE YOU SO WORKED UP ABOUT?
ISN'T HIBIYA WITH YOU?
Wait, is this ...?
Am I speaking with the big brother?
Where's your sister now?
HUH?
SHE RAN OFF. I'M OUT LOOKING FOR HER.
......
THAT'S BAD NEWS, MAN.
FOR REAL.
...WHAT DO YOU MEAN?

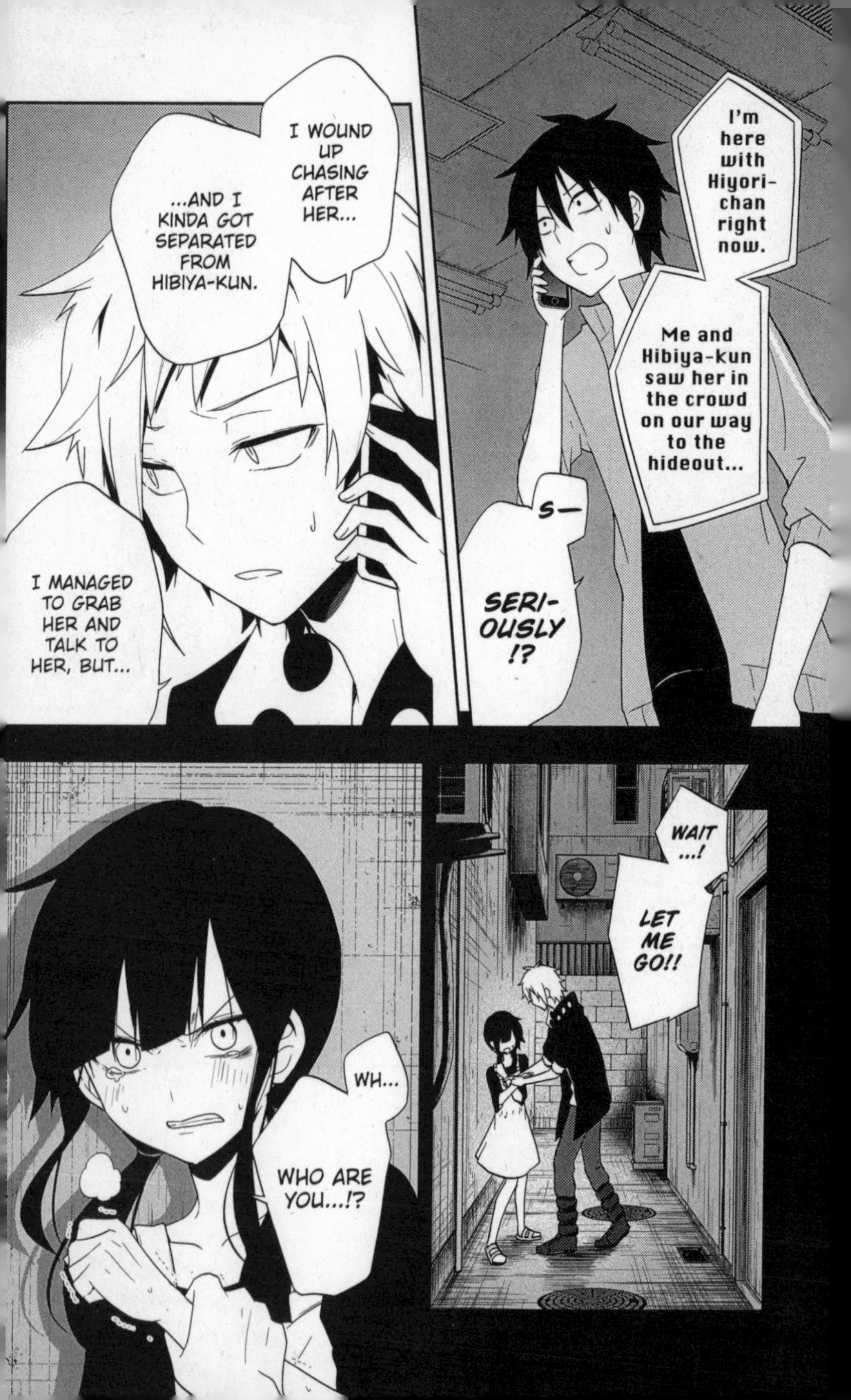
I'm here with Hiyori-chan right now.
Me and Hibiya-kun saw her in the crowd on our way to the hideout...
S—
SERI-OUSLY !?
I WOUND UP CHASING AFTER HER...
...AND I KINDA GOT SEPARATED FROM HIBIYA-KUN.
I MANAGED TO GRAB HER AND TALK TO HER, BUT...
WAIT ...!
LET ME GO!!
WH...
WHO ARE YOU...!?

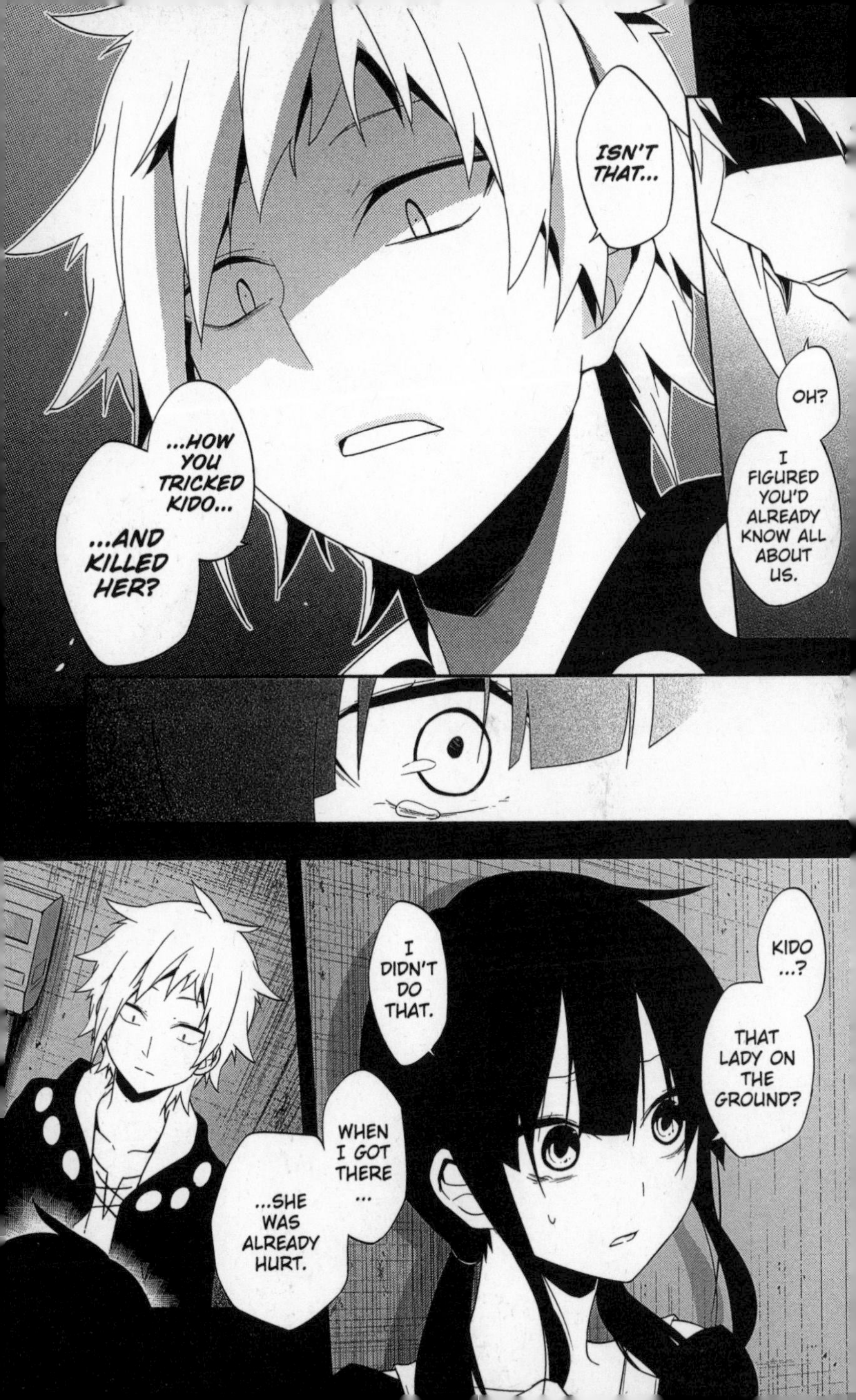
OH?
I FIGURED YOU'D ALREADY KNOW ALL ABOUT US.
ISN'T THAT...
...HOW YOU TRICKED KIDO...
...AND KILLED HER?
KIDO ...?
THAT LADY ON THE GROUND?
I DIDN'T DO THAT.
WHEN I GOT THERE ...
...SHE WAS ALREADY HURT.

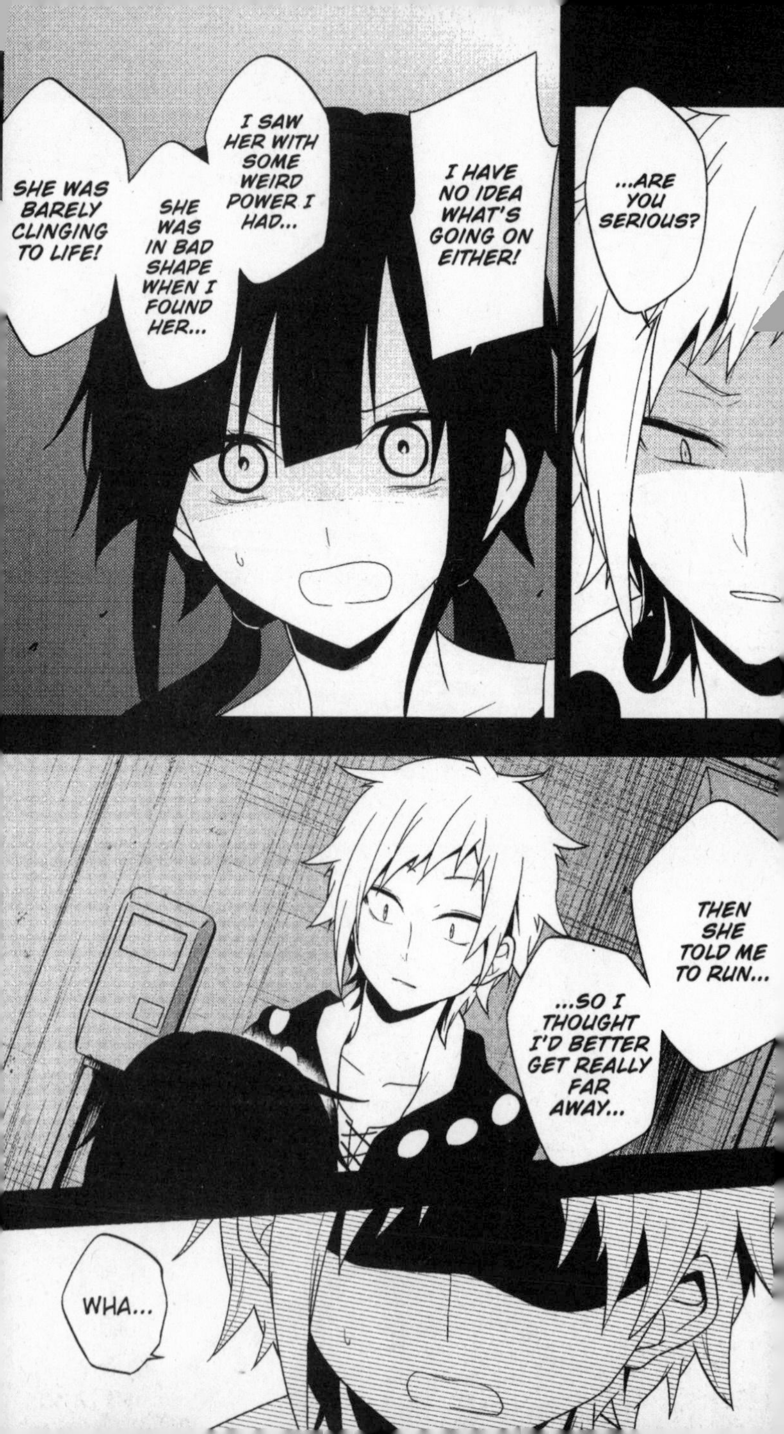
...ARE YOU SERIOUS?
I HAVE NO IDEA WHAT'S GOING ON EITHER!
I SAW HER WITH SOME WEIRD POWER I HAD...
SHE WAS IN BAD SHAPE WHEN I FOUND HER...
SHE WAS BARELY CLINGING TO LIFE!
THEN SHE TOLD ME TO RUN...
...SO I THOUGHT I'D BETTER GET REALLY FAR AWAY...
WHA...

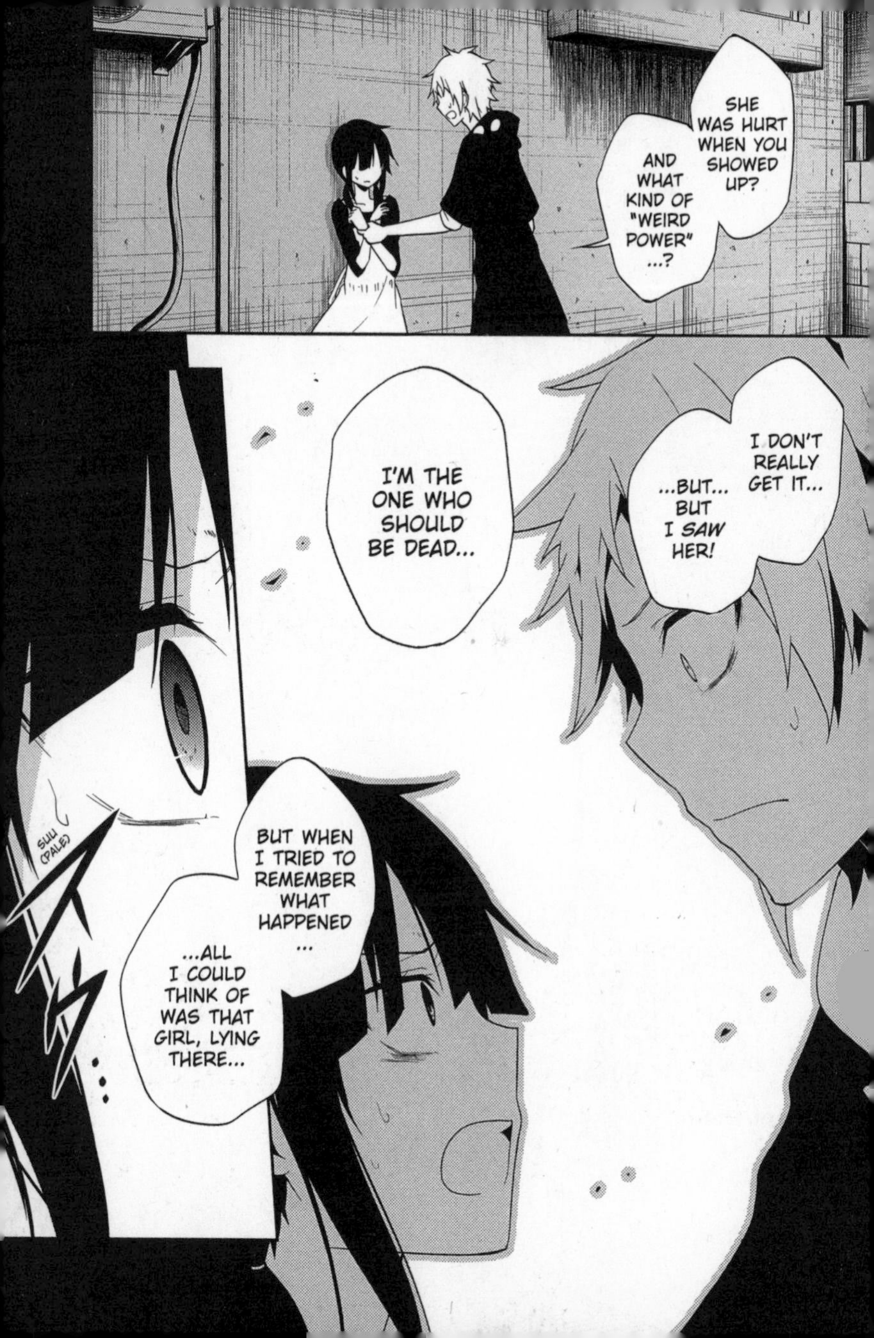
SHE WAS HURT WHEN YOU SHOWED UP?
AND WHAT KIND OF "WEIRD POWER" ...?
I DON'T REALLY GET IT...
...BUT... BUT I *SAW* HER!
I'M THE ONE WHO SHOULD BE DEAD...
BUT WHEN I TRIED TO REMEMBER WHAT HAPPENED ...
...ALL I COULD THINK OF WAS THAT GIRL, LYING THERE...
SUU (PALE)

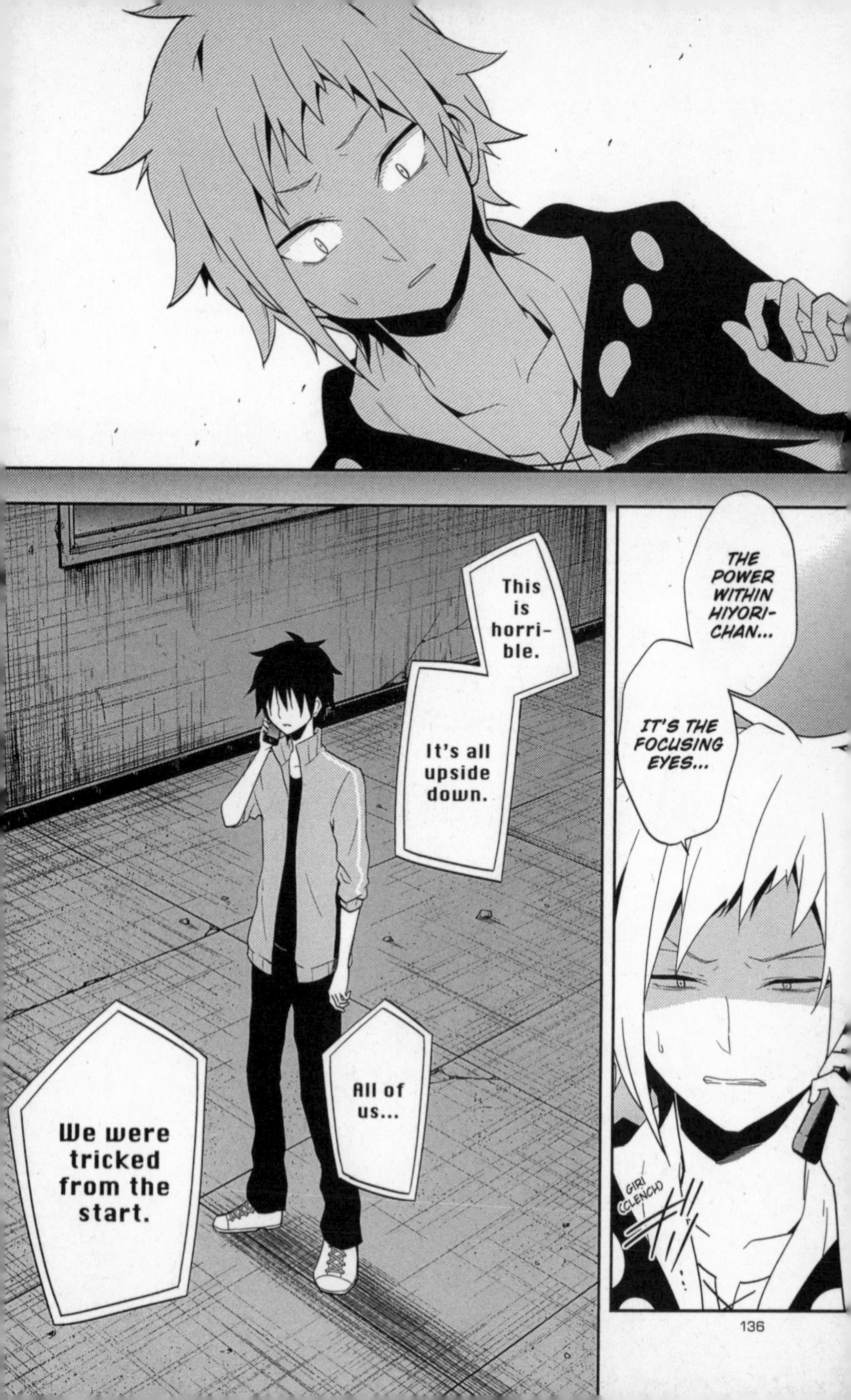
THE POWER WITHIN HIYORI-CHAN...
IT'S THE FOCUSING EYES...
GIRI (CLENCH)
This is horri-ble.
It's all upside down.
All of us...
We were tricked from the start.

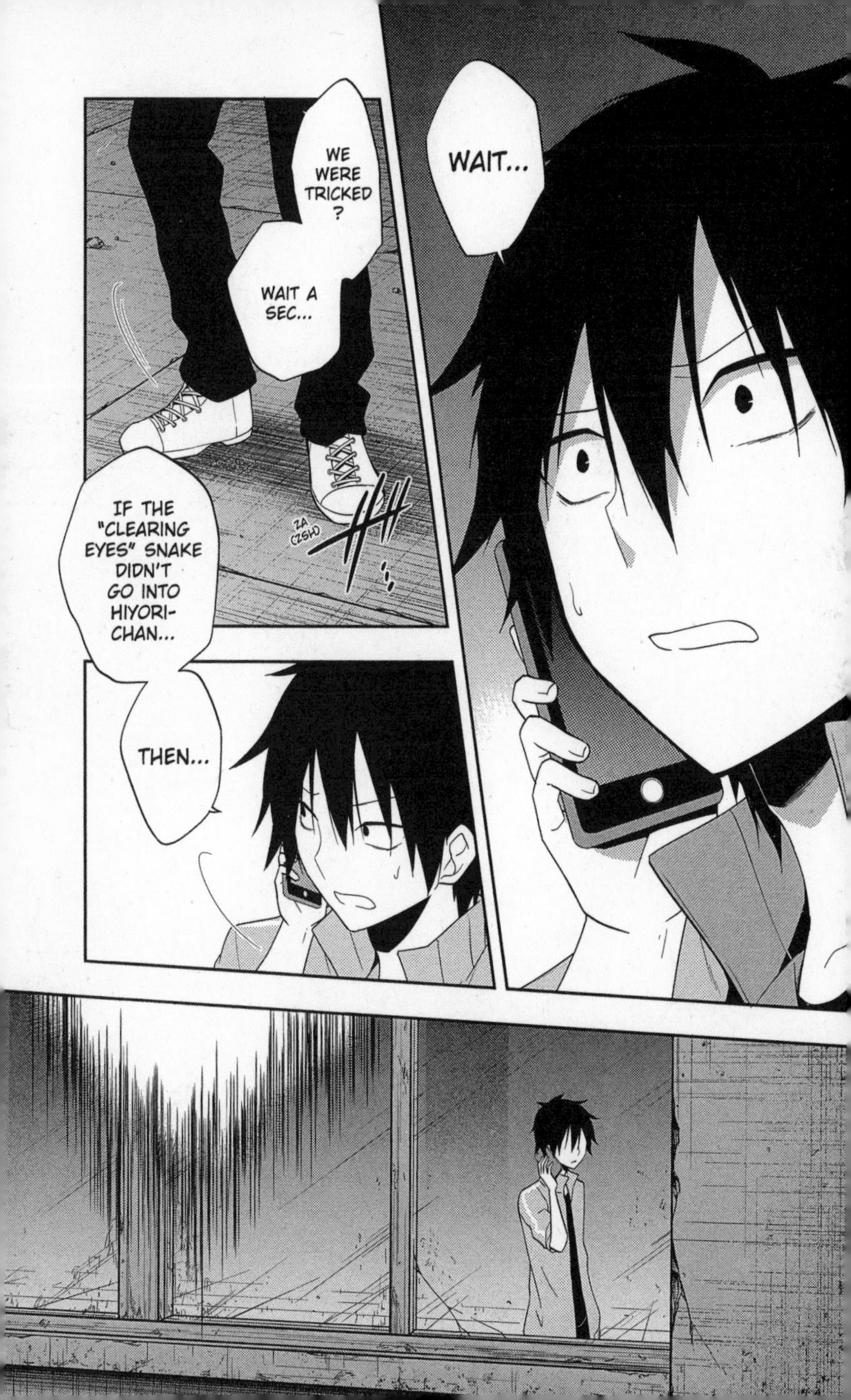
WAIT...
WE WERE TRICKED?
WAIT A SEC...
ZA (ZSH)
IF THE "CLEARING EYES" SNAKE DIDN'T GO INTO HIYORI-CHAN...
THEN...

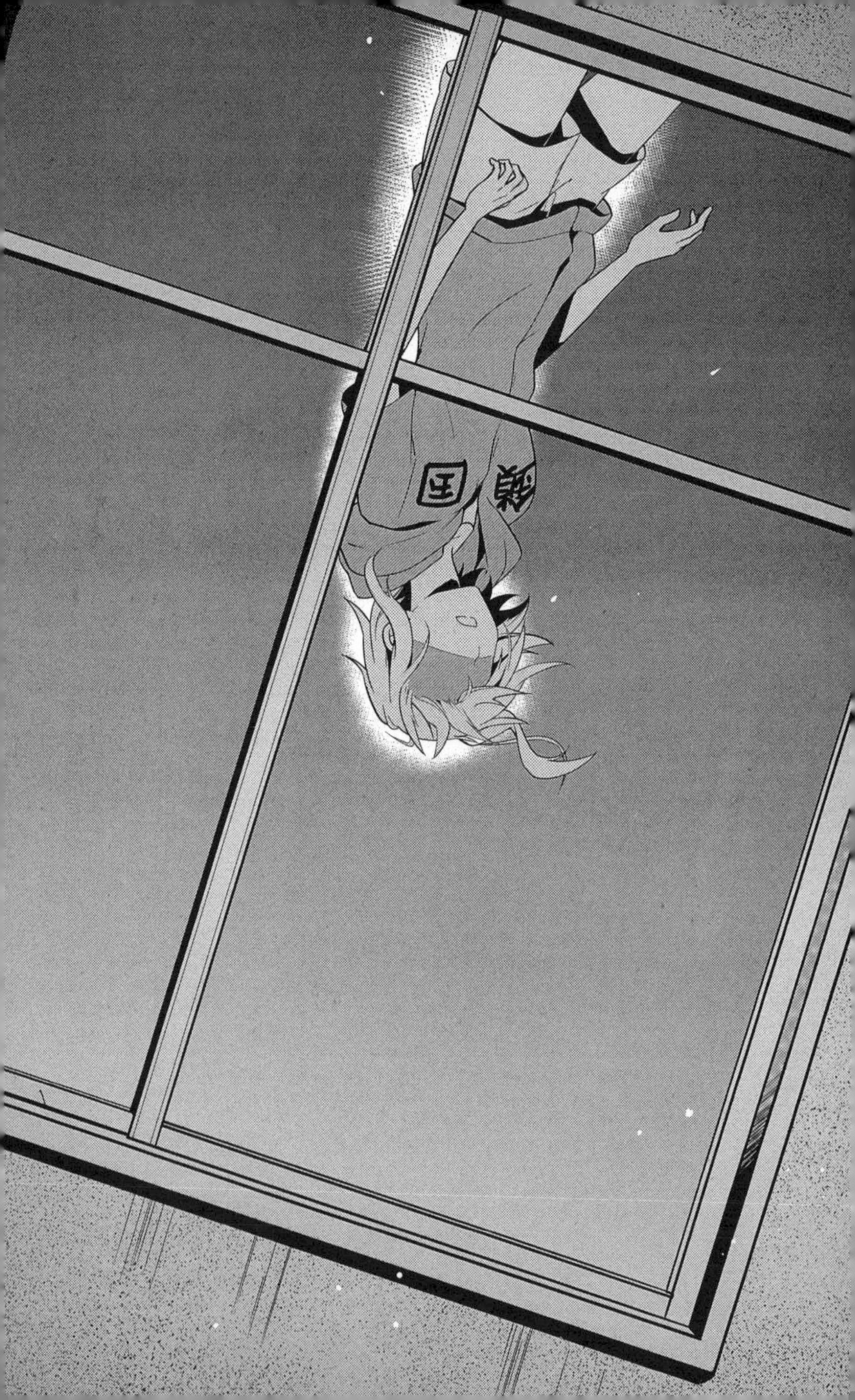

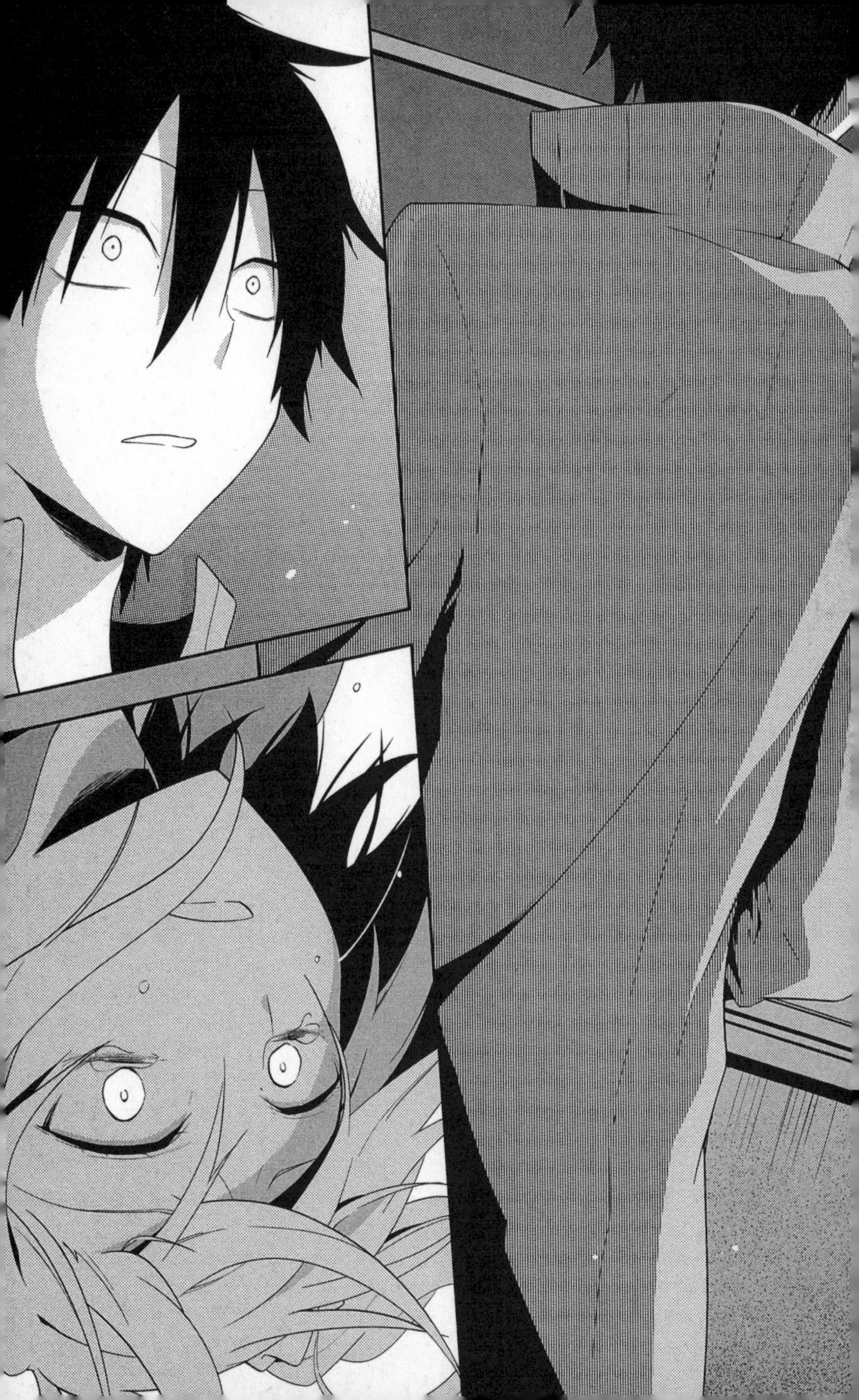

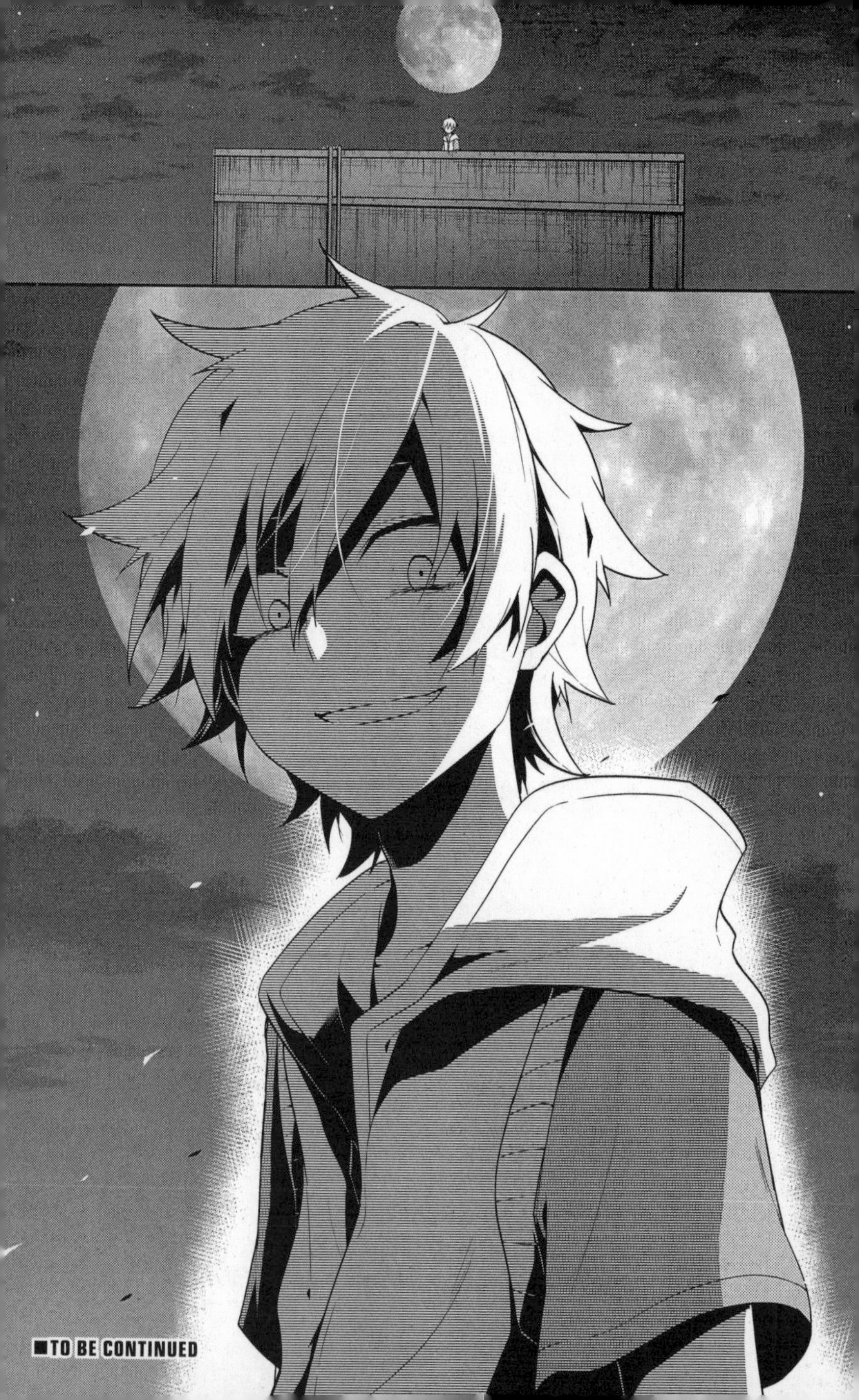
■TO BE CONTINUED

KAGEROU DAZE

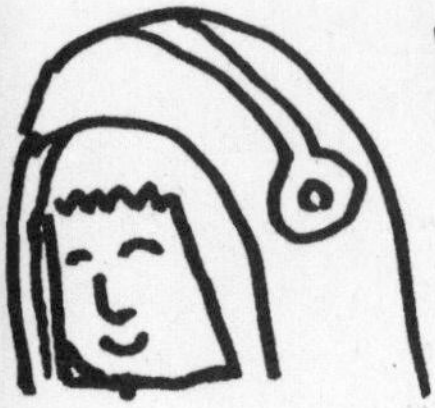

Manga VOL. 9 is out!

Congratulations.
And thank you too. Jin here.
The manga version of *Kagerou Daze* is finally at its ninth volume, and the story only gets darker and darker. I'd like to try bringing the characters in a brighter direction any way I can. I'll do my best on that.

Jin

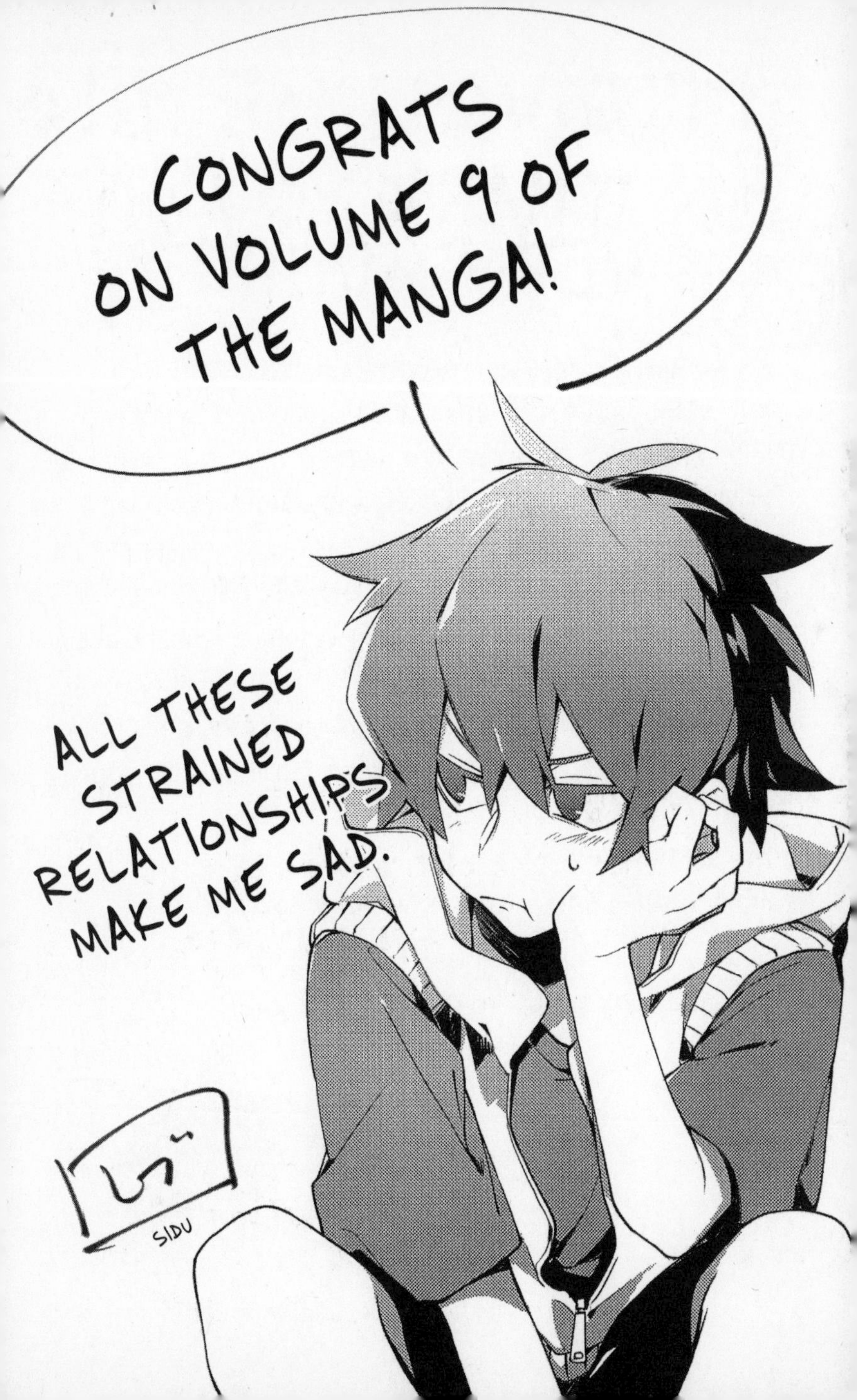
CONGRATS ON VOLUME 9 OF THE MANGA!
ALL THESE STRAINED RELATIONSHIPS MAKE ME SAD.
SIDU

IT'S VOLUME 9!!
THANK YOU
VERY MUCH!!

I'M SO HAPPY YOU PICKED UP THIS VOLUME! THANK YOU!!
I'VE BEEN UNDER THE WEATHER FOR A LOT OF THIS PAST
WINTER. GASTEROENTERITIS, THE FLU, CONJUNCTIVITIS...
IT WAS A SEASON OF SETBACKS AND COMEBACKS. THE
FEVER WAS PRETTY BAD...BUT I PULLED THROUGH! I SPENT
THE WHOLE TIME I WAS WORKING ON THIS COLLECTED
VOLUME WONDERING WHAT KIND OF ILLNESS WOULD GREET
ME NEXT, BUT LUCKILY VOLUME 9 RELEASED WITHOUT
ANYTHING HAPPENING. GOOD THING FOR THAT. GOOD
HEALTH IS DEFINITELY SOMETHING TO APPRECIATE, HUH?
TOO BAD I HAVE TO GO TO THE DENTIST NOW.
HOW DEPRESSING.
HERE'S HOPING ALL OF YOU REMAIN IN GOOD HEALTH!

MAHIRO
SATOU

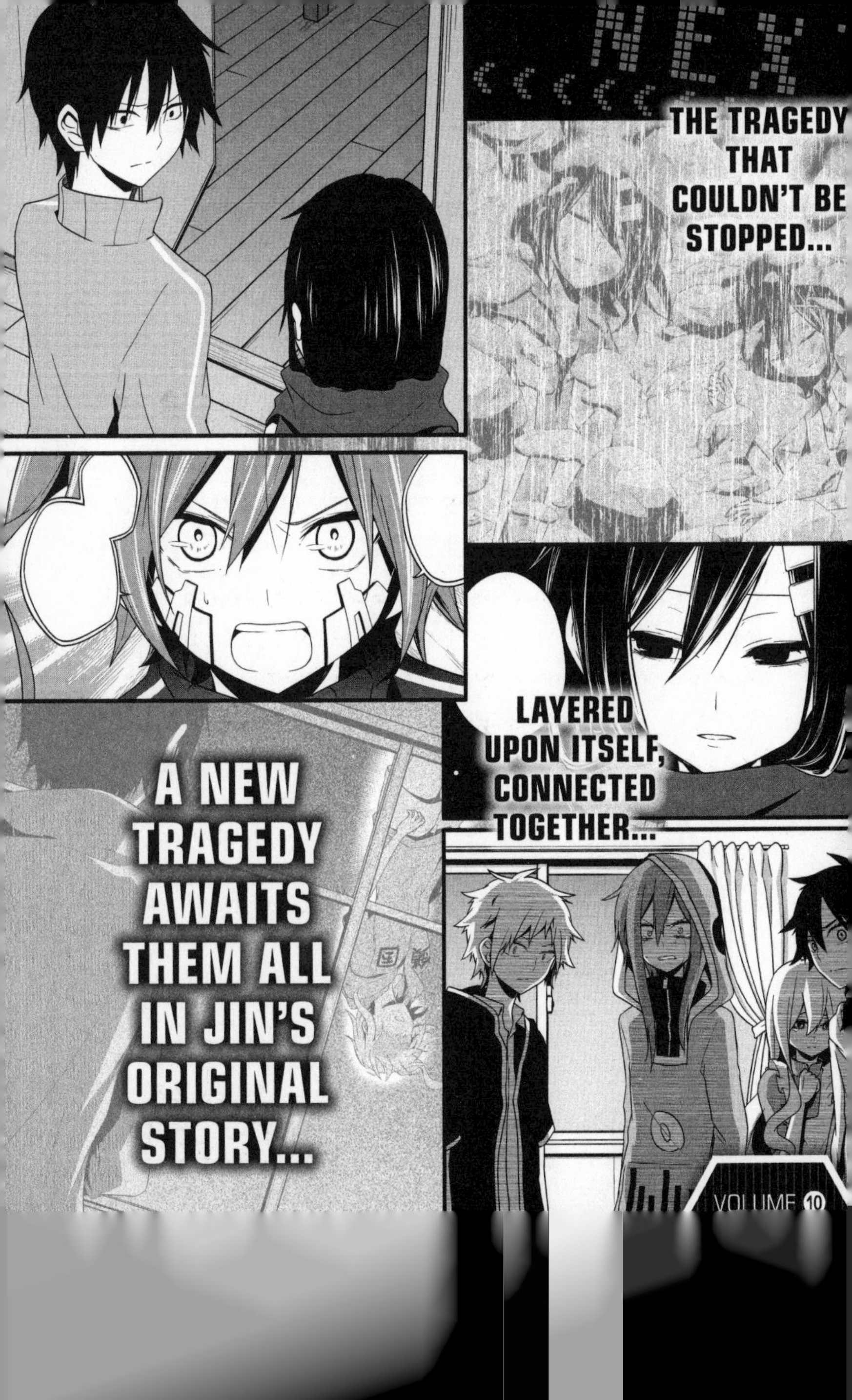
NEX
THE TRAGEDY THAT COULDN'T BE STOPPED...
LAYERED UPON ITSELF, CONNECTED TOGETHER...
A NEW TRAGEDY AWAITS THEM ALL IN JIN'S ORIGINAL STORY...
VOLUME 10

KAGEROU DAZE 09

MAHIRO SATOU
Original Story: JIN
(SHIZEN NO TEKI P)
Character Design: SIDU, WANNYANPOO

Translation: Kevin Gifford   •   Lettering: Abigail Blackman

KAGEROUDAZE Vol. 9
© Mahiro Satou 2017
© KAGEROU PROJECT / 1st PLACE
First published in Japan in 2017 by KADOKAWA CORPORATION, Tokyo.
English translation rights arranged with KADOKAWA CORPORATION, Tokyo through TUTTLE-MORI AGENCY, Inc., Tokyo.

English translation © 2018 by Yen Press, LLC

Yen Press
1290 Avenue of the Americas
New York, NY 10104

Visit us at yenpress.com
facebook.com/yenpress
twitter.com/yenpress
yenpress.tumblr.com
instagram.com/yenpress

First Yen Press Edition: March 2018

Yen Press is an imprint of Yen Press, LLC.
The Yen Press name and logo are trademarks of Yen Press, LLC.

Library of Congress Control Number: 2016297061

ISBNs: 978-0-316-52124-6 (paperback)
      978-0-316-52125-3 (ebook)

10 9 8 7 6 5 4 3 2 1

BVG

Printed in the United States of America